THE IMMIGRANT HERITAGE OF AMERICA SERIES

Cecyle S. Neidle, Editor

CONTEMPORARY AMERICAN IMMIGRATION

Interpretive Essays
(Non-European)

Edited by

Dennis Laurence Cuddy

TWAYNE PUBLISHERS

A DIVISION OF G. K. HALL & CO., BOSTON

Published in 1982 by Twayne Publishers,
A Division of G. K. Hall & Co.

All Rights Reserved

Printed on permanent/durable acid-free paper and bound
in the United States of America

First Printing

Library of Congress Cataloging in Publication Data

Contemporary American immigration.

(The Immigrant heritage of America series)
1. United States—Emigration and immigration—
Addresses, essays, lectures.   I. Cuddy, Dennis Laurence.
II. Series.
JV6450.C66   325.73   81–7130
ISBN 0–8057–8420–9   AACR2

Dedicated to
Joseph and Peggy Cuddy
to
Cecyle S. Neidle
and to
All the immigrants to the
United States of America,
who have contributed so
much toward the success
of this Republic.

Contents

Preface

This collection of essays on contemporary non-European immigration to the United States is one of two volumes, the first of which deals with European immigration. The concept behind these volumes was that while there have been numerous works on American immigration, very little has been done on the period since World War II. To fill that void, some of the leading figures in their respective areas have contributed essays on recent immigration to this country from non-European nations.

Although each contributor to this volume was allowed some freedom to develop his or her essay in a unique manner, each was asked to include six primary points of reference: (1) the history of the migration, (2) motives for leaving homeland (push factors), (3) reasons for selecting the United States (pull factors), (4) initial impressions of this country (including possible "culture shock," etc.), (5) later satisfaction or dissatisfaction with life in the United States (including ease of assimilation, acculturation, and other factors), and (6) possible return migration to homeland (motives, percentages if available, etc.).

As the reader can see, not every non-European country has been included in this volume. No essayist could be found, for example, who felt competent to write on immigration to this nation from Brazil. Also, the essayist who was to write on Jewish immigration to the United States suddenly was stricken with pneumonia, and unfortunately could not fulfill his commitment; and there remained insufficient time to find a replacement. Even so, most of the non-European countries from which large numbers of immigrants to the United States have come are included in this volume.

Finally, I would like to express special appreciation to Dr.

Cecyle Neidle, editor of Twayne's "Immigrant Heritage of America Series," for her comments, suggestions, and corrections.

DENNIS LAURENCE CUDDY

I

Chinese Immigration to the United States

By Betty Lee Sung

City College of the City University of New York

In 1969, earthlings navigated space and landed on the moon—a spectacular and history-making feat. Not too many centuries ago man navigated the oceans and landed on unknown continents. The date marking the discovery of America was 1492, and the credit for that discovery was given to Christopher Columbus; but when his flagship, the *Santa Maria*, touched these shores, the "discoverers" found inhabitants already living in the newfound land. Were these people native to the land, or had they also come from distant places and settled in America?

Prehistoric Immigration

There are many theories and much evidence to support the contention that some of the people on hand to greet Columbus were descendants of adventurers or shipwrecked seamen from the ancient Celestial Empire called China. Some historians maintain that the period of earliest contact by the Chinese was three centuries before Christ.[1] In his book, *Columbus Was Chinese*, Hans Breur, professor of anthropology at California State College, Pennsylvania, cites at great length the accumulated evidence that the transpacific contact of China with the American continents reaches back to at least 1000 B.C.[2] He wrote:

The seaworthy double canoes with the Venetian blind-like sails also point to China, where similar seacraft were used. In addition, the tribes of the northwest coast excelled in an art already mastered by the inhabitants of China: they produced superb cloth from the inner bark of the cedar which they traded with their neighbors at great profit. . . . If we compare the artistic motifs, the heads and figures, stacked on each other, immediately stand out. The Chinese at the time of the Shang Dynasty (1523–1027 B.C.) decorated bones with these figures. . . .[3]

Professor Breur goes on to point out other examples: the use of copper hammered into disks to which great value was attached; the appreciation of jade; the cult of the tiger in spite of the fact that no tigers exist on the American continents; the decorative motif of the two-headed dragon that originated in China at the time of the western Chou dynasty (1027–722 B.C.); the Asiatic features of the Olmec civilization in Mexico; and many other cultural similarities. Professor Breur firmly believes that if the cultural evolution of the aboriginal peoples of the Americas had not had an infusion from carriers of a more advanced culture, they could not have attained a cultural level within a time span of two thousand years. It took at least three to four times as long for the peoples on the Nile, the Euphrates, the Tigris, and Indus to reach that level.[4]

From his research and excavations, Professor Breur found that existing connections between China and the Americas broke off several times down through the ages. The severing of these contacts generally coincided with internal strife and struggles in China. The first of these break-offs occurred during the fifth century B.C. at the time of the Wu and Yueh Kingdoms. Contact resumed around 100 A.D. only to be discontinued a scant hundred years later, near the end of the later Han dynastic period (25– 220 A.D.).[5] After that, traces of Chinese influence faded out and did not resurface until the eighteenth century A.D. By that time, European maritime achievements were well advanced, and ships plying their trade over Pacific routes invariably carried in their holds Chinese silks, tea, lacquered wares, and porcelains. These goods were highly prized and brought handsome profits in the European markets. American participation in the China trade did not take place until 1784 when the first American ship, the *Empress of China*, set sail from New York to Canton carrying its cargo of ginseng—that root herb promising rejuvenation to all who drank it.[6]

Early American Contacts

Ships plying the China trade made their ports of call on the east coast and not the west coast of the American continent, which was yet to be settled and developed. Much fanfare accompanied the arrival of the Chinese junk, *Ke Ying*, owned by an English captain but manned by a Chinese crew when it sailed into New York harbor in 1847.[7] These transients and others came and went, leaving their footprints in the sands of time. Little is recorded about their sojourns.

A few students and merchants came as well. The earliest students studied at the foreign mission at Cornwall, Connecticut, in 1818. Yung Wing, who was to lead an entourage of others like himself, first arrived at the Monson Academy in Massachusetts in 1847. He went on to graduate from Yale College in 1854. He opted for American citizenship by becoming naturalized, but he returned to China, where he greatly affected the course of Chinese history.[8] Merchants came with their wares and when these were sold, they likewise departed American shores.

Fountainhead of the Immigrant Flow

It was not until the cry of gold went up in California that the Chinese arrived in larger numbers. A trickle came in with the "Forty-niners," but the following year, five hundred hardy adventurers traversed the Pacific ocean to seek their fortunes in the "Mountain of Gold." By 1851, it was estimated that 25,000 Chinese in California were engaged in placer mining, or manual and domestic labor.[9]

Strangely, the only ones who ventured abroad to the new land at that time came from a small area in the southern province of Kwangtung near the mouth of the Pearl River. The provincial capital, Canton, was the only port in the entire empire open to foreign ships, and news of the gold rush reached there quickly. Although the *Laws and Precedents of the Ching Dynasty* stated that any person caught leaving the country illegally whether to go out to sea, to trade, to live, or farm, would have his head severed from his body by one stroke of the executioner's axe, the prospect of finding gold was a strong magnet that offered the promise of quick wealth.

Reasons for Emigration

The push factors were equally strong. China's veneer of invincibility had just been shattered by defeat in the Opium War. Hong Kong was ceded to Great Britain, and the threat of further European imperialism hung heavy over the weakened nation. The Manchu government, then in power, was decadent and corrupt. A widespread revolt called the Taiping Rebellion was led by Hung Hsiu Chuan and lasted from 1851 to 1864. Estimates of lives lost ran as high as 20,000,000.[10] The country was ravaged and devastated. The revolt was finally put down by government forces with the aid of foreign powers, who had vested interests in seeing a weak emperor on the imperial throne.

Moreover, Kwangtung Province suffered internal strife between the Puntis (native people) and the Hakkas (guest people). The Hakkas from the north had attempted to push onto and settle on the coastal lands, but they were repelled and decimated by the Puntis. The fratricide lasted for two years between 1854 and 1856 and left more than 150,000 dead.[11] Thus bloodied and impoverished by war and rebellions, the discontented and more adventuresome looked beyond the oceans to a land that promised gold for what they thought was easy picking.

The Chinese Pioneers

The first immigrants were able-bodied males whose aim was to earn money to take back to China. Mostly small farmers, fishermen, and tradesmen, they came as "coolies." Coolie literally means bitter strength, and these newcomers brought no assets other than the strength of their bodies. At first they worked as gold miners, but they reverted to their former occupations as soon as the surface gold began to peter out. By the 1880s, 75 percent of all farmhands in California were Chinese. As fishermen, they brought up large hauls of fish, shrimp, and other seafood from San Francisco Bay to feed the hordes swarming to the West.

Having journeyed 7,000 miles across the Pacific to escape hard poverty, the Chinese were willing to work at jobs the whites scorned, and they were willing to work for less. As a result, they came to be associated with cheap labor. They took jobs building the first ships and homes in California. They made shoes and fabrics, dug mines, and drained ditches. During those gold rush days, there was hardly an industry in San Francisco in which they were not found in significant numbers.[12]

"When California was admitted as the thirty-first state to the Union in 1850, the Chinese took a prominent part in the ceremonies and the parade. The *Alta California*, a San Francisco newspaper said: "The China Boys will yet vote at the same polls, study at the same schools, and bow at the same altar as our countrymen." Governor McDougal recommended in 1852 a system of land grants to induce the further immigration and settlement of the Chinese whom he called, 'one of the most worthy of our newly adopted citizens.' "[13]

Work on Transcontinental Railroad

The year 1861 saw the United States embroiled in a civil war between North and South. The East and West were also separated by thousands of miles of unexplored territories. The continent threatened to break into sectional and factional interests under European spheres of influence. To bind this sprawling land mass into a single nation, Congress passed legislation in 1862 authorizing the building of a transcontinental railroad that would extend from coast to coast.[14]

The railroad was to be completed in fourteen years. At the end of the first year, only 56 miles of track had been laid. In the East, the men were engaged in war. In the West, labor was nowhere to be found. When the idea was first broached about using Chinese labor, the construction bosses were skeptical, but this skepticism was quickly dispelled. Eventually, the Chinese were to form the main labor force on the Western portion of the railroad, and by their labor, they were able to complete the transcontinental railroad in record time—seven years instead of fourteen—all done by backbreaking manual labor. The completion of the transcontinental railroad was called the engineering feat of the nineteenth century, and the record of miles of track laid in one day has yet to be surpassed, even with today's modern road-building machinery.[15] In testimony before Congress, Oscar Garrison Villard said:

I want to remind you of the things that Chinese labor did for us in opening up the western portion of this country. I am a son of the man who drove the first transcontinental railroad across the American Northwest, the first rail link from Minnesota to Oregon and the waters of the Puget Sound. I was near him when he drove the last spike and paid an eloquent tribute to the men who had built that railroad by their manual labor for there were no road-making machines in those days.

He never forgot and never failed to praise the Chinese among them of whom nearly 10,000 stormed the forest fastnesses, endured cold and heat and the risk of death at the hands of the hostile Indians to aid in the opening up of our great northwestern empire.

I have a dispatch from the chief engineer of the Northwestern Pacific, telling how the Chinese laborers went out into eight feet of snow with the temperature far below zero to carry on the work when no American dared face the conditions.[16]

The Chinese Must Go

The immediate aftermath of the completion of the railroad brought not prosperity but a depression. "Go West, young man, go West" was the slogan of the day, and eastern settlers poured into the West riding the rails put down by the Chinese. The latecomers came with the expectation of making it rich quick, and they were disappointed when the market became flooded with temporary surplus labor. Work was to be had, but not the kind of work they expected. In their frustrations, they found a convenient scapegoat in the Chinese whom they blamed for taking jobs away from whites. The Chinese were harassed and persecuted. They became the target of angry mobs aroused by the demagoguery of labor organizer Dennis Kearney. Many were murdered, lynched, put on ships for China, or hauled out to the wilderness to perish. To prevent more Chinese from entering the country, the first Chinese Exclusion Act was passed in 1882, thereby closing the gates to the Chinese four years before the Statue of Liberty proclaimed this land a haven for the poor and oppressed yearning to be free. During the next sixty-one years, Congress passed thirteen other laws that virtually sealed the doors against Chinese immigration. The number of immigrants dropped from 40,000 in 1882 to only ten persons five years later. For many years, the Chinese population in the United States—bolstered largely by illegal entrants—hovered around 60,000 to 80,000, a number that would fit comfortably in a modern football stadium like Miami's Orange Bowl.

Persecution

During this time, the Chinese were also taxed out, driven out, or kept out of many jobs. When the purge ended, they had nothing to do except what the whites did not want to do. These jobs were washing and ironing, cooking and serving food, and waiting on masters and mistresses—the kind of jobs that were labeled "women's work." Thus the Chinese were occupationally emasculated. They survived largely by operating restaurants and laundries.

Moreover, during exclusion, Chinese immigrants were not permitted to become citizens no matter how long they had lived here. They were forbidden by the Alien Land Act to own land, and many states also denied them the right to intermarry. Huddled together in Chinatowns, the immigrants had little incentive to adopt American ways. Those already in this country were afraid to leave because they might not be permitted to return, yet they could not send for their wives or children to join them. So the immigrants looked upon their stay in the United States only as a temporary interlude. They worked hard and saved their money, hoping only for the day when they could accumulate enough to go back to China.

A Trickle Allowed to Enter

World War II found the United States and China fighting a common enemy, and public opinion became more favorably disposed toward the Chinese. At the same time, it became indefensible for the United States government to discriminate against an ally-in-arms. In 1943, a gesture was made by repeal of the exclusion acts, but repeal meant little more than abolishing the offensive language of the laws saying in effect, "No Chinese admitted." A token quota of 105 per year was assigned to all Chinese wherever they may have come from or whatever nationality they may have held as long as they were Chinese. This was tantamount to exclusion and was so intended. The repeal act, however, did grant those Chinese already in the United States the right to become citizens. Thus, after almost a century of history in the United States, the Chinese finally gained the right to belong and to take their rightful place as citizens.

During the period of exclusion, and the two decades following in which 105 were admitted per year, it was a wonder that there were any Chinese at all in the United States. To preserve themselves against extinction, the Chinese resorted to inconspicuous circumvention of the immigration laws. To gain entry into this country meant better economic opportunity, but the venture was also a risky one. As a result, only men emigrated, leaving their wives and children behind. It was not until the War Brides Act of 1946 that Chinese women began to appear in any numbers on the American scene. This act permitted men who had served in the armed forces to bring their wives and children into the country outside of the quota. Following the passage of this act, from 1946 to the present, a large majority of Chinese immigrants have been female. (See Graph A and Table 1.)

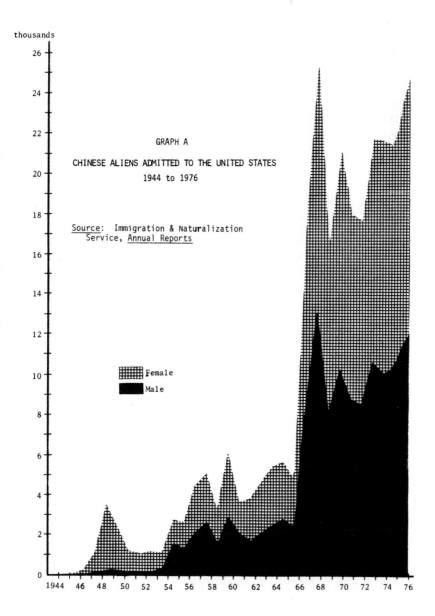

thousands

GRAPH A

CHINESE ALIENS ADMITTED TO THE UNITED STATES
1944 to 1976

Source: Immigration & Naturalization
Service, Annual Reports

Female
Male

Table 1

CHINESE IMMIGRANT ALIENS BY SEX, 1965-1977

Year	Male No.	%	Female No.	%	Annual Total
1965	2,242	47	2,527	53	4,769
1966	8,613	49	8,995	51	17,608
1967	12,811	51	12,285	49	25,096
1968	7,862	48	8,572	52	16,434
1969	10,001	48	10,892	52	20,893
1970	8,586	48	9,370	52	17,956
1971	8,287	47	9,335	53	17,622
1972	10,437	48	11,293	52	21,730
1973	9,937	46	11,719	54	21,656
1974	10,724	47	11,961	53	22,685
1975	11,179	48	12,248	52	23,427
1976	11,819	48	12,770	52	24,589
1977	12,176	48	13,220	52	25,396

Note: Figures reflect immigration from China (including Taiwan) and Hong Kong.

Source: Immigration and Naturalization Service, *Annual Reports* (Washington, D. C.: 1965–1977), table 9.

Repercussions of Sino-American Relations

In 1949, the government in China changed hands from Nationalist control to Communist control. Chiang Kai-shek fled to Taiwan and set himself up as head of the Republic of China. Mao Tse Tung firmly established his control over the Mainland and proceeded to root out vestiges of the old to establish a more equalitarian society. Since most of the families with members overseas in the United States lived in a very tiny region near Canton and were far removed from Peking, the Communist authorities had mistaken ideas about them. Because these families had continuously received remittances from the United States and because they had purchased land in China with their hard-earned money, they were looked upon as members of the bourgeois or landowners class. Their lands were confiscated, and they were persecuted. At that time the United States, China's arch enemy because of its support of Taiwan, sent the Seventh Fleet to blockade the Chinese coastal waters, took the lead in opposing China's admission to the United Nations, and refused to recognize Mao as the legitimate government of China.

Families with members overseas in the United States suffered on this score. They came under suspicion as counterrevolutionaries. They were afraid to write to their relatives in the United States, and relatives were afraid to send money to their families in China. With their ancestral homes and land confiscated and their remittances cut off, the families found themselves in a terrible predicament. The Chinese in the United States who had made it a practice to return to China for periodic visits were afraid to do so. Even those who were willing to go back and who had special skills were forbidden by the United States to return. At the same time, the Chinese government forbade anyone within its borders to emigrate. This was a period of great anguish and emotional stress for the Chinese in the United States and their severed families in China.

Some in China managed to cross the border into Kowloon or Hong Kong, and a number of refugee relief measures enacted by Congress in 1953, 1957, and 1959, opened American doors to somewhat less than 5,000 Chinese above the 105 annual quota. In May, 1962, in a puzzling anomaly of Chinese Communist behavior, 60,000 refugees were permitted to swarm across the Kwangtung borders into Hong Kong. This tiny British-held colony, already swollen with more than three and a half million persons, quickly strung up barbed wire, rounded up as many refugees as they could find, and sent them back to the Mainland. An uproar rose from an incensed American public, and President John F. Kennedy immediately invoked the provisions of existing legislation to permit the entry of additional refugees. From June, 1962, until the end of 1965, while the executive order remained in effect, over 15,000 refugees were paroled into the United States.[17]

Stranded Students and Political Refugees

Another group also found themselves stranded in the United States. These were elite students selected for study abroad in anticipation that their knowledge and skills would be needed in the postwar reconstruction. Thousands of these students had been sent from China after 1945 and either were unwilling to go home to a country embroiled in civil war or were not permitted to return to China by the United States government after the outbreak of the Korean War in 1950. At first, these students experienced terrible hardships. Their funds from China were cut off, but as students they were not permitted to seek employment. The American labor market, accustomed to seeing the Chinese only as laundrymen, restaurateurs, or domestics, could not accept the fact that Chinese could also be engineers, scientists, doctors, or other professionals. Employers, at first, were reluctant to hire this elite corps of intellectuals. Gradually, by dint of hard work and outstanding performance, these professionally trained individuals were able to prove themselves and to make substantial contributions in every field of human endeavor. As a highly educated group with origins in diverse geographic regions of China, these former students brought a diversity to the more homogeneous Chinese population, who were primarily from the Canton region.

The refugee group also added a new dimension to the Chinese population in the United States. Some of these refugees were former government officials or military men who sought political asylum. Some were businessmen, or of the monied class, who had somehow managed to escape. Although they had to start life anew, their backgrounds enabled them to pick up the pieces of their shattered lives within a short period of time.

The arrival of women and children brought balance and stability to the Chinese population. World War II had lowered the barriers of discrimination against the Chinese in employment and housing, and the Civil Rights movement gave further impetus to the process. Chinese families began buying homes and moving into the professions. Chinese children born in the

United States spoke only English and insisted that they were as American as their next-door neighbors. The trickle of newcomers was readily absorbed into the Chinese communities either through relatives or friends. But the continued separation of family members, some in China and some in the United States, remained unresolved until 1965 due to the stringency of the 105 annual quota.

Impact of 1965 Immigration Act

In October, 1965, the entire body of American immigration laws was overhauled. The national-origins quotas were abolished and immigrants from any one country were permitted entry up to a maximum of 20,000 on the basis of a six-point preference system, first come, first served. The Chinese quota, already "mortgaged" beyond the year 2000 under the former system, was immediately and fully utilized. Chinese immigrants increased more than fivefold, and in every year since then, Chinese immigration has remained at almost the maximum permitted under the law.

The sudden spurt in immigration has made a tremendous impact upon the Chinese communities in the United States. In 1960, the Chinese population was a mere 237,000 for the entire country. By 1970, this number had nearly doubled to 435,000.[18] The 1980 census figure undoubtedly will double again to exceed 900,000. This figure is a projection not only of immigrants originating from Hong Kong, Taiwan, or Mainland China, but it also includes ethnic Chinese from other parts of the world such as Indonesia, Brazil, Cuba, Panama, and most importantly Vietnam where the recent refugees have been largely persons of Chinese background. Although they may have come in as emigrants from their country of origin, they identify as Chinese ethnics when they arrive in this country.

As a reflection of the preference system of the 1965 Immigration Act, more of the new immigrants are from the professional occupational category. Lately, businessmen are increasing in numbers. (See Table 2.) By and large, however,

Table 2

IMMIGRANTS FROM CHINA AND HONG KONG AS REGION OF BIRTH, BY MAJOR OCCUPATION GROUP, 1970-1976

Major Occupation Group	1970	1971	1972	1973	1974	1975	1976	1977
Professional, Technical	3,924	4,292	4,263	2,952	2,796	2,915	2,835	3,672
Managers, Office Proprietors	580	482	718	1,042	1,273	1,535	1,573	1,939
Sales	155	155	217	204	243	250	323	354
Clerical	700	647	863	828	1,005	1,137	1,161	1,398
Craftsmen	347	361	480	467	465	541	530	503
Operatives	619	672	1,065	967	743	822	1,029	1,145
Service Workers	1,027	1,189	1,578	1,572	1,571	1,414	1,131	1,239
Farmers	16	16	22	13	324	156	329	174
Laborers	179	57	151	242	319	631	633	504
Wives, Children, No Occup.	10,168	9,617	12,139	13,223	13,704	13,899	14,970	14,548
TOTAL ADMITTED	17,961	17,622	21,730	21,656	22,685	23,427	24,589	25,396

Source: Immigration and Naturalization Service, *Annual Reports* (Washington, D.C.: 1970–1976), table 8.

Table 3

CITY OF INTENDED RESIDENCE OF CHINESE IMMIGRANTS, 1970-1977

Cities	1970	1971	1972	1973	1974	1975	1976	1977
San Francisco-Oakland	1,845	968	1,696	1,683	1,637	2,722	3,305	3,144
New York City-New Jersey	2,776	3,263	4,839	4,738	5,321	7,384	6,510	4,866
Honolulu	385	242	334	410	362	659	722	662
Los Angeles-Long Beach	743	802	930	914	1,286	1,406	1,210	1,534
Chicago	367	402	661	432	391	500	683	490
Boston-Cambridge	206	223	241	244	262	278	326	266
Sacramento	163	107	146	146	126	177	244	232
Washington, D.C.-Md.-Va.	609	583	873	958	1,038	1,077	666	167
San José	64	44	62	91	102	178	245	277
Seattle	158	150	199	198	210	338	376	361
Philadelphia	99	135	184	168	148	175	221	119
Houston	184	106	177	212	157	192	306	352
Total All Cities Above	7,599	7,025	10,342	10,194	11,040	15,086	14,814	12,470
Percent of Total U.S. Chinese Immigrants	54%	54%	60%	59%	61%	64%	60%	49%

Source: Immigration and Naturalization Service, *Annual Reports* (Washington, D. C.: 1970–1977) table 12A.

family reunification dominates the Chinese immigration pattern. If the wives and children had already joined their menfolk in this country, the families began to send for their parents and brothers and sisters. The skewed demographic profile of the past gradually became more normal in terms of sex, age, occupation, education, income, and social class.

Shifting Demographic Patterns

The destination of Chinese immigrants has also shifted from the West Coast and Pacific Islands to the East Coast and primarily to New York City. Former centers of Chinese population like San Francisco and Honolulu are getting many fewer immigrants than New York City. (See Table 3.) This shift and rapid influx have brought with them attendant problems. Immigrants tend to go where they will find others like themselves—which means in and around Chinatowns that prior to 1943 were heading for decline. Since the change in immigration law, the boundaries of all United States Chinatowns have expanded considerably, causing intense congestion and an acute demand for housing in the immediate areas. And Chinatowns have always been found in the inner core of urban centers, which are generally slum areas.

In New York City, Chinatown is located on the Lower East Side, which has seen wave after wave of immigrants come and go. The newest waves are the Chinese and the Puerto Ricans. In 1970, 64 percent of the Chinese in New York were foreign-born immigrants compared to California's 47 percent and Hawaii's 11 percent.[19] By 1980, New York's Chinese population may well be three fourths foreign-born, and the national total of foreign-born will rise dramatically as well, since immigration will be the overwhelming contributor to any population increase among the Chinese in the United States.[20] Thus, in spite of a history of more than 130 years in the United States, the Chinese are very much a first-generation group.

The immediate concerns of the immigrants, of course, are a place to live and a livelihood. Outright segregation and restrictive covenants no longer force the Chinese into ghettos, but the population distribution pattern still shows an extremely high concentration in urban centers of five states: California, New York, Hawaii, Massachusetts, and Illinois. In 1970, three out of every four Chinese in the United States were found in these five states. And within these states, the cities with the most Chinese are New York, San Francisco, Honolulu, Los Angeles, Boston, Chicago, and Sacramento. And within these cities, the Chinese tend to congregate in Chinatowns, so that they are highly visible in a few cities and nonexistent in most parts of the country.

Chinatowns

As mentioned previously, Chinatowns tend to be in the older sections of the core cities where the housing stock is old and dilapidated. But this does not deter the Chinese from crowding into the area, pushing the cost of housing sky-high. To add to the congestion, tourists come into the community by the busloads. Nonresident Chinese come from a wide radius in the surrounding areas. Although they do not live in the community, they shop, work, and socialize there. The overcrowding has led to a host of other problems such as lowered resistance to disease, increased stress and belligerency, unsanitary conditions, and even a lower birthrate.

At one time, Chinatowns were isolated, segregated, and self-contained communities. The larger society was hostile to their presence and sought to set them apart in ghettos. Since the testimony of Chinese persons was not accepted in courts, and since they could not exercise any political rights as citizens, they set up their own organizations and institutions to govern themselves. The organizations were formed along the lines of kinship or place of origin, and they provided mutual help and essential services in times of need. Since the number of Chinese in the United States was small, these simple organizations adequately served their purpose.

Problems of Adjustment

Since 1965, the huge influx of immigrants has overtaxed the

capacity of the traditional organizations. Set up to meet the needs of a group in a bygone era, the old institutions could not cope with the demands of a changed and changing situation. The young no longer want to submit to the traditional leadership of their elders. Old-timers with vested interests do not want to relinquish their privileges and their power. The Chinese communities are now in the throes of dynamic change. The organizations are undergoing reformation, and no doubt they will reemerge as more vital institutions. Meanwhile, the social service needs of this group are urgent and vital. By far, the most urgent of these is special help to overcome the language barrier. Adult English language classes, bilingual education, intensive language training, survival English classes or English as a second language are all programs that could help alleviate this problem.

The needs and life styles of an immigrant group are very much different from that of a native-born group. The language barrier poses an immediate and mammoth communication problem. Chinese is more difficult to bridge for the reason that the script is an ideographic one wholly different from the alphabetic one commonly found in Western scripts. The cultural chasm between Oriental and Occidental is much wider than that between Europeans and Americans. Culture is more than food and customs and festivals; it is fundamental attitudes and a way of thinking. It means deeply imbedded values. When cultural values conflict, dilemmas are created demanding painful decisions between what is already inculcated and what may be more expedient and rewarding in American society.

In spite of the fact that many of the new immigrants are skilled and educated persons, they must start all over again occupationally or economically. For many, their skills are non-transferrable. Professionals cannot practice in this country either because of the language handicap or because they do not have citizenship. Businessmen must establish their credit and rebuild their network of contacts. They must become familiar with American regulations and methods of doing business. Farmers are not likely to grow rice here. Midwives will find no demand for their services. Jobs formerly held in Hong Kong, Taiwan, or China cannot be practiced here; yet a livelihood and some means of subsistence are priority needs.

Most Chinese immigrants either find employment in restaurant work or garment factory work.[21] The men gravitate to jobs such as chef, waiter, bartender, dishwasher, restaurant manager, bookkeeper, and the like. The women go immediately into the hundreds of garment factories that dot the periphery of Chinatowns. These factories employ the women as seamstresses who are paid on a piecework basis. The rates run around 25 cents for a completed skirt, 80 cents for a completed dress, and $3.50 for a coat. The women work against the clock, and they put in long hard hours. Restaurant hours are even longer. As a result, parental presence and supervision is conspicuously absent from immigrant Chinese homes. In addition to suffering the absence of parents, the children are also confronted with cultural shock, language problems, and the demands of school work. It is therefore not surprising that juvenile delinquency, once unknown in the Chinese communities, now makes regular and sensational headlines.

Changing Cultural Patterns

Not only do occupations become outmoded, cultural values do too. Duty and obligation to the family become albatrosses rather than sources of comfort and security. A large family becomes an economic burden. Humility is a drawback rather than a virtue. In their insecurity, money becomes the ultimate pursuit.

Customs, traditions, and festivities are the cement that binds a group together. By sharing common beliefs and ways of doing things, by observing special occasions that evoke sentiment and emotions, by performing certain rituals, a people gain a sense of belonging and identity. The Chinese, more so than other groups, tend to hold on more steadfastly to their culture. But under the relentless pressure of time and the outward need to conform, the immigrants soon start to cast off their own ways, but never can completely embrace the new. Hence in many ways, they are marginal people.

Readjustment of Status and Roles

It is inevitable that the life style of Chinese immigrants must change in response to the conditions of life in the United States. When the parents are struggling to gain an economic toehold under alien ways they do not know how to cope with, they are under stress and strain. Their working hours are long and their working conditions far from desirable. Indubitably they have had to take lower-rung jobs from the ones they had in the home country.[22] The father who was respected by and responsible for his family now feels that he has lost status because the mother now also works outside of the home. Since her working hours are also long, much of the domestic work within the home must be shared, so that the traditional concept of masculine and feminine roles are altered. This process is also ongoing in many American homes, but the change does involve a more drastic realignment and readjustment of status and roles for the Chinese immigrants, because the males were more dominant and the females more submissive than is the custom in America.

The parent/child roles become altered when the parents come to lean more and more upon the offspring in their daily dealings with American society, primarily because the children overcome the language barrier more quickly and become more acculturated. When the child is called upon to lead and the parents to follow, the reversal of roles creates an upheaval that is difficult for both sides concerned. These are but a few of the myraid adjustments that immigrants must constantly make in their transplantation from China to the United States.

American Attitude Toward the Chinese

The American image of and receptivity toward the Chinese in this country generally tie in with economic conditions at the time or with international relations between China and the United States. Historically, it has been shown how the Chinese were first welcomed to help in the early development of the West and then driven out when their task was done. Pro-

Chinese sentiments resumed when the United States and China were allies during World War II; but public sentiment turned negative with the outbreak of the Korean War, and lingered with the Vietnam War. During the thirty years from 1949 to 1979, when there were no diplomatic ties between the two countries, Chinese-Americans had to continually assert that they were non-Communists and to proclaim this fact loudly so that they would not be suspected of being Communist agents. Those Chinese with relatives in China were denied jobs in the government or in any defense-related industry for fear that such an employee could be compromised by threats against his or her relatives. If any Chinese with any important technical or scientific skills had wanted to go back to China, he or she was forbidden to do so under the Internal Security Act of 1950.

The attitude of Americans toward the Chinese has always been ambivalent. On the one hand, the Chinese have been respected for their industry, their honesty, their intelligence, and other positive traits, but at the same time they were feared as economic competitors. Until recently, the Chinese have had one of the best law-abiding records of any minority group, but media stereotypes of the Chinese in the evil Fu Manchu image are common. Employers would love to hire Chinese because they are steady, reliable, and competent. As long as they are content to do the work and remain in the job for which they were hired, they are regarded with respect and affection. Once they start aspiring to upward mobility, however, racist attitudes set in. Although an unusually large proportion—almost a third of all Chinese males in 1970—are in the professions,[23] they are not as well situated as they seem to be. A closer look reveals that, by and large, they are or have remained at the entry level.

Hidden Discrimination

Nowadays, cases of overt discrimination against the Chinese are rare. In fact, the blatant practices of the past are illegal, outlawed by the Civil Rights Act, the Equal Employment Opportunity Act, and Affirmative Action measures. The Chinese suffer most because they are excluded from the special legislation enacted to aid minorities—or they are ignored altogether.

For example, in the early days of civil rights legislation, the term "minorities" was equated with the disadvantaged; and enforcement agencies interpreted minorities to mean black, Puerto Rican, Chicano, or American Indian. The presumption was that the Chinese, being law-abiding, highly educated, and upwardly mobile, were not disadvantaged and had no prolems. At that time, annual Chinese immigration was inconsequential, and the small numbers were readily absorbed into the community. In fact, the total Chinese population was so tiny as to be almost invisible and could be easily ignored. In essence, the Chinese at first were not beneficiaries of the special legislation enacted to help minorities. However, they were at an inherent and decided disadvantage when it came to competing with whites. And if employers had to fill minority quotas or goals, the Chinese found themselves squeezed out at both ends.

In federal legislation, the term "minority" eventually came to encompass Asians or Orientals, but the legislation of the various states is not uniform on this score. The universities in California do not want to consider Asians as minorities in their admission policies. Rulings by the courts in the state of New York say that Asians do not need special dispensations as minorities in construction-related jobs. Yet the total number of Asians in the entire building trades in the New York region for the year 1972 totaled only 229 men.[24]

Although the Chinese initiated and fought for bilingual education in the landmark decision of *Lau* v. *Nichols*, bilingual education classes for the Chinese in New York City were not instituted until the late 1970s, and they are still token concessions compared to bilingual education programs for other non-English-speaking groups. In 1979, the Small Business Administration wanted to exclude the Chinese from consideration under the Minority Business Enterprise provisions. It took a long, hard fight to reverse this decision.[25]

Being ignored or left out is almost as bad as being discriminated against. For example, most governmental statistics provide no data at all on the Chinese or other Asian groups. Until 1970, the census provided socioeconomic statistics for only three racial categories: black, white, and other. Hispanics were eventually added as a distinct group, but the 1980 census will provide more detailed information on the Asian groups. The Current Population Survey, the Bureau of Labor Statistics reports, health records, crime figures—none of these important statistical sources provide information on the Chinese. Consequently, when programs are to be funded or when decisions have to be made, information about the Chinese is unavailable.

The last two decades have seen drastic changes come about on the Chinese-American scene. The population has increased manyfold. The new immigrants are quite different from the ones that came before. The newcomers are more heterogeneous and lend balance and diversity to the ethnic group. They find themselves in a social climate that is more tolerant of other races and peoples. Although the Chinese tend to congregate in urban centers and specifically in and near Chinatowns, more and more are dispersing or forming satellite Chinatowns. The rapid influx has created problems, but these were inevitable. Given the proper and necessary transitional help, these prolems can be and should be alleviated. The difficulty at present is that the Chinese are generally overlooked and ignored.

A Look into the Future

In another five to ten years, the native-born children of this new immigrant wave of the 1960s and 1970s will come on the scene. Their outlook and their perspective will be entirely different from that of their parents, and the Chinese-American communities will again change direction. For the time being, immigrants continue to stream into the United States. With the normalization of relations, exit visas out of China have been easier to obtain, and immigration from the Mainland will no doubt increase. Taiwan, shorn of United States recognition and fearful of a Communist takeover, is allowing an ever-increasing number of people to go abroad. Usually the ones who get out of Taiwan are those with the resources to do so.

Perhaps the most spectacular increase in Chinese population in the United States will come from the "boat people," the ethnic Chinese driven out of Vietnam. Until June, 1979, the United States had committed itself to admitting 7,000 of these refugees per month. This number was doubled by President Carter when other countries refused permission for these people to go ashore. For example, countries like Malaysia towed the boats out to sea and abandoned the people to their fate. President Carter's humane act will enable them to start a new life in the United States. These boat people were ousted precisely because they were ethnic Chinese; and since they have suffered persecution from the Vietnamese, they will undoubtedly identify with the Chinese communities when they arrive. If so, they will swell the Chinese population dramatically. In addition to the usual problems experienced by immigrants in their transition, these refugees will have the nightmare and trauma of their banishment. Unless forethought and planning go into their reception and transition, their sheer numbers will spawn difficulties.

Reverse Migration a Possibility

To people the world over, America still symbolizes the land of opportunity. Chinese immigrants who have managed to get here consider themselves lucky beyond measure. They endure their hardships with patience and stoicism because they are happy to be here. They apply for American citizenship as quickly as possible, and they are grateful to the land that offers them haven and opportunity. But in the recesses of their hearts, there remains a warm sentiment for the land of their forefathers.

China, in its establishment of diplomatic relations with the United States, has now opened her doors wider to her former sons and daughters; and she is even anxious to call upon them for help in her industrial development. China needs the talent, the skills, the expertise, and the dedication that many Chinese in the United States can offer. There is a rich reservoir of human resources here, and the most important factor is that these people already possess the language facility and cultural affinity. China has put out feelers to tap this reservoir. In a drive to recruit teachers of English, the government placed an advertisement in the Chinese-American press; the remuneration offered was one hundred yen per month, which is equivalent to $65. In no way does such a paltry sum compare with salaries in the United States. Yet, for 100 positions available, 700 persons of Chinese ancestry responded.[26] Of course, most of these people do not want to go back to China permanently, but they are willing to do so for a short period of time. This is not to suggest that there will be any large-scale reverse migration in the near future, but this is a possibility if economic opportunities improve in China.

Future Chinese Emigration

In any mass movement of peoples across international boundaries, the push factors tend to be stronger than the pull factors. Economic opportunity may be a powerful lure, but war and disaster are the prime uprooters of people, and China has had ample doses of both in the past century. Under the new leadership in China, peace has been restored. Diplomatic relations have been established with the world community of nations. The new government in China is more receptive to an ideology different from its own, and it is reaching out and offering its hand in friendship and goodwill. Ambitious plans are under way to move the country ahead economically. These conditions are conducive to people staying within their own borders, because when they are content and satisfied, there is little incentive to go elsewhere.

NOTES

1. Betty J. Meggers and Clifford Evans, "A Transpacific Contact in 3000 B.C.," *Scientific American,* January, 1966; and Douglas S.

Watson, "Did the Chinese Discover America?" *California Historical Society Quarterly* 14, no. 1 (March, 1935).

2. New York: McGraw Hill, 1972.

3. Ibid., p. 270.

4. Ibid., p. 272.

5. Ibid., pp. 274–75.

6. T. W. Chinn, H. M. Lai, and P. P. Choy, *A History of the Chinese in California* (San Francisco: Chinese Historical Society, 1969), pp. 8–10.

7. H. M. Chapin, "The Chinese Junk at Providence," *Rhode Island Historical Society* 27, no. 1 (January, 1934).

8. Thomas Edward LaFargue, *China's First One Hundred* (Pullman: State College of Washington, 1942) and H. Mark Lai and Philip P. Choy, *Outlines: History of the Chinese in America* (San Francisco: Chinese American Studies Planning Group, 1973), p. 24.

9. Mary Coolidge, *Chinese Immigration* (New York: Henry Holt, 1909), p. 17.

10. Lai, p. 35.

11. Ibid., p. 36.

12. Betty Lee Sung and Gloria Stevenson, "New Directions for Chinatown," *Worklife,* March, 1976, pp. 2–8.

13. Betty Lee Sung, *Story of the Chinese in America* (New York: Colliers, 1971), pp. 27.

14. Ibid., p. 30.

15. Oscar Lewis, *The Big Four* (New York: Alfred Knopf, 1938), pp. 74–75.

16. O. G. Villard, "Justice for the Chinese," *Christian Century* 60 (May 26, 1943): 633–34.

17. Sung, *Story of the Chinese in America,* pp. 92–33.

18. Betty Lee Sung, *Statistical Profiles of the Chinese in the United States, 1970 Census* (New York: Arno Press, 1979).

19. Betty Lee Sung, *A Survey of Chinese American Manpower and Employment* (New York: Praeger, 1976) p. 21.

20. Surprisingly, the birthrate among the Chinese drops precipitously when they arrive at these shores. See Betty Lee Sung, *Transplanted Chinese Children, A Report to the Administration for Children, Youth and Family,* Department of Health, Education, and Welfare. (New York: Department of Asian Studies, City College of New York, 1979), p. 15.

21. Ibid., p. 20.

22. Ibid., p. 150.

23. Betty Lee Sung, *Survey of Chinese American Manpower and Employment,* p. 71–76.

24. Ibid., p 128.

25. *East/West: The Chinese American Journal* (San Francisco), May 30, 1979, p. 1.

26. Correspondence with a personal friend who answered the advertisement and went to China to accept a position as an English teacher.

II

Filipino, Korean, and Vietnamese Immigration to the United States

By H. Brett Melendy
San José State University

Any history of the immigration of Filipinos, Koreans, and Vietnamese to the United States after World War II must focus upon the late 1960s and 1970s. While there were some arrivals from Korea and the Philippines, and a lesser number from Southeast Asia between 1946 and 1965, it was the 1965 immigration legislation, as demonstrated in Table 1, which made possible such a rapid increase in the number of these Asian immigrants for the twelve years from 1965 to 1976.[1] At different times in the twentieth century, the Philippines, Korea, Vietnam, Cambodia, and Laos have all been involved in the Asian foreign policy of the United States and its wars in the Far East. The resulting changes caused by American involvement in the internal affairs of these countries stimulated emigration.

Table 1

IMMIGRANTS ADMITTED TO THE UNITED STATES, 1965-1976[a]

Year	Filipinos	Koreans	Vietnamese
1965	3,130	2,165	226
1966	6,093	2,492	275
1967	10,865	3,956	490
1968	16,731	3,811	590

1969	20,744	6,045	983
1970	31,203	9,314	1,450
1971	28,471	14,297	2,038
1972	29,376	18,876	3,412
1973	30,799	22,930	4,569
1974	32,857	28,028	3,192
1975	31,751	28,362	3,030
1976	37,281	30,803	3,048

aU. S. Dept. of Justice, Immigration and Naturalization Service, *Annual Reports, 1975*, pp. 6 and 65; *1976*, p. 89.

The 1975 report of the United States Immigration and Naturalization Service, summarized in Table 2 best shows the increase of immigrants from these three Asian countries and compares this influx with other areas of the world. When measured against other nations, only Mexico sent more immigrants annually to the United States than did the Philippines during the 1970s. Korea followed the Philippines as the next nation in the number of annual arrivals.

Table 2

IMMIGRANTS BY COUNTRY OR CONTINENT OF BIRTH, 1965 and 1975[a]

Country or Continent	1965	1975	Percentage of Change
Europe	113,424	73,996	−34.8
Asia	20,683	132,469	+540.5
Korea	2,165	28,362	+1210.0
Philippines	3,130	31,751	+914.4
Vietnam	226	3,039	+1244.7
North America	126,729	146,668	+15.7
Mexico	37,969	62,205	+63.8
South America	30,962	22,984	−25.8
Africa	3,383	6,729	+98.9
All Countries	296,697	386,194	+30.2

[a] U.S. Dept. of Justice, Immigration and Naturalization Service, *Annual Report*, 1975, p. 6.

One striking fact about Tables 1 and 2 is the bureaucratic lack of reference by the Immigration and Naturalization Service to refugees who fled from the wars of Southeast Asia, for these were not admitted under the provisions of existing immigration law. Between April, 1975, and March, 1977, almost 145,000 Indochinese refugees from Cambodia, Laos, and South Vietnam, not included in immigration statistics, settled in the United States. In the next few months following March, 1977, the United States admitted from 300 to 500 "boat cases" a month.[2]

Immigration from the Philippines to the United States first started in 1903. This initial influx, which lasted until World War II, consisted of students, most of whom returned to the Far Eastern islands. The second wave of Filipino immigrants, from 1907 until the 1930s, mostly Ilocanos from the island of Luzon, provided cheap labor for Hawaii and Pacific Coast states. In 1934, a United States statute virtually stopped all migration from the Philippines. The third, and largest, influx occurred after President Lyndon B. Johnson signed the 1965 immigration law, ending the national origins system.[3]

Korean immigrants first arrived in 1903 in Hawaii. This first wave, from 1903 through 1905, totaled only 7,226 because Korean immigration was involved closely with international affairs.[4] Japan, following the 1904 Russo-Japanese War, declared Korea a protectorate and closed the Korean Department of Immigration in November, 1905. The United States, recognizing Japan's imperial claim, considered Koreans as Japanese for immigration purposes. The Gentlemen's Agreement of 1907 thus applied to Koreans as well as Japanese and effectively curtailed most immigration. After 1907, a few Korean picture brides arrived in Hawaii and the West Coast, and some Korean political activists fled from Japanese imprisonment. The 1940 census recorded about 9,600 Koreans in the United States of whom 78 percent lived in Hawaii; in 1960 the census bureau reported that there were about 14,200 foreign-born Koreans living in the United States—there was no record of Korean-Americans.[5] The significance of the 1965 immigration law for Koreans is dramatically demonstrated by the 1970 census finding that their numbers had increased to more than 68,200.[6]

Increased Indochinese emigration, mostly Vietnamese, and some Cambodians and Laotians, resulted from the Vietnam War. Indochinese had been immigrating regularly to the United States since third-world quotas had been allocated in the 1950s. As Table 1 shows, the number of Vietnamese arrivals under the aegis of the immigration service had remained small even after 1965. But following the United States' decision to withdraw from South Vietnam in the 1970s, the number of immigrants increased rapidly. At the time of the confused and sudden mass evacuation in 1975, an estimated 30,000 South Vietnamese already lived in the United States, some of whom were Vietnamese war brides who had followed their American husbands to the United States.[7] During and following the Korean War era, the arrival of Korean war brides similarly added to the number of Koreans in the United States.

As Saigon fell in April, 1975, President Gerald Ford created the Interagency Task Force on Indochina Refugees which established reception centers at Guam and Wake Island. By June 30, 1975, over 106,000 refugees who had fled Vietnam within the short space of one week—April 25 to May 1—had passed through these Pacific centers to mainland reception centers at Camp Pendleton, California; Fort Chaffee, Arkansas; Eglin Air Force Base, Florida; and Indiantown Gap, Pennsylvania where they encountered varied American hostility and friendship.[8]

On April 22, 1975, Attorney General Edward H. Levi had utilized an obscure law which allowed him "to use his discretion to parole aliens temporarily into this country for emergent reasons." His orders applied to Vietnamese who were close relatives of American citizens and of permanent resident aliens; to "high risk" Vietnamese, such as past and present employees of the United States, and "significant political and intelligence figures" and their families; and to about 1,000 Cambodians who had been employed by the United States government. Some

Indochinese who worked for different American companies or their subsidiaries also sought and gained parole status.[9]

These refugees were a special group of immigrants. About 58 percent spoke some English and most were white-collar workers from Vietnam's middle and upper classes. Having abandoned their possessions and their professions in Vietnam, their common problem was to build new careers. Two thirds of the refugees came from urban areas while about half were Roman Catholics who had had considerable contact with Western civilization. The heads of these refugee households had considerable education; about 50 percent had completed secondary school and 23 percent held university degrees.[10]

On December 20, 1975, the Interagency Task Force on Indochina Refugees closed its last mainland relocation center at Fort Chaffee. In eight months, the agency had found homes in the United States for about 131,000 Indochinese—127,000 South Vietnamese and 4,000 Cambodians. The centers dispersed the refugees, according to federal plan, throughout the fifty states.[11] Private nonprofit agencies aided greatly, as did other federal agencies and state and local officials in the relocation enterprise. Additionally, 6,600 individuals were relocated in other countries, primarily Canada and France. In October, 1975, the agency provided a ship and supplies for 1,546 people who opted to return to Vietnam.[12]

The attorney general's parole program was extended in 1976 to admit another 11,000 Indochinese; the refugee clamor for sanctuary continued unabated throughout 1977. From April, 1975, through March, 1977, a total of 144,758 Indochinese refugees settled in the United States. Since March, 1977, some "boat people" have been admitted monthly. In August, 1977, the United States Department of State recommended paroling an additional 15,000 Indochinese immediately. In March, 1978, State Department officials testified that still another 7,000 needed to be included, an acknowledgment of the exacerbation of the problem, while Congress debated about permanent legislation for refugees.[13] By the end of 1978, an estimated 166,000 Indochinese, of whom 146,000 were Vietnamese, resided in the United States.

By July, 1979, according to revised estimates, there were 210,000 Indochinese refugees here. Seven thousand Vietnamese were then being admitted to the United States each month. In light of the growing crisis over the "boat people," President Carter announced in July, 1979, that the United States would double its monthly admittance rate to 14,000 Indochinese.[14] Since these people did not meet the conditions set forth in the 1965 immigration law, they were not eligible to begin the process of achieving citizenship. Each Indochinese family, or individual, had to have an American sponsor to be admitted. Again, nonprofit agencies labored to locate the required underwriters.

Thus, Levi's willingness to parole the Indochinese in 1975 had saved their lives but barred them from immediately beginning the process to qualify for citizenship. Furthermore, parolees could not be employed in most government jobs, work for firms holding government contracts, or join the armed services. The political and economic situation for most Indochinese therefore has remained uncertain.[15] Some even feared being forced to return to Vietnam when and if the United States and the new government of Vietnam resumed diplomatic relations.

Fear of reprisal because of political belief and uncertainty about government stability also led many Filipinos and Koreans to leave their homelands in the 1970s. Others left the Philippines and Korea for social and economic reasons. On September 23, 1972, President Ferdinand E. Marcos declared martial law in the Philippines, and early in 1973 proclaimed a new constitution which increased his powers at a time when it had become possible for Filipinos to enter the United States with ease. Political activists and some intellectuals took the opportunity to immigrate.[16]

A review of the annual reports of the United States Immigration and Naturalization Service suggests that 1976 was typical of the Filipino immigration trends of the 1970s. In 1976, over 7,000 "professional, technical and kindred workers" immigrated. There were significantly more females than male Filipinos crossing the Pacific in 1976—15,000 males and 22,300 females.[17] Most certainly, the changed sex ratio between the "old" and "new"

Filipino immigrants is striking. In 1930, the ratio of Filipino males to females was 14 to 1. This ratio slowly evened out so that by the early 1970s, with the recent preponderance of women immigrants, the ratio became 10 to 9.[18]

Most arrivals during the 1970s followed settlement patterns of earlier Filipino immigrants, concentrating largely in California and Hawaii. New York, Illinois, and Washington also received substantial numbers of new arrivals annually.[19] They flocked to major cities such as Los Angeles, Chicago, New York, and Honolulu and found jobs most often as janitors, waiters, construction workers, nurses' aides, and secretaries. The Filipinos initiated a chain migration, sending for relatives as soon as they could afford the airplane fare. The earlier arrivals then provided housing and assisted in locating jobs for their kin.

The Philippines, as well as Korea, experienced the "brain drain" phenomenon, the utilization of persons of high educational training and/or skills who were attracted from their native country to live and work in another. The Philippines, which ranked second in the world in the number of students attending college, produced graduates faster than that nation's economy could absorb them. Most graduates had developed life styles different from their parents, and most had higher economic expectations. Thus, in the wake of the 1965 immigration act, the Philippines became the largest supplier of professional and technical workers to the United States. By 1969, the Philippines replaced all European countries as the leading foreign source of engineers, physicians, and scientists for the United States.[20] The educational attainment of such immigrants was strikingly different from the Filipino agricultural workers of earlier years. About 15 percent of the men had college degrees, which was higher than the United States total of 13 percent, while the educational level for Filipino women during the post-1965 period was the highest of any immigrant group, male or female.[21]

Prior to World War II, following the first wave in 1903–1905, Korean immigration was virtually nonexistent. However, the aftermath of the Korean War and its impact upon South Korea led many to look upon the United States as a haven. Most were admitted as nonquota immigrants. In 1958, for example, of the 1,604 Koreans who entered American ports, 1,387 were classified as nonquota.[22] The Korean War solved nothing; political unrest, economic instability, and animosity between the two Koreas continued as before. During South Korea's later political reconstruction, General Park Chung Hee's tight control of the government after 1963 saw political dissidents either jailed for their views or seeking refuge in the United States.[23] During the 1970s, Park's authoritarian regime even followed such immigrants into the United States. In 1976, Koreans in California, critical of President Park, complained of harassment by the Korean CIA and overt pressures from the Korean government. Some received telephone threats and a few were beaten. Agents accosted a Korean minister for his opinions, delivered from his pulpit. An editor of a Los Angeles Korean language newspaper found that his advertisers had canceled their accounts, forcing him out of business.[24]

Tables 1 and 2 demonstrate how the number of Korean im migrants has increased dramatically since 1965. In 1976, of the 30,803 immigrants admitted, 20,011 entered under the numerical limitation, while 10,792 were exempt from such restrictions due to their relationship to United States citizens or permanent resident aliens. Those exempted were wives (4,276), children (4,375), and parents (1,239).[25] According to the 1970s immigration reports, which classified arrivals by major occupation, the largest Korean group (as it had been for the Filipinos) was "housewives, children, and others." In 1976, 223,319 persons were placed in this category while the second largest classification, "professional, technical, and kindred workers," numbered only 3,007.[26] Korea, with a large supply of college educated and highly trained people, experienced a "brain drain," just as the Philippines did. In one startling instance, of the 325 South Koreans who obtained doctorates in the United States in the early 1970s, only 64 returned home.[27]

Most Koreans immigrating during the 1970s fell into one of two large groups. One, composed of individuals in the middle and upper classes, sought better economic opportunities. Many were related to Korean war brides who had lived in the United States for some twenty years. The other large group leaving Korea in the mid-1970s was formed of well-to-do businessmen who did not oppose the Park regime but sought economic sanctuary for their investments in anticipation of Park's possible collapse.[28]

Korea's societal structure, based upon the concept of the extended family, meant a rising young employee without family connections could be squeezed out of a business establishment to make room for some relative of the owner. Many well-trained middle-class Koreans left their homeland because there was no economic future in working for another family's business.[29]

Another important "push" factor leading to emigration was the view of young parents that educational opportunities for their children were limited in Korea. Thus, parents suffered socioeconomic dislocations to provide their children with a better education. A Korean physics teacher in a Seoul high school immigrated to Los Angeles in 1971 with his wife and four children for such a chance. His first job in an electronics firm did not pay enough salary to support his family, so he quit and opened a hamburger stand, which made it possible to achieve the family goal of having the children attend school.[30] Similar aspirations for their children were frequently expressed by Filipinos and Vietnamese.[31]

While the repressions of President Park's South Korean government led many Koreans who opposed it to emigrate, that government encouraged emigration of less wealthy Koreans with the hope that these individuals might return wealthy or contribute to the cash flow into Korea. The Korean government aided potential Korean businessmen in Los Angeles through training classes and provided information about economic opportunities. More importantly, the Korean government utilized one of the two Korean banks in Los Angeles to provide capital for Korean immigrants.[32]

The government of the Philippines also encouraged immigration to the United States for national economic advantages.

Additionally, it provided inexpensive airfares and incentives to encourage return visits by recent emigrants who furnished first-hand information about opportunities in the United States. The cash flow from the United States to the Philippines supplied essential funds which paid taxes, purchased land, and sent relatives to college. The mayors of several Ilocos Norte towns reported throughout the 1970s that about $35,000 a month was being received through remittances by recent immigrants and from pension checks for the old *Hawaiianos* (returned Filipino contract laborers of the 1920s and 1930s) and the *pensionados* (returned retired agricultural workers).[33]

Similar to the Filipino immigrants, by the mid 1970s, the estimated 150,000 to 200,000 Koreans in the United States had concentrated in urban and industrial regions of California, Hawaii, and New York; but at the same time, they had dispersed more widely than had any other Asian group.[34] Table 3 indicates the location of the largest groups of Koreans. Cities in Pennsylvania, Ohio, Michigan, and New Jersey also had significant numbers of Koreans; very few resided in rural America.[35]

Table 3

METROPOLITAN AREAS RECORDING LARGE NUMBERS OF KOREAN RESIDENTS[a]

Los Angeles	40,000	New York	20,000
Honolulu	34,000	San Francisco	10,000
Chicago	20,000	Washington, D.C.	10,000

[a] Bok-Lim Kim, "Appraisal of Korean Immigrant Service Needs," *Social Casework* 57 (1976): 141–42.

Korean, Filipino and Indochinese immigrants all experienced traumatic disruptions in the life styles of their extended families, encountered American prejudice and discrimination, grappled with limited and dwindling financial resources, and faced the necessity of adapting to a new economic system. As they confronted their new environment in the United States, these newcomers often vented their feelings and frustrations over the difficulties they encountered as visible minorities with distinct social mannerisms which confirmed substantial cultural differences. But perhaps their biggest problem, since it affected directly the degree of economic success, was the inability to speak English with facility. All three immigrant groups expressed continuing apprehensions relative to language and culture shock, and articulated uneasiness about adapting to American modes.[36]

The "rice winners" of immigrant Asian families shared common concerns of finding employment to provide for their dependent members. That meant, of course, that these new arrivals had to interact immediately with the American culture, much of which ran counter to their own value systems. Each immigrant coped with his personal, emotional responses as he came to terms with the new life that surrounded him. Some were successful in this encounter, but most felt overwhelmed by the dominant culture.[37] The drive to succeed remained strong, however, even in the face of many frustrations and disappointments. Wrote a Honolulu newspaper reporter about this socioeconomic encounter:

They come here with great expectations and then find themselves crowded into slum houses. . . . They can't find jobs or are working at something far below their talent and training. Many are living on a pittance, some are dependent on welfare.

They struggle to communicate in a language they do not know. Often they are mocked by the unthinking and taken advantage of by the unscrupulous.

And yet, somehow, they endure.

Somehow they keep a sense of dignity and sometimes even a sense of humor. In time, most of them will make it. Very few will return home. They have a burning drive to succeed, many of them. They will lift themselves up, one halting step at a time, like the millions of immigrants to America who came before them.[38]

Perhaps the greatest culture shock for these recent Asian immigrants occurred as their children enrolled in American schools, learned different traditions and the dominant language —English. This in turn led to family tensions and, more often than not, a breakup of the group. In Los Angeles, for example, high-school age Koreans developed their own subculture, involving teenage gangs, drugs, juvenile delinquency, and sex. While these youths were set apart from American teenagers because of the language barrier, they adjusted more quickly to their new environment than did the adults, leading to a growing generational gap and conflict. The same pattern repeated itself in Honolulu among Filipinos.[39]

The ability of Vietnamese refugees to adapt to American life, not surprisingly, closely corresponded to their age and their degree of flexibility. The elderly, who had been heads of extended families and who had come to the United States as dependents of their adult children, more often than not withdrew from any contact with the dominant culture. Their children, who left home because of their status in Vietnam, usually had been professionals, businessmen, or high-ranking civil servants or military officers. Most had had substantial material assets, power, status, and prestige. Educated under the French colonial system, many did not speak English and encountered difficulties as they sought to adapt culturally and linguistically. Most of these refugees, not too far from the age of retirement, now found that they had to start anew in building their economic and social futures.

Vietnamese families here started disintegrating under the new set of daily pressures. Parents were frequently forced to rely upon their teenage children to serve as translators. These children, coming into daily contact with American culture at school, began to drift away from their own cultural values; some young people moved away from their families as quickly as possible in order to commence their own lives in the United States.[40] While many family groups managed to escape, some refugees were men who had to flee without their families; others were wives who came only with their children; and there were unaccompanied children.[41]

Vietnamese men experienced great frustration as the family structure broke down and they found their position as head of the household being challenged. Both Vietnamese and Korean men experienced severe disappointment in being severely underemployed. Several recent Vietnamese generals, for example, found employment as dish washers and chauffeurs while other men found jobs as janitors and in other menial tasks.[42]

One Vietnamese refugee, who had escaped with his wife and six children, worked in a Virginia restaurant for about thirty-two or thirty-five hours a week. His wife worked about six hours a week, cleaning a doctor's office. Together they earned about $450 a month.[43]

The former chief of counterintelligence in the Mekong Delta for twelve years worked in southern California as a maintenance man while his wife was a chambermaid at a hotel. Five other family members worked at assorted jobs. By 1977, this family thought it was winning its economic battle and planned on sending two sons to college.[44]

Two years after arriving in the United States, another member of the Vietnamese elite, a Confucian scholar who had studied economics and sociology in Paris, worked in a boiler room for $600 a month and attended evening school to improve his knowledge of English. In addition to finding a position commensurate with his prior training, his dream, the one shared by most immigrants as noted earlier, was to have his children succeed in America.[45]

Post-1965 Filipino immigrants underwent experiences similar to those of the Vietnamese and Koreans, but their adaptation was both aided and hampered by their encounter with the second and subsequent generations of Filipino-Americans. There was a wide gulf between the two groups. According to Antonio J. A. Pido's study, "The early immigrants perceived the new immigrants as upstarts and snobs who are now reaping the benefits of what they had sowed at a great cost in anguish and deprivation. The new immigrants look upon and treat the old immigrants patronizingly or even with disdain and as equivalent to 'hillbillies.' "[46] Those Filipinos who contributed to the "brain drain" accommodated more quickly to life in America than did those with less education. While many Filipinos felt they assimilated more easily into American life, most experienced the frustration of being underemployed and of living in substandard housing which led to social disorganization and growing personal conflict over cultural traditions.[47]

A considerable number of Filipinos who arrived in the United States were unable to communicate in English. In Hawaii, social service centers taught them English by showing them how to shop in supermarkets and how to order in restaurants.[48] Filipinos crowded with recent arrivals from Korea and Samoa into the ghetto areas of Kalihi, Palama, and Chinatown in Honolulu, or in one of the outlying farming centers such as Waipahu or Ewa. Although housing in Waipahu was dilapidated and unsanitary, the tenants made no complaints, fearing that landlords would evict troublemakers. They paid $30 a month to live in shacks constructed from scrap lumber and sheet iron. There was no hot water, no bathroom, and no stove—cooking had to be done on hot plates. Honolulu's Chinatown apartments had one toilet and shower per floor.[49]

Since unskilled and untrained people found employment virtually impossible, a special training program for Filipino teenagers was devised in Honolulu during the early 1970s to provide entry-level skills.[50] Young Koreans and Vietnamese with language problems and no occupational skills had similar difficulties.

Conversely, being overqualified was also a real predicament for some of these recent Asian immigrants. In many instances, licensing requirements for most professions required passing satisfactorily a state examination in order to practice in a particular state. Frequently, an additional requirement demanded that the professional degree be awarded by an American university. Such barriers made it impossible to pursue one's profession. One Filipino doctor who had received his M.D. degree in Manila in 1954 worked as a janitor in a Honolulu drive-in. A lawyer who was kept from practicing because he was not a graduate of an American law school was a sales clerk in Hono-lulu.[51]

A curious dilemma thus confronted these Korean and Filipino professionals who, given admission preference by the United States immigration service because of their skills, found after entry that they could not take state licensing examinations, partly because of the language problem, partly because of the requirement to complete additional training in the United States, and partly because of state laws regulating particular professions.[52]

In New York City, about 300 Koreans became green grocers because their professions were closed to them. Their stores— family affairs—employed from ten to twenty relatives. Most of the merchants had formerly been chemists and engineers. Other professions represented were dentistry, medicine, and the military. One of these merchants had been a chemical engineer and his wife a nurse. Two of his younger brothers worked in the store while another attended medical school in Switzerland. One of his sisters was an aerodynamics engineer and another was a chemist. Not able to find employment equal to his train-ing, the storeowner operated his fruit and vegetable business to enable his family to subsist in New York City.[53]

A Korean couple in Los Angeles, who operated a sandwich shop in 1977, had been professionals in Korea—the husband a doctor and the wife a pharmacist. With five children, two of whom were in college, the husband and wife could not afford the time or the expense of attending American universities to prepare and qualify for the licensing examinations.[54]

Another example of the problem was a thirty-six-year-old woman, a practicing pharmacist in Korea. In Los Angeles, she worked as a knitting machine operator in a factory where 90 percent of the work force was Korean. She had spent seven months futilely trying to get the California Board of Pharmacy to recognize her professional training. She and about 200 other Korean pharmicists in the Los Angeles area, stopped by state regulations, were underemployed.[55]

As increasing numbers of Koreans continued to immigrate during the 1970s, each new arrival confronted problems faced by earlier immigrants. In addition to the Manhattan green grocers, large numbers of Koreans settled in the New York area; one substantial contingent lived in Flushing. To offset their problems of adjustment, this group utilized the Korean Community Action Center which offered extensive services, ranging from finding jobs to marriage counseling. Of the 2,000 families helped by the center, none had had to seek welfare benefits in order to survive. Most of these families found it necessary for both parents to work. While they commenced at a low combined total income level of less than $5,000 a year, the center found that after two years, they had moved from these jobs to more remunerative ones. Once English-language skills were mastered, employment opportunities improved. Thus, the center's clients, who had been professional people and who had lived comfortably in Korea, were currently employed in sewing and baking shops in Queens.[56]

Koreans in Chicago reported similar experiences. A study of 181 Korean families found that most were young parents with small children. They had lived in Chicago for three years or less. Seventy-one percent of the men were employed and 60 percent of the women also worked outside the home. More than half of the working women were professionals—mostly nurses. Over 83 percent of these families had incomes in excess of $5,000.[57] These Koreans, as did Filipinos in Chicago, encountered employment discrimination and found that they had to take lower level jobs than they had held in their homeland. Both Koreans and Filipinos reported additional discrimination as they sought housing.[58]

Los Angeles attracted most of the Korean immigrants during the 1970s. In a short span of three years, some 70,000 Koreans transformed a decrepit part of that city, bounded by Olympic Boulevard and Western, Eighth, and Vermont Avenues, into a bustling area of small shops and service-related businesses. Southern California's Koreans flourished and prospered at a time when the United States was enduring a recession. Called

"Second Seoul," "Little Seoul," or "Korea Town," this largest Korean center in the United States in 1976 had over 1,000 small businesses, five newspapers, and hundreds of community organizations, churches, and interest groups.[59] The Los Angeles telephone book that year listed over 1,000 subscribers named Kim, the most common of the Korean surnames. (Honolulu's 1979 telephone book listed over 2,800 Kims, indicative of that city's long-time Korean community with its four generations.)

Although Los Angeles's Olympic Boulevard community appeared well-managed, it reported problems common to new immigrant groups. Youths were largely underemployed; the area had a worrisome high crime rate, and juvenile delinquency was increasing. Koreans in Los Angeles, additionally, had difficulties with the English language and in accommodating to American life.[60] While Los Angeles' Korean community had phenomenal success in launching grocery and liquor stores, small shops, service stations, and restaurants, many Koreans (especially the most recent arrivals) lived in abject poverty.[61]

Koreans sought to move up the economic ladder by first opening a service station or a wig shop. At the second entrepreneurial level were grocery stores; liquor stores and restaurants appeared to be at a third level; dealing in and selling real estate seemed to them to be the pinnacle of economic achievement.[62] Four factors underlay Korean success—thrift, communal resources, public resources, and the Korean government. Thrifty Koreans accumulated capital by working long hours and by saving their earnings. Although the South Korean government restricted the outflow of capital—with a legal limit of $1,400— considerable funds were smuggled out. It has been reported that several Koreans dipped into paper bags for cash to pay for houses in the $100,000 range and above.[63] But generally, most arrived in Los Angeles without funds, as was the case for thirty-six-year-old Ki Duk Lee, a college graduate. For three years, he worked as a can inspector and then as a welder while his wife found employment as a nurse. Together they saved some $18,000. Borrowing additional capital, Lee opened the Olympic Market. After a difficult initial period, he developed a brisk business and by 1976 had launched a second business—a restaurant.[64] Arriving Koreans with little money worked very hard while maintaining a minimal standard of living to gather their desired capital. But hard work did not end with the attainment of a small business whose survival depended upon unpaid family labor. The hours of work remained long and usually included seven days a week.

The Koreans also pooled capital through a rotating credit association called a *gae*, a method familiar to Chinese and Japanese. A *gae*'s fiscal resources were given interest free to one member of the group who used the capital to start his business. The *gae*, dependent upon trust and honor, operated until each member of the association had an opportunity to utilize the money.[65]

The Los Angeles Korean community, unlike other Asian groups, eagerly sought public resources and utilized, for example, the services of the Small Business Administration. And, as already noted, the Korean government assisted immigrants to launch businesses through loans by the Korean bank which had a branch in Los Angeles.[66] Through hard work by the family, many Koreans by the end of the 1970s had achieved a measure of financial independence and had secured educational opportunities for their children.

Koreans everywhere in the United States faced daily the exigencies of the American way of life. Still to be answered was whether they would be eventually overwhelmed by the dominant culture or whether they could adapt and maintain their own cultural standards. The alienation of their children was a time of turmoil for the parents. The "Americanization" of second and third generations in Hawaii suggests the eventual outcome.[67]

Throughout most of the twentieth century, Filipinos had continuous and easy access to the United States. By the 1970s there were four generations of Filipino-Americans. The first generation, mostly men, were sixty-five years old or older who lived in crowded quarters in San Francisco's and Honolulu's Chinatowns or near the two states' agricultural areas. They relied upon monthly social security checks to survive as best they could. Interviews with these elderly men reveal that most still cherished the dream of returning to the Philippines but, for one reason or another, postponed the ultimate decision. Truly, these aging first generation Filipino immigrants had become men without a country, captive in what was to have been a temporary home.[68] Several of these men, together with second generation Filipinos, continued to provide a substantial number of workers for California and Hawaii agribusinesses. In both states, Filipinos took leading roles in organizing farm labor.[69] Another occupational career pursued by many Filipino men, particularly those residing in the Philippines, was that of United States Navy mess steward. The steward's pay was higher than most jobs in the islands and an honorable discharge provided the chance for American citizenship.[70]

Filipinos who lived in the United States prior to the 1965 immigration act had entered all levels of employment, but those in California and Hawaii remained in the socioeconomic group which consistently had the lowest median income.[71] During the 1970s, while many professionals of the Philippine "brain drain" attained the higher salaried ranges, large numbers of Filipinos barely subsisted. A 1976 estimate guessed that 40 percent of the 350,000 Filipinos in the United States earned less than $4,000 a year, 25 percent lived in poverty, and such persons tended to remain fixed at low income and low achievement levels. Both "old" and "new" immigrants with minimal education found employment opportunities limited; and their low incomes dictated, in part, what type of housing they could own or rent. Even though civil rights legislation and court rulings had removed several legal constraints, de facto segregation remained very real for Filipinos and other Asians.[72]

Filipinos who had arrived prior to 1965 and their children, as well as newer immigrants, usually formed community groups based upon language, the groups to whom their relatives belonged, or their home village or area in the Philippines. These kinship organizations tended to keep the Filipinos fragmented, making it difficult to present a common front when dealing with economic, political, and social problems in the United States. Those immigrants from the Philippines' rural provinces with no professional training and limited educational skills (particularly the Ilocanos who settled in Hawaii and California) sought refuge in remaining Filipino, speaking their native tongue, eating familiar Filipino foods, and conducting illegal cock fights— a major legal recreation in the Philippines.[73]

In contrast to such immigrants were many of the 75,000 Filipinos in the New York City metropolitan area, of whom an estimated 35,000 lived in New York City itself. New York City's Ninth Avenue provided a Filipino center of small shops selling Filipino foods and a restaurant or two—a place where one could keep in touch with the familiar culture. Filipinos settled in Queens and Westchester in New York and in Jersey City, Riverdale, and Bergen County in New Jersey, but there was no identifiable ethnic enclave such as West Coast or Hawaiian Filipinos had developed. New York area Filipinos claimed to be mostly professionals—bankers, doctors, insurance salesmen, lawyers, nurses, and secretaries. Middle class and college educated, they were fluent in English when they arrived in the United States. According to the *New York Times*, Filipinos in the New York metropolitan area were not clearly regarded as a distinct ethnic group but rather as part of a larger amorphous Asian group.[74]

While many Filipinos, particularly members of the older first generation immigrants, dreamed about returning to the Philippines, the situation was changing for the younger ones. Like immigrants from all nations, while they were continually interested in the welfare of their homeland and many returned home for visits and momentous family events, Filipinos were becoming established in the United States where their children had become acculturated to American life. While the children had problems and learning difficulties in school, they no longer had the same ties to the Philippines as did their parents. The same circumstance happened among Koreans, for most children of the first generation saw themselves as Americans. While proud of their cultural heritage, most did not consider the prospect of returning to the land of their parents. Nevertheless, Korean-

Americans and Filipino-Americans have identified strongly with their inherited cultures, as evidenced by flourishing ethnic programs in the United States for these two, as well as other, Asian groups.

As had happened to Koreans and Filipinos, by the end of 1978, most of the 1975 Vietnamese refugees had made considerable adjustment to life in the United States. They overcame, for example, the explicit federal policy of dispersing the refugees throughout all fifty states. The policy had aimed at minimizing racial hostility and economic problems at a time when American unemployment was at a high level. As part of this policy, for example, about 175 Vietnamese, comprised of thirty-seven families and several single men, were relocated in and around Lexington, Kentucky. Most of these people knew English, had had contact with Americans in Vietnam, and had both employable skills and adequate financial resources. Most quickly found employment while a few enrolled in college to gain professional training.[75]

As the Vietnamese gained economic security, they thwarted the federal plan by moving to California, Texas, Pennsylvania, northern Virginia near the District of Columbia, and Louisiana.[76] In northern Virginia, for instance, the heads of some fifty families decided that there was no rush to adopt American ways. These refugees still observed, as had the Filipinos and Koreans, their own native holidays, enjoyed Vietnamese food, and listened to the music of their homeland on cassettes.[77]

The approximately 8,000 Vietnamese attracted to New Orleans encountered growing numbers of resentful comments, particularly from blacks who saw immigrants taking scarce jobs and occupying even scarcer spaces in public housing. Louisiana, with the third largest number of Vietnamese, discovered in 1978 that success had been achieved in the job market. The fact that these new immigrants had a higher employment rate than the state and national averages led to a growing hostility in many areas—Kansas City, Missouri; Augusta, Maine; Pensacola, Florida; and Louisiana.[78]

The migrating Vietnamese sought out locales with a wide range of job opportunities, liberal welfare programs, and agreeable climates. By mid-1977, an estimated 18,000 to 50,000 Vietnamese had settled in the metropolitan Los Angeles area. (Obviously, such a disparity showed that no one was certain about an exact number.) Orange County with from 11,000 to 15,000 Vietnamese had two columns of the Vietnamese name Nguyen in its 1977 telephone book.[79]

The fact that the Vietnamese were aware of welfare benefits became a major concern in some places, particularly in southern California's Orange County where the welfare rolls escalated sharply. In 1977, Orange County spent about two million dollars on Indochinese recipients. Twenty percent of the Vietnamese in southern California were reported on welfare.[80] This, of course, was not unexpected, for as the Vietnamese moved from their first place of resettlement to California, they sought federal welfare while looking for employment. According to the Department of Health, Education, and Welfare, by late 1977, only 11 percent of all Vietnamese refugee families were totally dependent upon welfare while 32 percent were either eligible for, or were receiving, cash assistance. The Vietnamese unemployment rate was 5.5 percent as compared to 6.4 percent nationally.[81] Thus, it appears that the bulk of those who entered the United States during 1975 made a good start in their new environment.

Meanwhile, the United States and other nations were confronted with the continuing plight of the "boat people" who were fleeing from Vietnam at the rate of 65,000 a month. In many instances, the Vietnamese were expelled from their homes by the Vietnam government and no other Asian country would accept them. By mid-1979, 300,000 homeless Indochinese had been turned away by other Asian nations, such as Malaysia and Thailand.[82] These refugees differed greatly from the first refugees both in education and financial resources. In the first months of 1979, those who constituted the 7,000-a-month new arrivals to the United States found it very difficult to locate employment and encountered rising resentment because of competition for jobs and because they tended to rely heavily upon public and private social services.

On the one hand, immigrants from the Philippines, Korea, and Vietnam have stood out as color-visible minorities and appeared to American labor as a threat in the job market. On the other hand, these immigrants demonstrated positively that they shared many characteristics of the American way of life that is so valued by the citizens of the United States. The recent Asian immigrants have held education in high regard, considering it to be the significant means of gaining economic independence. Most have also demonstrated that nineteenth-century virtue—self-reliance—and have sought to make their own way. These American goals are pursued by these new immigrants with varying degrees of success, but just as is the case for other Americans, not all of the new Asian immigrants are successful. In truth, many remained at poverty levels and found themselves entrapped in urban ghettos. Regardless of personal preference, they were dependent upon social services. A comparison of the immigrants from the Philippines, Korea, and Indochina with immigrants and residents of similar socioeconomic circumstances shows that these new arrivals have adapted fairly well to their new life in the United States, and in some cases have succeeded better than previous immigrants who confronted similar cultural and economic problems.

NOTES

1. For a general historical background on Filipino and Korean immigration to the United States, see H. Brett Melendy, *Asians in America: Filipinos, Koreans, and East Indians* (Boston: Twayne Publishers, 1977).

2. *U.S. News & World Report*, June 13, 1977, p. 46.

3. *U.S. Statutes at Large*, 48: 456–65; ibid., 79: 911–22; Mary Dorita Clifford, "The Hawaiian Sugar Planters' Association and Filipino Exclusion," in *The Filipino Exclusion Movement, 1927–1935* (Quezon City, Philippines: Institute of Asian Studies, Occasional

Community," *Proceeding . . . Migration from the Philippines, 1974*; Harold J. McArthur, Jr., "Hawaiianos: A Study of Noninnovative Behavior," in ibid.

34. Melendy, pp. 130–31; Hyung-chan Kim, "Some Aspects of Social Demography," in *The Korean Diaspora*, pp. 123–25; Jai P. Ryu, "Koreans in America," in ibid., pp. 212–13.

35. Hyung-chan Kim, pp. 123–26; Ryu, p. 213.

36. *Honolulu Star-Bulletin*, November 29, 1974, p. A–2; *Chicago Tribune*, November 20, 1975, p. vii–16; *New Yorker*, July 4, 1977, pp. 20–23.

37. Ibid., *Human Organization* 37 (Spring 1978): 95–100.

38. *Honolulu Advertiser & Star-Bulletin*, November 25, 1973, p. F–36.

39. Interviews with Paul Chun and Sam Bom Woo; *Honolulu Star-Bulletin*, June 12, 1975, p. B–14.

40. Nguyen Dang Liem and Dean F. Kehmeier, "The Vietnamese," in *People and Cultures in Hawaii*, ed. John F. McDermott, Jr. et al. (Honolulu: University of Hawaii Press, 1980), pp. 202–217.

41. *Washington Post*, May 1, 1977, p. 1.

42. Ibid., April 5, 1976, p. C–1; May 1, 1977, p. 1.

43. Ibid., May 10, 1976, p. B–3.

44. Ibid., May 2, 1977, p. 1.

45. Ibid., July 10, 1977, pp. 1, 11.

46. Pido, p. 53.

47. Lott, p. 172.

48. *Honolulu Advertiser*, November 24, 1971, p. B–1.

49. Ibid., November 22, 1971, p. A–10.

50. Ibid., January 11, 1971, p. A–1.

51. Ibid., November 22, 1971, A–10; January 11, 1971, p. A–1; Melendy, pp. 107, 171–72.

52. Bonacich, Light, and Wong, "Koreans in Business," pp. 58–59.

53. *New Yorker*, July 4, 1977, pp. 20–23.

54. *Los Angeles Times*, May 11, 1977, Sect. IV, p. 1.

55. Ibid., February 1, 1976, Sect. IV, p. 10.

56. *New York Times*, August 26, 1973, p. 102.

57. Bok-Lim C. Kim, pp. 144–46.

58. *Chicago Tribune*, November 20, 1975, Sect. VII, p. 17.

59. *Los Angeles Times*, February 1, 1976, Sect. IV, pp. 1, 11; David S. Kim and Charles Choy Wong, "Business Development in Koreatown, Los Angeles," in *The Korean Diaspora*, pp. 229–43.

60. *New York Times*, October 30, 1976, p. 3; Won H. Chang, "Communication and Acculturation," in *The Korean Diaspora*, pp. 135–53.

61. Bonacich, Light, and Wong, "Koreans in Business," p. 58; David Kim and Charles Wong, pp. 231–32.

62. Bonacich, Light, and Wong, p. 59; Kim and Wong, p. 242.

63. *New York Times*, October 30, 1976, p. 1.

64. *Los Angeles Times*, February 1, 1976, Sect. IV, p. 1.

65. Bonacich, Light, and Wong, p. 56.

66. Ibid., 57.

67. Won H. Chang, pp. 135–53; Chae-kun Yu, "The Correlates of Cultural Assimilation of Korean Immigrants in the United States," in *The Korean Diaspora*, pp. 167–75.

68. Melendy, pp. 96–101; Lillian Galedo and Theresa Mar, "Filipinos in a Farm Labor Camp," in *Letters in Exile* (Los Angeles: Asian American Studies Center, University of California, 1976), pp. 96–111; Chris Braga and Barbara Morita, "Agbayani Villiage," in *Letters in Exile*, pp. 141–45.

69. Melendy, pp. 92–98, 100–102.

70. *Newsweek*, November 9, 1970, pp. 32–33; Alfredo N. Munroz, *The Filipinos in America* (Los Angeles: Mountainview Publishers, 1971), pp. 107–13; Jesse G. Quinsaat, "How to Join the Navy and Still Not See the World," in *Letters in Exile*, pp. 96–111.

71. California Department of Industrial Relations, *Californians of Japanese, Chinese and Filipino Ancestry* (San Francisco, 1965), pp. 12, 14; Andrew Lind, *Hawaii's People*, 3d ed. (Honolulu: University of Hawaii Press, 1967), pp. 75–78, 100.

72. Lott, pp. 165–66, 170; "Anti-Miscegenation Laws and the Filipino," *Letters in Exile*, pp. 63–71; Evelyn Hernandez, "The Makibaka Movement: A Filipino Protest and Struggle," in *Proceedings . . . Migration from the Philippines, 1974.*

73. Honolulu Advertiser, September 8, 1970, p. A–7; Ruben R. Alcantara, "The Filipinos in an Hawaiian Plantation Town," in *Proceedings . . . Migration from the Philippines, 1974;* F. Landa Jocano, "Stages of Adaptation among Filipino Immigrants in Hawaii," in ibid.; Moreno C. Requiza, "The Role of Social Networks in Filipino Immigration to the East Coast of the United States," in ibid.

74. *New York Times*, December 30, 1976, p. 27. See too Precios M. Nicanos, *Profiles of Notable Americans in the U.S.A.* (New York: Per-Mar, 1963).

75. *Human Organization* 33 (Spring, 1978): 95–100.

76. *U.S. News & World Report*, June 13, 1977, p. 46.

77. *Washington Post*, July 10, 1977, p. 1.

78. *Newsweek*, September 11, 1978, p. 36; *Time*, August 28, 1978, pp. 4–5.

79. *U.S. News & World Report*, June 13, 1977, p. 46; *Washington Post*, May 2, 1977, p. 1.

80. *Washington Post*, May 2, 1977, p. 1.

81. *Bridge* 6 (Spring, 1978): 60.

82. *Time*, July 2, 1979, p. 38.

III

Japanese Immigration to the United States

By Harry H. L. Kitano and
Cynthia Kadonaga
University of California, Los Angeles

Japanese immigration to the United States began in significant numbers during the 1890s, reached its peak between 1900
and 1920, then came to an abrupt halt with passage of the 1924
Immigration Act. It was not until 1952, when the McCarran-
Walter Act was passed, that the Japanese could again legally
immigrate to America and become naturalized American citizens.
These circumstances resulted in clear-cut divisions among the
generations, with the Issei, or first-generation immigrants, arriving primarily between 1890 and 1924, and their children, the
Nisei, generally being born in America from 1910 to 1940. The
children of the Nisei, born mostly since World War II, are the
Sansei, or third generation of Japanese ancestry in the United
States.

Each generation may be further distinguished by its cultural
and adaptive patterns. These patterns stem in part from the
prejudice and discrimination faced by the Issei, Nisei, and Sansei during different eras. This presentation thus will be based
on generations, with the understanding that a multitude of other
factors—including area of residence, social class, ethnic and
community identity, and personality also has affected the lives
of the Japanese in America.

The relatively homogeneous Issei have spawned a multigen-
erational, multicultural population with a wide range of atti-

tudes and behaviors. To further complicate generalizations about Japanese-Americans, new groups of Japanese immigrants have been arriving since 1954, bringing with them the experiences and expectations of people from an industrialized, urbanized nation, far removed from the Japan of the late nineteenth and early twentieth century.

Issei

The first Japanese immigrants to form an American colony settled north of Sacramento in 1869. Except for the gravestone of a nineteen-year-old woman known only as Okei, there is no trace of the lost colony of Wakamatsu, established by 27 Issei under the leadership of a European named Schnell. Okei is believed to be the first Japanese woman to die in America.

From 1891 through 1924, 295,820 Japanese immigrants flocked to the United States, in addition to others who came as illegal and unrecorded entries from Canada and Mexico. Because an unknown number of these Issei came and left several times, their actual number during the period was somewhat lower.

The Issei came from a country experiencing the turmoil of Western development. They were products of the Meiji era (1868–1912), a period associated with the rapid growth of Japan from an isolated, technologically backward nation to an international power. The direct influence of this change on Japanese immigrants is difficult to assess. However, most Issei had completed six compulsory years of school, appreciated the importance of money and banking, and were, in time, desirous of acquiring their own land and businesses.

The Issei influx, sparked by the need for cheap labor in America and in the independent monarchy of Hawaii, came almost immediately after the halt of Chinese immigration. Anti-Asian sentiments on the West Coast fueled fears of a "yellow peril," and these fears increased as the Japanese began advancing in agriculture, an area which required little capital and fitted into the past experiences of many Issei. Other initial entry jobs included working on the railroad, in canneries, logging, mining, fishing, and meatpacking.

By 1909, there were approximately 30,000 Japanese working on farms, often in collectives or in labor gangs managed by agents. The Issei began as agricultural laborers, progressing to contract farming, share tenancy, cash leasing, and finally, land ownership. But the increasing number of Issei farmers led to legal efforts aimed at curbing their advancement. In 1922, the United States Supreme Court ruled in the Takao Ozawa case that Japanese immigrants could be denied American citizenship, since it was a right limited to "free white persons" and those of African descent. One year later, the California legislature passed an alien land act, making Issei ineligible for citizenship and unable to own land. The law not only prevented ownership, but also barred the Issei from bequeathing or selling their farms to one another, and limited any leases obtained to three years. Despite these efforts, the amount of land owned by Japanese farmers dropped only slightly between 1920 and 1930 because many Issei registered their deeds in the names of their Nisei children, who were American citizens by birth.

In addition to being farmers and industrial laborers, many Issei found domestic service jobs, or opened curio shops, cafes, laundries, dry cleaning establishments, rooming houses, grocery stores, and barber shops. The businesses were often connected by an interdependent ethnic network so that an Issei rooming house, for example, catered to Issei customers and relied on Issei workers and suppliers. These Japanese entrepreneurs also served other ethnic minorities, such as blacks and Filipinos; and these small businesses quickly became the cornerstone of Issei economic strength in urban areas.

Another source of strength was in the ability of the Japanese to develop parallel structures in the face of discrimination. For example, when California banks refused to grant loans or offered prohibitive terms, the Issei turned to relatives and friends, and also to the "tanomoshi," which was an investment pool of money which served as an alternative banking system. Similarly, when Issei doctors could not find appropriate hospital facilities for themselves and their patients, they developed the Japanese hospitals, some of which exist (in modified form) to the present day.

Although there were innumerable instances of overt prejudice and discrimination against individual Issei, the most far-reaching actions occurred in the legal area. For example, between 1910 and 1920, proposed California legislation would have barred Japanese immigrants from employing white women and inheriting land, and would have established higher fishing license fees for Asians. State Attorney General Ulysses S. Webb said in 1913:

The fundamental basis of all legislation has been, and is, race undesirability. It seeks to limit (the Japanese) presence by curtailing their privileges which they may enjoy here, for they will not come in large unmbers and long abide with us if they may not acquire land. And it seeks to limit the number who will come by limiting the opportunities for activity here when they arrive.[1]

Discrimination, the denial of American citizenship, and cultural and language barriers forced many Issei to seek relief through the Japanese Consulate. In 1906, Issei complaints concerning San Francisco's segregated schools led Japan to protest the unequal treatment of its citizens to President Theodore Roosevelt. Roosevelt convinced the city school board to rescind its segregation order, partly to avoid a confrontation with Japan, which had just won a war with Russia and was emerging as a world power.

The 1924 Immigration Act totally barred the immigration of Japanese and other Asians to the United States. It was a violation of the Gentleman's Agreement of 1906, since it was a discriminatory law aimed at the Japanese, but protests from Japanese were ignored.

Discrimination against the Japanese residing in the United States continued. One result of this hostility was the strengthening of the ethnic community. It was difficult for Issei to merge and be accepted by the dominant community; therefore they turned to their own. The ethnic community provided comfort and protection; opportunities were available to satisfy social, religious, recreational, and health needs. Groceries and other stores provided familiar foods and goods. These segregated communities acquired such names as Little Tokyo (in Los Angeles) and Little Osaka (in San Francisco). Ethnocentrism, nationalism, and cultural factors were also important in maintaining these communities.

The most important social organization was the "kenjinkai," or prefectural association. According to Bradford Smith:

In a rural culture like Japan's, differences of habit and custom might vary considerably from one part of the country to another. It was natural enough that those who had come this far from home enjoyed the company of their own kin-folk, with whom they shared the same dialect, the same birth and marriage customs, and often the same Buddhist sect. Doubtless the kenjinkai also served as a means of self-aggrandizement for those . . . [with] qualities of leadership who could find no scope or acceptance in the larger community surrounding the Japanese. For the children, the kenjinkai was chiefly useful as the sponsor of a summer picnic—a wonderful affair of games, soda pop, speeches, sweets, exhibitions of wrestling and fencing, and more soda pop.[2]

The Japanese Association, with activities ranging from disciplining community members to sponsoring July Fourth parade floats, was the most influential Issei group. The association advocated behavior to enhance the image of Japanese immigrants, making the community an important reference group. The association also urged that immigrant families not become "too American too fast," a motto that helped discourage Issei acculturation and alienated many Nisei.

In addition to these groups, the Issei also depended on their families for support. Issei men, many of whom had married "picture brides" from 1910 to 1924, took comfort in patriarchal families that emphasized solidarity, helpfulness, and filial piety. The potentially unfavorable aspects of these arranged marriages between strangers was endured with the help of norms stressing adaptiveness to both fixed positions and external realities. This adaptiveness, which reflected an emphasis on duty and obligation, as well as values of conformity and obedience, also guided the Issei outside the ethnic community.

The Issei avoided direct confrontation with the white majority culture, seeking instead to become as invisible as possible. Competing on equal terms with whites usually meant additional discriminatory treatment, so that the major strategy was to keep a low profile. As a result, Issei life styles were conservative, and actions ranging from crime to flashy dressing and conspicuous consumption were discouraged.

The strategy was reinforced by the Japanese "enryo" syndrome, under which social inferiors were expected to show reserve, deference, self-abnegation, and denial before their superiors. Enryo served to reinforce an overtly submissive posture to the dominant society. Manifestations of enryo include hesitancy to speak out, willingness to accept a less desired object, and automatic refusal to accept offers of help or assistance. Another important norm was "amae" which served to soften power relationships through acknowledging dependency and weakness. Through amae, younger employees could display meekness and confusion in order to give their superiors a chance to offer paternal advice and to reinforce their more powerful role. Japanese were encouraged to form strong bonds of loyalty, trust, and cohesiveness, whether in the company, community, or family. Other important norms emphasized indirectness and deflection as opposed to confrontation and speaking out; the internalization of problems and stress; a recognition of the hierarchy of roles and positions; and a group rather than an individualistic orientation.

In addition to these norms, the Issei brought with them an almost reverential attitude toward work. In a crowded island nation with limited natural resources, diligence and self-discipline were encouraged. The moral imperative to work hard was complemented by traditional Japanese attitudes encouraging resiliency in the face of setbacks. The Buddhist dicta of "gaman"

–don't give up–and "gambatte"–don't let it bother you–stressed hiding frustration and disappointment, and the need to carry on.

Issei attitudes and norms were valuable assets in a country where their ignorance of English, lack of capital and technical skills, and minimal education combined with hostility from the majority group served to sharply curtail advancement in America. Their training helped them cope with the hostile environment. Nonetheless they believed that the environment would prove beneficial for their American-born children, the Nisei.

The Issei, like many other immigrants to America, could be labeled a "sacrifical generation" in that most gave up their own chances for further educational, occupational, and economic mobility and placed their expectations and hopes on their American-born Nisei children. The spirit is described by Dennis Ogawa in a book titled *Kodomo No Tame Ni,* or "for the sake of the children," a phrase familiar to all Japanese.[3]

The Nisei now are in a position to care for many of the surviving Issei. But the number of these aging pioneers is rapidly diminishing; and by the end of the century, there will be no more. According to data based on the 1970 census, Issei comprised less than ten percent of the Japanese-American population, with 26,654 women and 20,505 men over 65 years of age. The census also showed that 7.5 percent of the 588,300 Japanese-Americans in the United States had incomes below the poverty level, and that of this group 20.8 percent were at least 65 years old. Therefore, although many Issei are spending their last years in the comfortable knowledge that they have helped their children achieve a degree of economic success in the United States, others are finding poverty and hardship their reward for a lifetime of hard work and low wages. The Japanese community has, often with the aid of federal funds, developed retirement housing such as the Little Tokyo Towers in Los Angeles, and social service activities for the elderly have been developed with public and private funds.

Nisei

Before World War II, the Nisei found themselves in the marginal position of being Americans with Japanese faces. If they attempted to join American organizations, they were accused of not knowing their place, and if they lived in their own ethnic communities, they were said to be clannish. Although many Nisei attended college and some went on to graduate schools, professionals were generally confined to employment within the Japanese-American community; elective and civil service jobs were virtually closed; and teaching positions were almost impossible to obtain in public schools. Consequently, Issei occupations—including gardening, farming, small business, and service work—were taken up by the Nisei, especially during the Depression.

The majority of Nisei were law-abiding citizens, very much identified with America, but from 1920 to 1941, West Coast newspapers and civic groups such as the American Legion and the Native Sons and Daughters of the Golden West warned that Japanese-Americans were a threat to national security. These warnings intensified even after a 1929 Carnegie Corporation study concluded that the Nisei had low rates of crime and delinquency.[4]

The $40,000 study, based on 9,690 interviews in California, also showed that Nisei scored as high as whites on standardized intelligence tests, and that Japanese-American employment problems stemmed from discrimination rather than from low academic achievement. The Nisei were concerned about their marginal position in American society, and worried about how and where to earn a living.

Some Nisei decided to leave the United States for Japan, but most, like their Issei parents, turned to the ethnic community for support. Unlike the Issei, however, the Nisei patterned their organizations and recreational and social activities on American rather than Japanese models. Nisei shunned their parents' Japanese associations, for example, forming instead the Japanese

American Citizens Leagues that became the group's most influential national organization in 1931.

Nisei athletic leagues, sponsored by the YWCA, YMCA, Boy and Girl Scouts, church and other community groups, participated like their white counterparts in state and national championships for various sports. The competitions gave the Nisei a chance to travel, plan, and develop social and leadership skills.

Although many Nisei attended Japanese language schools on weekday afternoons and Saturdays, most never learned their lessons well. Nisei attending Protestant and Buddhist churches preferred Sunday services in English, for example, while their parents went to separate Japanese services. The Issei often complained that their children skipped classes and talked back to teachers at the Japanese schools, but were models of good behavior in American schools. Some Issei interpreted this as a rejection of their Japanese heritage.

Then, on December 7, 1941, Japan bombed Pearl Harbor, an event that led to the wartime upheaval of 110,000 persons of Japanese ancestry on the West Coast. Under President Franklin Roosevelt's Executive Order 9066, the evacuees—64 percent of whom were American citizens—left home, businesses, and pre-war life styles for crowded barracks in isolated camps scattered across five states. The order, signed February 19, 1942, gave the military power to remove "dangerous persons" from designated areas, and relocate them in camps at Manzanar and Tule Lake, California; Heart Mountain, Wyoming; Granada, Colorado; Topaz, Utah; Poston, Arizona; and Rowher and Jerome, Arkansas. Most remained in these camps ringed by barbed wire until January 2, 1945, when a United States Supreme Court ruling reversing the evacuation order went into effect.

The relocation resulted from several circumstances, the most important being anti-Japanese sentiment, economic gain coupled with the disorganization in the Japanese-American community and Japanese cultural values.

First, the war sparked a move to solve California's "Japanese problem," by removing the threat of sabotage by Issei and Nisei presumed loyal to Japan. The solution urged by state officials, congressmen, farmers' associations, and patriotic organizations was the mass evacuation of Japanese-Americans from California, Oregon, and Washington. Although there never was any evidence supporting Japanese-American subversion, California Attorney General Earl Warren, in a damaging statement toward fair treatment of the group, said on February 21, 1942, "Many . . . are of the opinion that because we have had no sabotage . . . none [has] been planned for us. But I take the view that is the most ominous sign in the whole situation."[5] Warren went on to become chief justice of the United States Supreme Court.

This anti-Japanese climate was aggravated by a lack of support from liberal and civil rights groups, which, instead, joined international efforts aimed at eliminating overseas Facism. Although some helped establish humane conditions in the camps, few questioned the legitimacy of the evacuation.

In addition, the Japanese-American community was politically powerless and disorganized. Most Nisei were just reaching voting age and their Issei parents would not be allowed American citizenship until 1952. Issei leaders in the community had been arrested by the Federal Bureau of Investigation; and the Japanese-American Citizens League, the only national Nisei group, advocated cooperating with the relocation.

Economically, most Japanese-Americans had no choice but to follow that advice. Shortly before the evacuation order took effect, Issei and Nisei were given the opportunity of moving to the East and Midwest. The majority, however, were too poor to do so. Business owners, for example, could not afford the financial risk of leaving the interdependent ethnic network of customers, workers, and suppliers who comprised the major support of their livelihoods.

Another factor contributing to the group's cooperation was a set of norms emphasizing conformity and obedience. These norms were reinforced by beliefs that the relocation was inevitable ("shi ka ta ga nai"), and that cooperation would prove Japanese-American loyalty to the United States.

The evacuation order did not apply to people of Japanese descent living in Hawaii, even though the island was more likely strategically to be invaded than the mainland. Instead, the island was put under martial law, and ethnocultural institutions such as Buddhist churches and Japanese language schools were closed.

A proposal was made to relocate 150,000 Japanese-Americans in Hawaii to Molakai Island, but no ships were available for the transport; and neither the war effort nor the Hawaiian economy could afford the loss of half the state's population. In addition, racially mixed Hawaiians were more tolerant of ethnic diversity than were Californians.

Concentration was a monotony of barracks, mess halls, long lines, and led to a stifling existence. There were riots, strikes, and fights among inmates who complained constantly about the food, neighbors, living conditions, and administrators. Frustrations sometimes were vented in attacks on leaders of the Japanese-American Citizens League, which had urged cooperation with the evacuation. Tensions between American and Japanese loyalists also resulted in violence. Nisei who had been sent to Japan to be raised by relatives (Kibei) found that their Japanese nationalism antagonized Nisei reared in the United States.

On the other hand, camp life also meant that the basic necessities were taken care of by the United States government, so that for one of the few times in their lives, Japanese-Americans had leisure time. Many of them, especially the Issei, participated in cultural and educational activities.

Enlisting in the armed services was one way of leaving the relocation camps. Another was resettlement in the East and Midwest. About 35,000 Nisei left the camps to attend college or take jobs along the East Coast and in Midwestern cities such as Chicago, Cleveland, and Minneapolis. In their own way, these Japanese-Americans were "new" immigrants, and many found that the Midwest and East were more racially tolerant than the Pacific Coast. As one consequence, the previously concentrated Japanese-American population began to take on a much more national distribution. However, by the end of World War II, there was a gradual drift of the group back to the Pacific Coast.

The camps were ordered to close by the Supreme Court decision in the Endo case in 1944. By 1945, the evacuation camp era came to an end. However, some inmates were reluctant to leave the camps.

A few had adapted completely to camp life, while others feared anti-Japanese terrorism outside the guarded enclosures. By May, 1945, terrorist incidents against Japanese-Americans returning to the West Coast had been reported. Nonviolent instances of racism also were recorded, including the American Legion's removal of sixteen Nisei soldiers from the Hood River, Oregon honor roll. Four of the soldiers had been killed in battle, and ten others had been awarded the Purple Heart. Community sentiment was summarized in a headline of the *Hood River Sun* on February 2, 1945: "So sorry please, Japanese not wanted in Hood River."

These incidents, combined with the loss of homes, farms, and businesses due to the evacuation, provided little incentive for Japanese-Americans to return to the Pacific Coast. But the majority did, especially to California. By 1950, 85,000 of the 168,000 Japanese-Americans living on the mainland resided in California, with that number increasing to 157,000 in 1960.

The Postwar Era

The period after World War II can be viewed as the new Nisei era. The Nisei were now at the age of assuming leadership. They had gone through the wartime evacuation; an estimated 35,000 Nisei had been cleared and left the camps to live in the Midwest and the East; others had served in the armed services and experienced life in Europe and Asia; and the schools and colleges enrolled a large number of Nisei students. The G.I. Bill was one source of assistance; Issei parents were also helpful, even though they themselves were starting off anew since many had lost much of their material possessions during the evacuation.

West Coast Issei and Nisei returned to what seemed a different place than the one they had left. Thousands of people from the South and Midwest, drawn west by wartime industry, remained after the end of the fighting. In addition, a growing number of blacks and Mexicans in the area helped absorb some of the racial antagonism which was previously directly against the Japanese-Americans. This more tolerant racial and ethnic climate, together with a distinguished Nisei war record, feelings of guilt over the relocation, and elimination of Japan as a military power, led to California's defeat of a 1946 ballot proposition aimed at allowing a state takeover of Issei lands bequeathed to the Nisei.

The Nisei also had changed. Ironically, the relocation camps provided job opportunities that had been unavailable to Japanese-Americans prior to the war. For example, Nisei teachers who had been unsuccessful in finding public school positions in California were recruited to lead camp classes. The experience helped them find teaching jobs in East Coast cities under the wartime resettlement program.

Nisei competed against Nisei based on education, training, and ability to fill every job required by the camp communities, with the exception of administrative posts reserved for whites. The jobs paid only $16 to $19 a month, but gave the Nisei confidence they could function in varied and important roles. After the war, the expectations raised by this experience met with increased job availability, and many Nisei found employment in once closed fields, including the civil service.

The transition from camp to civilian life was aided by United States government relocation offices, churches, and volunteer groups. The government also began to repay some of the $400 million lost by the evacuees. When the last claim was adjudicated on October 1, 1964, the government had authorized payment of $38 million to 26,560 claimants. Many Japanese-Americans viewed the settlement, which amounted to ten cents per dollar, as a gesture of government sympathy and remorse, but pitifully inadequate.

The occupational picture for the Japanese-American did not shift significantly upon their return to the West Coast. Many used occupations such as gardening as a temporary transition toward other endeavors, while others returned to agriculture and small business. Especially popular were real estate and furniture and appliance stores. There was a great need on the part of Japanese-Americans to start anew with the purchase of homes and home furnishings so that much of the clientele was drawn from the ethnic community. However, the greatest impact in terms of future occupations was the high proportion of Nisei attending schools and colleges in preparation for professional careers.

The upward mobility can be seen by comparing United States Census figures for 1940 and 1960. In 1940, more than 25 percent of Japanese-American males were classified as laborers, but in 1960, the figure had dropped to five percent. Conversely, in 1940, only 3.8 percent were professionals, but in 1960, the figure had risen to 25 percent.

In 1952, the McCarran-Walter Immigration Act was passed. Although the bill was generally considered a restrictive bill by liberal organizations, it was favored by many Japanese-Americans because for the first time it provided an opportunity for the naturalization of the Issei and also included a token quota for Japanese immigration.

The New Immigrants

There were several special groups of Japanese immigrants during the postwar era. The most prominent were the Japanese war brides, products of the American occupation. An estimated 25,000 war brides were in the states by 1960. They were a heterogeneous group in terms of background and in terms of their motivation for marrying out of the Japanese culture, but homogeneous in terms of sex and age.

The experiences of this group varied. Some married Nisei and merged imperceptibly into the ethnic community. Others scattered throughout the country to the homes of their husbands. Many found employment in the Japanese restaurants and bars which were springing up in West Coast cities. Individual tales of hardship, separation, and divorce were circulated widely in the ethnic community but were probably atypical of the general experiences of the majority of the group. Data on the war brides and their families is scarce.

The total number of Japanese immigrants to the United States after World War II has been small. Immigration department figures indicate 113,987 Japanese immigrants from 1950 through 1978. The influx has been gradual; from 1950 to 1960, 44,399; from 1961 to 1970, 38,905; and from 1971 to 1978, 30,683. The impact of these new immigrants has been slight, partly because they came in small groups, merged into already established Japanese-American communities, and were readily absorbed into the American economy. Most of them did not have to face the overt prejudice and discrimination that were a part of the lives of the Issei, Nisei, and Sansei.

The Sansei

Although the influence of the Nisei and even some Issei, still lingers in the Japanese-American communities, the period from the 1960s can be viewed as the Sansei era. Their experiences have been widely varied—some were born in the World War II concentration camps, others in the Midwest and East. However, the majority were products of California and the West Coast.

The relative homogeneity of the Issei and Nisei has given way to a wide range of behavior, expectations, and life styles among the Sansei. By most measures of acculturation, including test scores, achievement, interests, and social values, the Sansei are nearly identical to the white group. In general, their education is oriented toward "secure" professions such as teaching and engineering. Few have faced overt discrimination, and employment has been based on education, training, and the overall job market. Although some evidence indicates a slightly higher rate of deviant behavior among Sansei compared to previous generations, this trend is congruent with an acculturative process in which juvenile delinquency is generally higher among the American-born children of immigrants.

The most dramatic trend which symbolized Sansei acculturation has been in the area of interracial marriage. The model of immigration, acculturation, integration, and assimilation has generally been viewed as inevitable especially for those of European background, but has not fitted the experiences of most nonwhite groups. Antimiscegenation laws and other discriminatory actions have systematically discouraged intimate contact across racial lines. As early as 1661, the colony of Maryland passed laws to control intermarriage between white female servants and black slaves. The fear of the "mongrelization" of the races has been such that it took until 1967, in the case of *Loving* v. *Virginia* to overturn the legal barriers concerning interracial marriages.

The trend in terms of interracial marriage for the Japanese-Americans can be linked to generations. For example, in Los Angeles County, the period prior to 1924 (the Issei) showed only two percent of the Japanese outmarrying. The figures of outmarriage for the 1930s, 1940s, and mid-1950s (the Nisei) showed a rate between 11 and 17 percent. The outmarriage rates for 1971 and 1972 (the Sansei) were at the 50 percent level, and similar outmarriage rates were also found in San Francisco and Fresno. Therefore, one of the most visible changes among the current Japanese-Americans is that of marrying out of the group.[6]

The majority of the marriages were to Caucasians. There was also an early trend of more females marrying out of the group than males, but the latest figures indicate a more even distribution, with 55 percent of the exogamous outmarriages by females.

There are a number of hypotheses which help to explain the phenomenon. One of the most salient relates to the opportunity for increased contact, which is a function of the breakup of the ethnic ghetto, the housing dispersion of Japanese-Americans, and socioeconomic mobility. Another is the relatively small population base of the group, especially in areas away from Hawaii and the California cities which encourage nonethnic marital choices. The breakup of the ethnic family, changes in family and ethnic identity, and the inability of the family to exert social control over individual members combine to form other reasons for outmarriage. Finally, there has been a combination of length of time in the country, acculturation, and the changing attitudes of the majority of Sansei which had led to the current rates of outmarriage.

There are a wide variety of opportunities open to the Sansei, especially in comparison to the Nisei and Issei generations. The earlier generations had fewer voluntary choices in terms of jobs, social relationships, and ethnic identity. Sansei can and do socialize across racial lines. Others may prefer ethnic groups and can join all-Asian fraternities and sororities. The trend of increased interracial dating and marriage is likely to continue. These acculturative trends are true even in Hawaii, where Japanese influences remain strong. Hawaiian Sansei have blended ethnic group traditions with the islands' cosmopolitan culture—a mixture that has resulted in an Asian, Euro-American, and Polynesian assortment of foods, games, behavior, entertainment, and folklore. Island Sansei retain some allegiance to their ethnic culture, but see themselves primarily as "locals."

The experiences of the Japanese in Hawaii are different enough to warrant a special section. For example, in 1980, the governor and the two state senators were Japanese-American Nisei. Japanese-Americans also held prominent positions in other political and economic structures of the state.

The Japanese first immigrated to Hawaii in 1868 as contract laborers for sugar plantations. Their numbers were limited by the Japanese government, which screened workers from the agricultural regions of Hiroshima, Yamaguchi, and Kumamoto in an effort to avoid making Japan a storehouse for cheap labor similar to China in the mid-1880s. Japanese immigration to the Hawaiian Islands increased from 1891 to 1920, and by 1920, there were 109,294 Issei.

The Issei established their own ethnic communities adjoining the Hawaiian plantations, a practice that supported the planters' policy of separate living areas for Japanese, Chinese, Portuguese, and Filipino workers. This isolation resulted in the reproduction of Japanese village life in Hawaii, a trend that was further encouraged by the islands' geographic closeness to Japan.

The single most important difference between the Japanese in Hawaii and their peers on the mainland United States was that of numbers. Rather than a small minority in a vast area such as along the Pacific Coast, the Japanese in Hawaii were a large group in a small area, even achieving numerical majority group status at certain periods. However, because the Issei were denied the right to become American citizens until well after World War II, the ability to translate their numbers into political power has been of relatively recent origin.

During World War II, Japanese-Americans in Hawaii joined those on the mainland to form the famed 442nd Combat Team and the 100th Battalion. These units, the most decorated in American history, suffered more than 9,000 casualties and 600 deaths among their 33,000 men.

Hawaii has been the site of dramatic progress by Japanese-American politicians. In 1950, Japanese-Americans comprised 37 percent of Hawaii's population, giving them a clear electoral advantage. This advantage was enhanced in 1952, when Issei were allowed United States citizenship and earned the right to vote. The newly enfranchised Issei joined the Nisei, who had come of age, and a growing, multiethnic coalition of dissident Democrats led by John Burns and Nisei war veteran Daniel Inouye. In 1954, the coalition supporting Nisei politicians took control of both houses in the territorial legislature, ending the long years of Republican conservative white rule.

Hawaiian Nisei expanded their political power after the islands achieved statehood in 1959. In 1962, Spark Matsunaga and Patsy Takemoto Mink were elected to the U.S. House of Representatives, while Inouye won a U.S. Senate seat. Within the next decade, Matsunaga joined Inouye in the Senate. By 1974, George Ariyoushi and Nelson Doi had been elected governor and lieutenant governor, respectively, of Hawaii. At about the same time, half the state's representatives and senators were Japanese-Americans, with Nisei also dominating the Hawaii Department of Education and other departments.

This rise in Nisei political power has caused anxiety among some Hawaiians fearing a Japanese-American "takeover." This apprehension has been intensified by a recent flood of Japanese tourists, and by the purchase by Japanese businessmen of prominent Waikiki hotels.

The postwar years also brought a growing tourist industry that provided new jobs and stimulated business. Japanese-Americans, now one of the power groups in Hawaii's multiethnic society, filled the ranks of professionals with doctors, dentists, lawyers, teachers, and engineers. But the growth of Hawaii has also created problems of overcrowding and pollution so that there have been attempts to control the islands' growth. One novel, but clearly unconstitutional, suggestion by Governor Ariyoushi concerned the restriction of immigration to the state.

Japanese-Americans also have been elected to public office in California, despite that state's history of anti-Japanese sentiment. Norman Mineta, former mayor of San Jose, was elected Congressman in 1972; S. I. Hayakawa, a retired college president, won a U.S. Senate seat in 1976, but did not receive strong support from younger Japanese-American voters; and Robert Matusi was elected to the House of Representatives in 1978.

Japanese-American names can also be seen on the ballot for local offices, especially in California. Since the group seldom has a large numerical base (with the exception of Hawaii), it can be interpreted as a possible sign of political acceptability. However, physical identifiability also remains salient, especially during the adolescent dating period. Many Sansei relate stories of felt discrimination especially as they begin to date and become more seriously involved with non-Japanese. There also remain strong stereotypes of these Americans with Japanese faces. For example, Sansei are expected to know about Japan and the Japanese culture, and when well-meaning Americans comment on the Sansei's marvelous ability to speak English, they unintentionally are questioning the Sansei's "acceptability" as "real Americans." During the "save the whales" campaigns of the late 1970s, young Sansei and Yonsei (the fourth generation) were often identified by their American peers with the nation that shot the mammals.

Intermarriage and acculturation have not diminished the importance of the Japanese-American community, which continues to serve as a focal point for social activities and civic affairs. For example, the Gardena Community Center in suburban Los Angeles offers judo, kendo, and other martial arts classes, financial support for social and counseling services, Little League baseball, fishing derbies, Japanese language courses, and gardening exhibitions. Gardena, however, is expectional in its high concentration of Japanese-Americans. Those in other areas generally participate in more racially integrated facilities.

The Japanese-American community has become a heterogenenous enclave of political positions, interest groups, economic roles, and cultural styles. This heterogeneity was illustrated in community reactions to a Los Angeles redevelopment project in the 1970s that caused the removal of Japanese-American businesses and the eviction of old people from low-income hotels. Some Japanese-Americans got together to bid for redevelopment sites in competition with Japanese capital from Japan, while others, primarily the younger generation, opposed the idea of moving out the elderly Issei as inhumane and unnecessary. Some Japanese-Americans were active as federal housing administrators, while others represented the forces of law and order. The Little Tokyo project is symptomatic of a rekindling of Sansei interest in the ethnic community, a concern that has sparked many to enroll in ethnic study courses and reassess their Japanese-American identity in relation to the "melting pot." Others have visited Japan on vacations, while some young Sansei are going to live in Japan.

Interest in Japan also has been stimulated by a recent influx of Japanese immigrants. Japanese brides began arriving from American-occupied Japan in the early 1950s; and beginning in 1950, other Japanese—including students, businessmen, consular officials, and United Nations representatives—began arriving in increasing numbers under nonquota immigration categories.

Most of the new immigrant Issei have settled into American society with little difficulty. Friends, relatives, and the ethnic community have helped in easing the adjustment, and the immigrants themselves sometimes appear to be more "modern" in their attitudes and dress than Japanese-Americans. Although Sansei often criticize these immigrants as being "fresh off the boat," the new Issei defy easy description. For example, whereas many Sansei are still somewhat reserved and hesitate to bring out ideas openly, some of the new Issei are more outspoken and direct, which reflects the changes in the home country.

Many of the new permanent immigrant Issei have found employment similar to the Japanese immigrants of years past. Farming and agricultural work, as well as gardening are initial entry positions which require hard work but little knowledge of English and minimal capital investment. The major difference between today and yesterday appears to be the level of acceptance. Whereas Japanese of a previous era faced resistance on almost every level, today's worker finds that bank loans and other forms of financing are open and that racially discriminatory laws are nonexistent. Successful Nisei nursery men have told us that the new Issei do not seem to appreciate that their lot has been made easier because of the hard work and enterprise exhibited by the Nisei.

Employees of large Japanese companies form extensive transient groups, particularly in Los Angeles and New York. Members of these "kai-sha," or business groups, have limited social contact with the Japanese-American community. They operate as business people with other businessmen at clubs, restaurants, and golf courses. Their presence, however, reminds Japanese-Americans of Japan's importance in world affairs. In addition, increasing numbers of Japanese-Americans are employed at American branches of Japanese firms, although chances for advancement are slim. The firms normally fill executive posts with Japanese from Japan or whites.

With the exception of gardening and agriculture, Sansei employment has followed that of the Nisei in terms of occupations. Overall, the third generation of Japanese-Americans has experienced little or none of the overt job discrimination that confronted their forebears, and an overwhelming number of Sansei have attended college. They are overrepresented in the college population. Although Japanese-Americans constituted only 0.8

percent of United States residents, they represented one percent of undergraduate students and two percent of graduate school enrollment.

Despite these high education levels, many Sansei face the possibility of downward mobility. Nisei achievements have in some cases made Sansei expectations of equaling or surpassing their parents both unrealistic and undesirable.

Sansei also have acculturated in terms of American attitudes. Their egoistic behavior and emphasis on personal rather than group advancement have developed to such an extent that on a question regarding family and the nation, Sansei displayed a more individualistic position than non-Japanese-Americans.

Additionally, the Sansei reflected American standards of discipline and values. The degree of acculturation prompted Mamoru Iga to say in 1966:

[The Sansei] desire to be assimilated appears to be so complete and their knowledge of Japanese culture so minimal that we cannot anticipate their return to traditional cultural interests, (and) the only factor which prevents them from complete assimilation seems to be the combination of their physical visibility and racial prejudice on the part of dominant group members.[7]

Iga's observation was made before the recent interest in ethnic identity among many Sansei.

The juvenile crime rate among Sansei is itself another indicator of acculturation. According to Donald Cressey, delinquency is higher among the American-born children of immigrants than among the immigrant group. Although the Sansei surpass the Nisei in the rate of juvenile crime, they remain below the rates of their non-Japanese peers.

The types of crime committed by Japanese-Americans also have varied according to the generations. Drunkenness and gambling were the highest offenses among the Issei, and Nisei crimes were similar. But for the Sansei, drug-related offenses are among the most common, which is reflective of the overall changes in the American society. But the overall rate of

Japanese-American crime as measured by official statistics remains extremely low in comparison to other groups. Similarly, the rates for hospitalization for mental illness also remain low.[8]

The 1970 census provides the following demographic picture of the Japanese-Americans. The median age was 29.5 years for the males and 33.2 for the females. More than 68 percent were high school graduates (one of the highest for all groups in the United States) and the rates of separation and divorce were four percent for the male and six percent for the female. Only 7.5 percent had incomes below the poverty level (as defined by the U.S. Census), with a high proportion of low incomes in the 65 years or older age group. General income statistics indicate that Japanese-American family income ranks among the highest of all ethnic groups. Part of the explanation for the high family income is related to the employment of several family members.

The overall demographic picture indicates an ethnic group that is competitive in America in terms of education and income. But very few have achieved positions in the most powerful sectors of the American economy (corporate directors, leaders of industry, responsible administrative and managerial positions) leading Kitano to ask whether the Japanese have become a middleman minority.[9]

Finally, the area of values provides some of the most interesting data concerning changes and acculturation among the various Japanese generations. The major psychological and behavioral orientations in the Japanese society during the time of the Issei immigration included an emphasis on collectivity, as against an individualistic orientation; on duty and obligation, as opposed to individual desires and motivation; a recognition of a hierarchical order of social relationships, rather than one based on a more egalitarian model; and dependency, rather than the more American perspective of aggressiveness and independence. A study by John Connor (1977) indicates the changes in these values by each generation from a "Japanese value system" toward the American way of looking at the world, although it should also be noted that some Issei had also acquired some American perspectives.[10] It is expected that the longer the group remains in America the more acculturated they will become, so that variables such as geographic area of residence, social class, and reference groups will become more important than ethnicity in determining their behavior. Nevertheless, as long as physical visibility remains, a Japanese element will persist as part of their identity.

The most interesting development for the Japanese-Americans at the start of 1980 was the reawakening of World War II issues. For several decades after World War II, events such as the trial of Tokyo Rose and the wartime evacuation were repressed topics, and the general feeling among Japanese-Americans was to ignore and forget this period. However, during the late 1970s, the suddenly "quiet" Japanese-Americans became involved in actions heretofore considered taboo. One was a successful effort to pardon "Tokyo Rose," a Japanese-American convicted as a traitor for alleged anti-American comments over Japanese radio during World War II. The most ambitious drive was an attempt to gain redress from the United States government for the forced evacuation into the World War II concentration camps. At the time of this paper, the outcome of the redress campaign is in doubt, but the very fact of bringing up the issue is symptomatic of the change among Japanese-Americans.

NOTES

1. Sidney Gulick, *The American-Japanese Problem* (New York: Charles Scribner, 1914), p. 189.

2. Bradford Smith, *Americans from Japan* (Philadelphia: J. B. Lippincott, 1948), p. 47.

3. Dennis Ogawa, *Kodomo No Tame Ni* (Honolulu: University of Hawaii Press, 1978).

4. Edward Strong, Jr., *The Second Generation Japanese Problem* (Stanford: Stanford University Press, 1934).

5. See *Congressional Record,* February 21, 1942.

6. Akemi Kikumura and Harry H. L. Kitano, "Interracial Marriage: A Picture of the Japanese Americans," *Journal of Social Issues* 29, no. 2 (1973): 67–81.

7. Mamoru Iga, "Changes in Value Orientation of Japanese Americans," paper read at the Western Psychological Association Meeting, April 28, 1966, Long Beach, California.

8. Harry Kitano, *Japanese Americans: The Evolution of a Subculture* (Englewood Cliffs, N.J.: Prentice-Hall, 1976), chap. 9.

9. Harry Kitano, "Japanese Americans: The Development of a Middleman Minority?" *Pacific Historical Review* 43, no. 4 (November, 1974): 500–519.

10. John Connor, *Tradition and Change in Three Generations of Japanese Americans* (Chicago: Nelson Hall, 1977).

IV

The Mexican-Americans

By Carey McWilliams
The Nation

The Spanish-speaking people in the United States are clearly on their way to becoming this country's largest minority, a fact most Americans find hard to believe. Nor do they fully appreciate the extent to which the experience of the Spanish-speaking people differs from that of other immigrant minorities. I use the term Spanish-speaking as a matter of convenience, although "Hispanic" is coming into more common usage. The Spanish-speaking never constituted a thoroughly homogeneous minority; what its various components have in common is an identification with the Spanish language and ancestral ties with the peoples of Spanish-speaking lands and islands.

Today the Spanish-speaking minority includes descendants of Spanish settlers who were living in territories now part of the United States before the war with Mexico; Mexican-Americans who are citizens through birth or naturalization; Mexican immigrants both legal and illegal; and a large eastern seaboard contingent made up of Puerto Ricans, Dominicans, Cubans, and people from various Central and South American countries. Until fairly recently there had been little contact between Mexican-Americans, who are mostly concentrated in the Southwest (sixty percent reside there), and other Spanish-speaking elements. Differences are to be noted in the background and experience of these two main divisions of the Spanish-speaking. Under the Jones Act of 1917, for example, Puerto Ricans are citizens. What the Spanish-speaking share is a language—with a variety of ac-

91

cents—and a heritage. The Mexican-American experience is exceptional in that it does not fit the familiar pattern of immigration. In the Southwest, demographic, historical, geographical, and economic factors have combined to shape a special relationship between Hispanics and Anglos (another term of convenience used here to designate the non-Spanish-speaking majority).

Setting and Background

At the time of the signing of the Treaty of Guadalupe Hidalgo (1848), four small colonies of Spanish-speaking people were to be found in what is now the United States. Long isolated in time and distance, these settlements were located in California, Arizona, New Mexico, and Texas, with a combined population of perhaps 80,000. Of this total, fewer than 14,000 had been born in Mexico; the rest were of Spanish-Indian origin. Given the fact that the treaty ceded to the United States approximately half the land area of Mexico (an additional acquisition came with the Gadsden Purchase), one might have thought that the settlers would want to return to Mexico or resettle there. But they had deep roots in the areas where they lived and, under the treaty, had been given formal assurances that their rights would be protected. Some did return, but what probably kept most of the others in the borderlands was the more or less simultaneous discovery of gold in California; the discovery was made a few days before the treaty was signed. Word of the discovery stimulated an influx of Mexicans from Sonora, many of whom had mining experience and still others who performed valuable services for mining communities in northern California by operating packtrains and serving as guides. Also, many of the emigrant wagon trains passed through New Mexico en route to the gold fields, and supplying these trains became a profitable form of endeavor for the resident Spanish-speaking people.

Given this background, Spanish-speaking people had little reason to think of themselves as "immigrants"; in their eyes, the Anglos were the outsiders. The area "North From Mexico" was similar to that from which the first Mexican immigrants had come; the terrain was much the same. Spanish was spoken wherever there were settlements; and the Hispanic imprint remains clear to this day throughout the vast territory which Mexico ceded to the United States. States, rivers, mountains, cities, and towns retain the names given them by the first Spanish-speaking settlers. Historic trails crossed what later became the border and branched out into different parts of the ceded territory. The border itself was defined without much regard for natural barriers of which there are few. In an arid or semi-arid region, a river such as the Rio Grande does not separate those living on either side so much as it draws them to its banks. Actually, the international line was drawn up the middle of the river which has constantly shifted its course.

From Brownsville and Matamoros on the Gulf Coast to San Diego and Tijuana on the Pacific, the bilingual and bicultural border towns (about 700 in number) are linked like the beads of a double-strand necklace. Economically, the sister cities and towns are inextricably interlocked; they accept each other's currencies and often share the same telephone service and tap the same water sources. Nowadays, Tijuana and San Diego are described as "two cities as close together as a kitchen and a dining room," symbiotically interdependent. Tijuana and San Diego—with respective populations of 850,000 and 800,000—constitute one of the largest urban complexes on the West Coast. In 1978, Mexican visitors spent an estimated $220,000,000 on retail purchases in San Diego.[1] Disturbances in relations between the United States and Mexico, such as the devaluation of the peso, have an immediate impact on the economies of the American border cities and towns. Total annual border crossings are now estimated at 200 million. Some 82 million crossings were tallied at the El Paso–Juarez entry point in 1978: about 250,000 a day, 10,000 an hour.[2] An estimated 50,000 residents of Juarez are regular, authorized commuters to El Paso.

Recent economic developments have tightened the ties between the twin border cities. Caught by Mexican fishing boats in Mexican waters, shrimps are brought to Brownsville from Matamoras by truck, sorted, frozen, and stored. If cleaning is desired, the shrimps are then trucked back to Matamoras and processed by

poorly paid Mexican women workers and returned to Brownsville ("the shrimp capital of the world") for packaging and
shipping. Despite the fiction of a "border" separating Brownsville from Matamoras, this is essentially a single, integrated
economic operation. Since 1966, American corporations have
been induced to open labor-intensive assembly plants in the
Mexican border cities where labor is plentiful and cheap, and
duties are paid only on the labor-added value. A newspaper report estimates that there are 450 of these so-called *maguiladoras,*
or assembly plants, employing perhaps 80,000 workers, mostly
women between the ages of 17 and 34. Juarez alone has about
100 such plants, where electronic parts, toys, garments, radios,
calculators, and other products are assembled.[3] And today
Sinaloa, on the west coast of Mexico, has become a huge "winter
garden," where large corporations, many with home bases in
California, raise produce (tomatoes, bell peppers, cucumbers,
squash, eggplant, etc.), which is trucked to Nogales, Arizona,
on a major new highway and then shipped to large urban markets in the United States. Some 2,000 Mexican growers, working
with large American canning and produce corporations, employ
an estimated 200,000 workers in these operations.[4]

The 1,000-mile Transpeninsular Highway down the coast of
Baja California, completed in December, 1974, has greatly stimulated traffic, tourism, trade, and migration. As many as 5,000
Mexicans a month have been making their way to Tijuana, seeking jobs there or some means of getting across the border to
California. In fact, Baja California is by way of becoming
another Southern California, dotted with rich resort hotels and
seaside subdivisions; perhaps as many as 10,000 Americans
have purchased real estate along the coast.[5] And, of course, the
stretch of the west coast of Mexico from the border to Acapulco
is dotted with resorts and communities that each year attract more
and more American visitors and homeseekers.

Developments of this sort have greatly increased the population of the Mexican border cities and towns. The population
of the six Mexican border states has increased from 5.5 million
in 1960 to a projected estimate of 14 million for 1980. Popula-

tion in the Tijuana zone increased from 377,308 in 1970 to 636,114 by the end of 1978; and in the Mexicali zone from 263,498 to 583,585 in the same period.[6] Migration to the Mexican border cities has provided jobs for some immigrants, but it has also intensified the "push" factors and increased the number of illegal border crossings. The border has never been strictly policed. An indeterminate number of cub planes now dart back and forth across the line with the greatest ease. Experts have estimated the number of such unscheduled flights as high as 150 a day, in certain seasons. Flights of this sort are used to smuggle drugs and "illegals" into the states. In point of fact, the border is a sieve. Only forty or so miles have topographical barriers of a kind that might hinder illegal crossings by land routes. Only twenty-seven miles of the border are fenced and patrols cover less than ten percent of its reach, one officer for approximately every ten miles. And "illegals" also enter this country in small boats.

It should be kept in mind that the border between the United States and Mexico, so casually drawn, is nearly 2,000 miles in length (1,952 miles to be exact). From 1850 to 1900, Mexican immigration was constant but of limited volume with most of the immigrants being drawn from areas about 100 miles south of the border. It was, of course, easy then to cross and recross the international line; the Border Patrol was not established until 1924. Immigrants just walked or rode across the border and returned when they felt like it. But construction of rail lines from the interior of Mexico, beginning in the 1900s, enabled more immigrants to make their way north in search of work. Railroad construction and maintenance, mining, and agricultural developments in areas immediately north of the border—activities in which Mexican labor played a key role—drew increasingly large numbers of immigrants into the United States. And the flow of new arrivals was stepped up after the displacement of Diaz in 1910 and the upheaval caused by the Mexican Revolution. The inception of World War I and the curtailment of European immigration that resulted also stimulated migration from Mexico. Between 1911 and 1930, some 678,291 immigrants crossed into the United States. Yet the back-and-forth movement of Mexicans remained so easy and informal—it had become so much a matter of custom—that the Immigration Service did not begin to report the number of immigrants until 1908. Actually, in some places the border is almost literally nonexistent. For example, one 75-mile stretch is largely ignored by the Border Patrol for the reason that half of the Papago Indian ancestral lands are on one side of the border, half on the other. The Papagos continue to move back and forth as though the border did not exist. "We were here first," they say, "before there was a Mexico or a United States."

A combination of unusually strong "push" and "pull" factors has been responsible for the continued heavy migration from Mexico. A high birthrate, lack of economic development, and a paucity of jobs in Mexico have combined with equally strong "pull" factors in the United States, including nowadays a strong demand for "cheap" labor in many urban industries and service occupations. Today, in fact, the bulk of the Spanish-speaking population here is concentrated in urban areas.

At certain periods—the history is much too long to detail— Mexicans have been encouraged to move across the border by the thousands while the Immigration Service has obligingly looked the other way. At periods, such as during and after World War II, thousands of farm workers, the so-called *braceros*, have been imported under contract with the approval of both governments to work for limited periods. The cessation of this program gave an immediate impetus to the so-called "wetback" or illegal immigration. To curb the influx of wetbacks, which soon reached flood proportions, the Immigration Service began to stage major dragnet raids or sweeps in which thousands of Mexican nationals were rounded up—"apprehended" is the word most frequently used—and unceremoniously returned to Mexico. In fact, this has become a continuous process. For example, in Tacna, Arizona, some 1,300 illegals are returned to Mexico each week during the harvest season; and in El Paso, an estimated 10,000 to 11,000 illegals are returned every month (even so, the Immigration Service believes that many more just disappear into urban areas to the north and west).[7]

Continuous in both directions, the traffic has served to fashion a single expanded labor market with an exceptional degree of interdependence. Mexico provides a major market for American products, and in 1977 the United States accounted for 66 percent of Mexico's four billion dollar export trade.[8] Today it would take a Berlin Wall to curb the constant movement of Mexican migrants across the border. Pregnant Mexican women often manage to slip across the border so that their children may be born in this country. In Tijuana, many of the thousands of Mexicans who apply for visas do so on the ground that they have American-born children. At the same time, the adoption of Mexican babies by childless American couples has become a minor growth industry. On occasion the babies are simply brought back across the border in the arms of one or another of the adopting parents. An attorney in San Diego was quoted in the *New York Times* of November 13, 1978, as saying that there are places in South Tijuana "sort of like a supermarket" where American couples can pick a baby for adoption from a roomful of prospects.

Of recent years, the subject of "illegals" or "undocumented" workers has attracted a great deal of attention. The Immigration Service and various special interests like to manipulate the figures on "illegals" to suit their own purposes. For example, the Immigration Service has estimated that there may be more than eight million "illegals" in this country, and in the last fiscal year it reported that 1,070,000 illegals had been "apprehended." But there is no way to determine how many of those apprehended were "repeaters," that is, illegals who had been deported more than once in the same period. Nor do the figures tell us how many of those "apprehended" agreed to leave the country voluntarily. Most of the apprehensions take place near the border and the same individual may be deported several times in the same year. For those and other reasons, the official figures on "illegals" are notoriously unreliable. As an indication of the uncertainty that prevails about numbers, two Latin American scholars recently were quoted as saying that there are "some three to six million Mexican immigrants in the United States at any given time," which is quite a wide range of variation.[9]

Currently, Washington is considering a number of proposals for dealing with the problem of "illegals," such as reorganizing the Immigration Service, establishing a fair quota for Mexican Immigration (the quota was arbitrarily cut from 40,000 to 20,000 in the last days of the Ford administration), granting an amnesty for aliens who have resided in this country for seven years, barring employment of recently arrived illegals, and building a higher fence along certain sections of the border! Clearly, the effect of illegals on the economy of the American border states needs far more study than it has received. It is fairly easy to determine the impact employment of illegals at substandard rates may have on wages in a particular industry; but the overall effect of illegals on the general economy is more difficult to assay. Local labor, including resident native-born Mexicans, are not interested in many of the jobs illegals are glad to accept. Some experts find little evidence of large-scale displacement of local resident workers by illegals. Nor is it true that illegals necessarily depress wage scales and lower working standards. In one study of illegals, 73 percent were found to have had federal income taxes deducted from their paychecks, 77 percent had paid social security taxes, only .06 percent had received welfare payments, and only 1.05 percent had accepted food stamps.[10]

But there is an abundance of evidence of harsh border realities: violent "incidents" are quite common; bodies of immigrants who have attempted to swim the Rio Grande are frequently washed ashore; families are separated; and, on occasion, the border patrol has engaged in pitched battles with immigrants seeking to cross the border. Illegals often live as fugitives in constant fear of the *migra* (Immigration officials); they are frequently rounded up in large dragnet raids and shipped like cattle to points in the interior of Mexico; and most of them live in miserable housing and are to be found in the lowest paying, most menial positions. Most of them are law-abiding, hard-working individuals in desperate need of employment who would have preferred to stay in Zacatecas or Jalisco if jobs had been available.[11]

The total number of the Spanish-speaking in the United States today is not known with any accuracy. For one thing, the illegals are not counted when they cross the border; then, too, many return to Mexico, either voluntarily or involuntarily. A 1977 estimate offered these figures: 7.2 million Mexican-Americans; 1.8 million Puerto Rican-Americans; 700,000 Cubans; and 2.4 million individuals from a heterogeneous collection of countries with a Spanish-speaking heritage.[12] To these estimates should be added an indeterminate number of illegals—800,000 to 1,000,000 would be a minimum estimate—mostly of Mexican origin. But these are only estimates; the exact totals are not known.

Today, sizable Spanish-speaking communities can be found in the St. Paul–Minneapolis area; in Seattle; in Kansas City (perhaps 50,000); in Chicago (an estimated 700,000); in Newark; in the Miami area (an estimated 1.6 million); and small contingents can be found in such unlikely places as Lancaster, Pennsylvania and Hanover, New Hampshire.[13] Texas, according to the Census, has at least 2.2 million Hispanic residents, about 20 percent of the state's population; San Antonio has a Spanish-speaking majority. California's Spanish-speaking population may be as high as four million (including illegals), about 17 percent of the state's total population. The New York City area has about 1.7 million Spanish-speaking, mostly Puerto Ricans but including contingents from the Dominican Republic (51,231), Cuba (63,043), and Colombia (22,581). Only 3,541 Mexicans and Mexican-Americans were tabulated in the New York City count. For the most part, Mexican-Americans stay fairly close to the border. Chicago, in fact, is the one urban area where Mexican-Americans as well as other Spanish-speaking elements are to be found in large numbers.[14]

One uncertainty in regard to the number of Spanish-speaking people is that the 1970 census, which was supposed to be the most accurate taken up to that time, undercounted Hispanics in California alone by an estimated 643,000. In general, the 1970 census failed to count one out of every seven Hispanics.[15] Since the population is young, with high birthrates, the Spanish-speaking will soon constitute 20 percent of California's population. Already, the Hispanic population is estimated to be roughly 22.4 percent of the total in the city of Los Angeles. Fifty percent of the children in kindergarten schools in Los Angeles claim Spanish as their first language. Spanish surnamed students are now the largest single ethnic group in the Los Angeles schools (34.6 percent of those enrolled). In Los Angeles County, the number of Spanish surnamed individuals rose from 9.9 percent to 18.1 percent between 1960 and 1970 and will probably reach 28 percent in 1980. In many Sun Belt communities, Mexicans outnumber Anglos; in the states of the Southwest they constitute something like 30 percent of the population—40 percent in New Mexico.

The special experience of the Spanish-speaking in the years subsequent to 1848 has been a key factor in shaping the attitudes of both Anglos and Hispanics in the Southwest. Most Mexican immigrants (legal and illegal) have settled in Spanish-speaking *barrios* or neighborhoods where Mexican cultural traditions prevail. Many have lived in labor camps where they associated, traveled, and worked with other Spanish-speaking people, often under the supervision of a Spanish-speaking labor contractor.

Not surprisingly, therefore, Mexican immigrants have not shown as active an interest in acquiring American citizenship as some European immigrant groups. For illegals, the process of regularizing their status has been both expensive and difficult. And since so few have applied for citizenship (only two petitions were filed in El Paso in one year during the 1950s), they have been ineligible for many benefits and have lacked political power to correct a variety of discriminations. Their "alien" status also has encouraged elements of the Anglo community to regard them as outsiders who could be imposed upon and, if necessary, pushed around. Residual hostilities dating from the Mexican-

American War have been a factor in creating and maintaining these attitudes. Continuous immigration, much of it illegal, has handicapped resident native-born Mexican-Americans who have had to compete, in some instances, with illegals in some job categories. According to Barry R. Chiswick, a senior fellow at the Hoover Institution at Stanford, it takes on an average about 10 to 15 years for foreign-born white male workers to match the earnings of those with comparable backgrounds born in the United States. For these and other reasons, the experience of Spanish-speaking immigrants, particularly those from Mexico, does not in all respects resemble the familiar pattern of European immigration.[16]

"Not Counting Mexicans"

Against this setting and background, it is not surprising that Mexican-Americans should have remained a submerged subclass in the Southwest for nearly a century. Identified with a nation defeated in a war of conquest that had resulted in large annexations, they could hardly be expected to be joyful over the prospects of "Americanization." Along the border and particularly in Texas, the Mexican-American War left a heritage of bitterness and ill-will which has not entirely vanished to this day. Border feuds were waged, on a limited scale, long after the treaty was signed and the feuding accelerated during and immediately after the 1910 Revolution in Mexico; sections of the border in Texas remained a zone of lawlessness for many years. The legendary Texas Rangers came into being in part to serve as a constabulary to police resident Mexicans. The historian T. R. Fehrenbach quotes a reputable Anglo witness who testified at a public hearing that hundreds of Mexicans had been executed without a trial by the Texas Rangers.[17] King Fisher, the famous Texas gunman, when asked how many notches he had on his gun, replied: "Thirty-seven, not counting Mexicans." Hostile attitudes were most pronounced in Texas but were not unknown in Arizona, parts of New Mexico, and California, where native-born and alien Mexicans were driven from the gold mining areas and a kind of guerrilla warfare prevailed for some years after

1848. The effect was to leave a heritage of ill-will and distrust which survived well into the present century. European immigrants did not face a comparable situation. For years the Southwest was polarized between "gringos" (Anglos) and "greasers" (Hispanics). The *Century Dictionary* defined "greaser" as referring to "a native Mexican . . . originally applied contemptuously by the Americans of the Southwestern United States to Mexicans." But there always were, of course, a few areas and relationships in which Anglos and Hispanics got along quite well even in the early period. New Mexico, where Spanish-speaking people were deeply entrenchd, was one of these areas, but even there "incidents" were reported from time to time.

It should also be noted that the Hispanics were Catholics by inheritance, while the Anglos of the Southwest were, in the early period, predominantly Protestants. Mexicans have not figured prominently in the Catholic hierarchy of the Southwest until recent years. In 1970, for example, there were no Spanish surnamed bishops in the region; and as late as 1979, there were only six. For years the Spanish language was not used in the celebration of the mass. Today approximately one third of some 50 million American Catholics are Spanish-speaking and, quite naturally, the attitude of the church toward them is undergoing a remarkable change. Originally, the church was of little assistance to Mexican-Americans who could not afford to send their children to parochial schools; today it is becoming an important ally in furthering their advancement. With European Catholic immigrants, the church was from the outset an important factor in their experience; with the Spanish-speaking, it was a minor influence for many years.

In accounting for the handicapped status of the Spanish-speaking relative to other immigrants, it should also be noted that, except in New Mexico, Mexican-Americans exerted little political influence in the Southwestern states until after World War II. Even today their influence does not correlate with their potential voting strength. For example, California has an estimated 800,000 Spanish surnamed registered voters, but the potential is 1.7 million; Hispanics constitute 20 percent of the population in San

Francisco, but 80 percent are not registered to vote. By comparison with other immigrant groups, Spanish-speaking immigrants were slow to develop a middle class which could assert political leadership. In New Mexico, middle-class elements were fairly common but tended to think of themselves as "Spanish" and were often fully accepted by the Anglo elites. Both there and in California, the large landowning families frequently intermarried with Anglos. The reluctance of this privileged minority-within-a-minority to assert active leadership helps explain the delayed politicization of the Spanish-speaking immigrants.

It would be a mistake, however, to conclude that during the long years of their submergence Hispanics were entirely docile or apathetic. On the contrary, Mexicans played a prominent role in the early history of the trade union movement and showed remarkable courage and tenacity in asserting their rights although they won few of the struggles in which they participated.[18] In the years from 1848 to 1950 it has been estimated that Spanish-speaking immigrants launched, at different times, some 500 Spanish language newspapers, although few survived for any length of time. If the organizational efforts of these people had met with a more sympathetic response from the Anglo trade union movement, their economic and political submergence might have been less prolonged. But here again, language was an important barrier to understanding and cooperation. Throughout these years, Mexican-Americans were at a disadvantage even when compared with blacks. Philip Ortega has explained why:

The socio-economic plight of Mexican-Americans is made even more glaring by the strident progress of Negro Americans. But the same solution cannot be proposed for the two sets of problems. Negroes don't come into this country as Mexicans do. There is no Negro language to penalize the Negro. There is no Negro country contiguous to the United States across whose border the Negro may travel at will. The daily intercourse across the border is like an umbilicus that keeps the fetus dependent upon the mother. *La Patria*, the homeland, is just across the border for the more recently arrived.

As one generation moves out of the zone another moves in to take its place.

This then is the real problem of the Mexican-American situation in the United States. For if the Americanization of the immigrant groups from overseas takes, let us say, one or two generations, the Americanization of the Mexican immigrant, if it occurs at all, takes three, four or five generations. And because the Mexican immigration is into high density Mexican-American zones, there is always a surplus of cheap labor. The newly arrived will work for peanuts, because whatever they earn looks like a "fortune" by comparison to what they earn back home. And where labor is so abundant wages are correspondingly low.[19]

For many young Mexican-Americans the complex and special experience which they face in the Southwest has created a persistent identity problem. For example, one young Chicano was quoted recently in the *Los Angeles Times* (January 18, 1977) as saying: "I couldn't value myself as a person. I could hardly value myself as a Chicano. I didn't realize that the reason I couldn't have a high opinion of myself was because I didn't have a high opinion of Mexicans." In an effort to resolve the problem, he went to Mexico to see, as he put it, if he belonged there; but he soon returned to Los Angeles where he now teaches in one of the state colleges. He had discovered, he says, that he did not belong in Mexico "any more than I belong here." Many Chicanos have experienced some variation of this same problem. One of them commented at length in the *Los Angeles Times* of June 1, 1976, on the irony of feeling rootless in a land that once belonged to Mexico. Most young Mexican-Americans have grown up in Spanish-speaking communities within an extended family system, an experience which has emphasized "the Mexican connection." Of them as a group, it has been observed that they do not reject the parental culture as quickly or to the same degree as other first generation children born here of immigrant parents.

The East Coast Spanish-speaking immigrants face a somewhat similar identity problem. Not so long ago, for example, 55 young Cuban-Americans, all born in Cuba but sent here at an early age, were permitted to visit the land of their birth. On returning, the consensus among them seemed to be that while they would not want to live in Cuba, the visit had helped them achieve, as one put it, "a sense of credibility."[20] And Puerto Ricans, who move back and forth between the mainland and the island, frequently face an even more complex problem. Divorced Puerto Rican women with children often take them back to Puerto Rico, as they put it, "to straighten them out," that is, to help them achieve a sense of identity. But the issue is not easily settled. Such children are known in the island as "Neo-Ricans" and many confess confusion about their identity and where they belong. Large numbers of Puerto Rican men—34 percent in one sample taken in New York City—live with or marry women who are not Puerto Ricans; the same sample showed that 32 percent of the second generation Puerto Rican women had married or were living with men who were not of Puerto Rican origin. Such a high degree of intermarriage doubtless contributes to the "credibility" problem faced by the children of such unions.

In areas close to the border, there are many Mexican-American families whose culture remains more Mexican than American. In contrast, there are Mexican-American families, usually at some distance from the border, who make a point of speaking only English in the home and would have one believe that they have broken most of their ties with Mexico. Those in the first category refer to the second as *agringados*, whereas those in the second refer to the others as *pelados* (i.e., "backward types"), much as some Anglos might refer to other Anglos as "poor whites." This social and cultural division has been, to some extent, a factor in minimizing the political power of the Spanish-speaking immigrant. With Mexican-Americans as with other immigrant groups, upward mobility has a tendency to erode ethnic solidarity. Even more of a factor is the division between Mexican-Americans in the Southwest and the East Coast Spanish-speaking; the two groups have shown little interest in joint action until quite recently.[21]

Rapid increase in the Mexican population after 1920 created a problem for which Anglo educators and school administrators in the Southwest were unprepared. Coincident with the large influx of immigrants, educational theorists became intensely interested in devising tests to determine intelligence differences which were assumed to be innate. These tests often proved to be a severe handicap for students from Spanish-speaking homes. Segregation of Mexican-American students was also a factor in retarding their advancement. By and large, the public schools of the region were opposed to bilingual programs. For fifty-one years (prior to 1969), the use of any language other than English in public school instruction was prohibited by law in Texas. Slight wonder, then, that Spanish-speaking first graders were at a distinct disadvantage. And only six of every ten Spanish-speaking students, on an average, went on to graduate from high school.

Prevailing educational practices had even wider implications. In 1969, State Senator Jose Bernal of Texas told the United States Commission on Civil Rights that by "trying to take away our language" the public schools had deprived Mexican-American students of a sense of pride in their Spanish-Mexican heritage. Indeed, most of the Anglo teachers knew little about this heritage and few of them were bilingual.

The condescension in educational practices reflects the prevailing social bias. To cite one of many illustrations: on September 2, 1969, a Superior Court judge in San Jose, California, announced from the bench that Mexican-Americans were "lower than animals . . . just miserable, lousy, rotten people" who should not be allowed to live in a civilized society. Later, this judge was censured by the State Judicial Council, but such comments reflect a widespread bias. A lawsuit had to be filed in the federal district court to open the public swimming pools of San Bernardino County, California, to Mexican-American youngsters. In such a social environment, educators felt it appropriate to set up special programs for "neighborhood" schools, that is, schools in which a large measure of *de facto* segregation existed. These programs often emphasized vocational training which, however, did little to open up new opportunities for

Spanish-speaking people, since discrimination barred their entry into many trades and vocations. And the general level of education in these schools was inferior. On an average, Mexican-Americans are older than other students of the same grade and have a higher dropout rate.

In retrospect, it is obvious that many Anglo educators in the Southwest, as Dr. Thomas P. Carter and Dr. Roberto D. Segura have pointed out, shared the community's view of Mexican-Americans "as outsiders who were never expected to participate fully in American life. Attitudes were tinged with racial prejudice; literature emphasized the inadequacies of the child of Mexican descent. The typically lowest scores of the children were considered evidence of innate intellectual inferiority, which in turn was thought to justify school segregation. Mexicans were said to be capable only of manual labor; in fact, some Anglos were afraid that education would make them useless for farm labor."[22]

The social sciences reflected a similar bias. If Mexicans were treated differently, it was because they were genetically "inferior." Sociologists devoted much research to measuring the "social distance" between Hispanics and Anglos in various relationships without attempting to find out what had created the distance in the first place. What Dr. E. Franklin Frazier once said of social science theory in relation to blacks could also be said of it in relation to Mexican-Americans, namely, that it tended to rationalize the existing ethnic status quo. The effect, of course, was to confirm popular prejudices. And this in turn had a two-fold consequence: it strengthened the mistaken "image" which the Anglo majority had of the Hispanic minority as "inferior" and "undesirable," and by so doing made it difficult for Mexican-Americans to advance at a rate comparable to many European immigrants. The prevailing stereotypes not only handicapped Mexican-Americans; they also fostered deep resentment. But the status of Mexican-Americans began to change once these stereotypes were successfully challenged. This process dates from World War II.

The Coming of Change

With World War II, Anglo-Hispanic relations began to change. The removal of Japanese-Americans (126,000, citizens and aliens alike), from the West Coast states intensified the manpower crisis brought on by the war. Once again, Mexicans began to cross the border in large numbers; during the depression many had been "repatriated" or had voluntarily returned to Mexico. In cities such as Los Angeles, rationing coupled with an acute shortage of housing sharpened group tensions. Also, Mexican-Americans had a special grievance in that a disproportionate number were called into the services since they did not hold jobs that would have entitled them to draft-deferral. Soldiers and sailors, by the thousands, passed through the city en route to the Pacific, and many were looking for a little excitement. With workers in demand, even Mexican-Americans began to have a bit more money to spend and were drawn to downtown shopping districts they had not previously frequented in large numbers. Inevitably, tensions began to mount between Anglos and Hispanics. Two "incidents" of the period were of major importance in marking a change in relationships.

In August, 1942, a group of Mexican-Americans, all minors, were charged with the murder of another young Mexican-American. Since the death occurred near an abandoned East Los Angeles gravel pit which had been dubbed "Sleepy Lagoon," after a motion picture of that title, the case became known as "The Sleepy Lagoon Murder Case." The case against the defendants was inherently weak, and their trial was a travesty of justice. For one thing, the local press had whipped up a frenzy of excitement about Mexican-American youth "gangs." All nineteen of the defendants were convicted after one of the longest and largest mass murder trials in the history of the county. But on October 4, 1944, the District Court of Appeals, in a unanimous decision, reversed the convictions and castigated the trial judge for misconduct.

I served as chairman of the Sleepy Lagoon Defense Committee, which had raised funds for the appeal. The committee was composed of Anglos, blacks, and Hispanics. The reversal of the convictions represented the first time in the history of the state that Mexican-Americans had won a victory of this significance in the courts. In a sense, the Chicano insurgency of the 1960s really dates from this victory which had aroused a new sense of pride and self-confidence. Today, the case has become a legend: the subject of theses, dissertations, pamphlets, articles, and books.

In the spring of 1943, the so-called "zoot suit" riots occurred in Los Angeles. The riots, which came in the wake of the Sleepy Lagoon arrests, began as a clash between sailors and young Mexican-Americans and lasted for nearly a week. These were, in fact, the first of the "race riots" of that year. Since Mexico had by then declared war against the Axis powers (May 22, 1942), the riots were a source of acute embarrassment to federal and state officials. A committee was appointed by Governor Earl Warren which promptly issued a report—I wrote the draft copy —which brought about a significant modification in the tone of the press. Concurrently, the Office of Inter-American Affairs, headed by the late Nelson Rockefeller, sent representatives to the Southwest to help ease tensions and foster better Anglo-Hispanic relationships. A fascinating play, "Zoot Suit," by Luis Valdez was presented with great success in Los Angeles (it also had a limited run in New York and is now to be made into a motion picture).

Gradually some of the barriers against the Spanish-speaking began to be lowered. Segregation of Mexican-Americans in the public schools was successfully challenged when Judge Paul McCormick of the Federal District Court in California ruled (on February 18, 1946) that the practice was unconstitutional, and the decision was affirmed on appeal. The Delgado case in Texas resulted in a similar ruling on June 15, 1948, and other actions were quickly initiated.[23] Wartime considerations were a factor in bringing about these changes, but more important were the emerging new attitudes. A minority in the Anglo community began to take a more favorable view of Mexican-Americans who, in turn, started to assert their rights with a new confidence. The splendid performance of Mexican-Americans in the armed services also helped to speed the abandonment of old stereotypes and clichés.

The Civil Rights movement, which began in 1955, opened up new vistas for Chicanos as well as for blacks. What the Montgomery Bus Boycott was for blacks, the eight-months-long grape pickers strike and boycott, which began on September 8, 1965, was for Mexican-Americans. Cesar Chavez, offering the same charismatic nonviolent leadership as Dr. Martin Luther King, Jr., evoked a similar response. With the support of church groups, young social activists, and some labor leaders, the United Farm Workers Union began the long march toward the future. Despite reversals and setbacks, the Chavez movement has worked a remarkable change in attitudes. Using the new civil rights legislation, Mexican-Americans began to eliminate some of the discriminations which had denied them equal employment, voting, housing, and educational opportunities.

One of the first major Mexican-American protests against unfair educational practices took place in Los Angeles on March 8, 1968, when students in five high schools with a large Chicano enrollment staged what came to be known as "the East Los Angeles blow-out."[24] This dramatic protest by about 4,000 students forced federal, state, and local officials to examine practices that had long gone unchallenged; for the first time Chicano students, as a vocal, assertive minority; made it known that they were no longer willing to accept a third- or fourth-rate education.

In the middle 1960s, the Chicano Rebellion—the increasing use of the term "Chicano" marked a milestone in the social and cultural history of Spanish-speaking people—began to have widespread repercussions on campuses throughout the Southwest. Campus organizations of Mexican-American students were formed to demand more emphasis on Chicano studies, an enlarged Chicano faculty, and a larger Spanish-speaking enrollment. In the first century of its existence, the University of California had enrolled scarcely any Mexican-Americans, but responding to the new pressures, the university created an Equal

Opportunity Program in 1965. Ten years later, approximately 3,000 Chicanos were enrolled throughout the state university system. From twenty Chicanos enrolled in graduate programs at Stanford in 1968, the number increased to 235 in 1973.[25]

In *Cisneros* v. *Corpus Christi* and *Serna* v. *Portales,* both decided in 1972, the courts ruled that Spanish-speaking students were entitled to equal educational opportunities as a constitutional right. These rulings were reenforced by the Supreme Court's decision in *Lau* v. *Nichols* in 1974, in which it was ruled that a Chinese non-English-speaking student had been denied the equal protection of the law. In the wake of these decisions, a new emphasis has been placed on bilingual education in the early grades as a means of overcoming the language handicap of students who come from Spanish-speaking homes and neighborhoods. Studies have shown that those who usually speak Spanish in the home are from two to three years behind their age group in high school, and a large number become dropouts. Among Hispanics who habitually speak Spanish, 18 percent were found to be two or more years behind in school and showed a dropout rate of 15 percent.[26] Of recent years, progress has been made in introducing bilingual programs which are often based on federal grants made for this purpose. Unfortunately, many of these programs have been hastily conceived, inefficiently administered, inadequately staffed, and based on meager research. In some instances, federal funds have simply been misused for purposes other than the furtherance of bilingual education.

Despite significant improvements, Mexican-Americans are still seriously handicapped in the field of higher education. Fred E. Crossland's 1971 study for the Ford Foundation lists some of the barriers: (1) The Test Barrier, that is, the way admission tests have discriminated against the Spanish-speaking; (2) The Barrier of Poor Preparation, that is, not as many Mexican-Americans as other groups complete high school, and have either elected or have been counseled into taking nonacademic, vocational, and technical programs in high schools; (3) The Money Barrier, that is, the average Hispanic-American family income in 1968 was only 63 percent of what the "whites" or Anglos earned in the same year (as late as 1977, it was only 68 percent as high); (4) The Distance Barrier, that is, minority students usually have to travel greater distances to attend colleges and universities; and (5) The Motivational Barrier, that is, fewer inducements are offered Mexican-Americans than other students to complete their education.[27]

Yet few minorities have made such rapid and dramatic gains as the Spanish-speaking since the middle 1960s. The founding of such interesting and scholarly journals as *El Grito* in 1967, and the *Journal of Mexican-American History* (edited by Joseph and Kathleen Navarro) in 1970, reflects a new intellectual maturity and sophistication. Since 1965, young Chicano scholars have published a library of books about the Spanish-speaking people, and Chicano studies programs have burgeoned on many campuses. As might be expected, a new middle class is emerging as more and more Mexican-Americans have entered the professions and other middle-class employments. Spanish-speaking persons figure prominently in the popular mass culture and are making impressive gains also in radio, the recording, television, and motion picture industries, as well as on the stage.

No longer a silent or invisible minority, Hispanics are becoming an increasingly important element in American politics. The election of Edward W. Roybal to the City Council in Los Angeles in 1949 was a sign of changing times, as he was the first Mexican-American to serve in that body. Later, he was elected to the Congress where he still serves. In 1953, Ruben Ayala of Chino was the first Hispanic to be elected to a school board in California; in 1964 he became mayor and in 1973 was elected to the State Senate. Julian Nava, a distinguished senior member of the Los Angeles Board of Education, was first elected in May, 1967. Of recent decades, Spanish-speaking persons have been elected to the United States Senate and House of Representatives, and as governors, mayors, judges, and members of state legislatures and city councils throughout the Southwest. Today, five of San Antonio's eleven city councilmen are

Spanish-speaking, and with 400,000 Spanish-speaking residents, the city may soon have a Mexican-American mayor. Nationally, the growing political influence of the Spanish-speaking dates from formation of the *Viva Kennedy* groups in 1960. In 1977, the first Hispanic caucus was formed in Congress, made up of such representatives as Badillo, Roybal, de la Garza, Gonzales, Lujan, and others.

Brutal incidents in which Spanish-speaking individuals have been mistreated by police still occur, but prosecutions based on civil rights legislation have had a restraining influence. In one recent year alone, nine Southwest law enforcement officers were arrested and tried on charges of police violence which resulted in the deaths of Mexican-Americans. That police have been forced to stand trial on such charges in Texas is in itself a notable advance. Even so, such crimes continue; in the past few years some fifteen Mexican-Americans have been the victims of police violence of a kind that reflects a strong bias.[28] But Mexicans in the Southwest are no longer the easy and safe targets they once were. At its tenth annual meeting in San Francisco on June 14, 1978, the Mexican-American Legal Defense and Educational Fund (MALDEF) heard its counsel state that "conditions have changed tremendously since 1968."

Already one of the largest American minorities, with from 12 to 14 million in all categories—Mexican-Americans, Puerto Ricans, Cubans, and other Latin Americans including illegals—the Spanish-speaking population could reach a much larger total by the year 2000. Dr. Dudley Kirk, a demographer at the Stanford Food Research Institute, foresees an Hispanic population of 25 million by then if illegal migration continues.[29] Admittedly, many imponderable factors are involved: the extent to which Mexico can achieve a better balance of resources and population and employment opportunities; the extent to which Mexican birthrates can be reduced; what measures will be taken by both governments to create more jobs in Mexico for those seeking work; how much longer the economic expansion of the

Sun Belt states (largely based on Mexican labor) will continue; the effect a major recession in the United States might have on migration; as well as other factors. But the expansion of the Spanish-speaking minority is likely to continue, if at a slower pace, into the foreseeable future. Spanish-speaking America will soon constitute the fourth largest Spanish-speaking "nation" in the hemisphere. Without firing a shot, Hispanics are establishing their presence as the largest minority in the vast region acquired from Mexico in 1848.

Today the Spanish-speaking borderlands (i.e., the lands extending both immediately north and south of the present border for a distance of a hundred miles or more) have become a region of unique historical, economic, and cultural importance. In this region, Hispanic and Anglo elements are fusing to form a new bicultural entity or zone of influence. Currently, commentators are fumbling for a phrase to describe this zone; it is being referred to, for example, as MexAmerica and, on occasion, Amer-Mex.

It should be noted also that nowadays the Canadian border presents a not dissimilar picture. Drawn in 1842, the Canadian-American border is approximately 3,986 miles in length, and like the Mexican-American border, was defined in a haphazard fashion. In some places, for example, the border cuts through kitchen walls, divides communities, and has spawned twin towns such as Piney, Manitoba, and Pinecreek, Minnesota. Similar to its Mexican counterpart, the Canadian-American border is "a porous line" which in 1978 saw barely monitored crossings by 70 million people.[30] Americans from south of the border rank second in number to immigrants from the British Isles in Canada; and Canadians constitute the fourth largest (332,949) group of registered aliens in this country, after Mexicans, West Indians, and Cubans. Three fourths of the Canadian population, incidentally, is concentrated within a 100-mile zone immediately to the north of the international boundary. This zone closely resembles, in its interlocking of social and economic interests, the Mexican-American border zone. "The Canadian-American border," writes Andrew H. Malcolm (*New York Times*, May 17, 1979), "is different, for it seems to unite rather than divide. The unusual situation has created a special culture—almost a narrow third country where nationality matters less than personality, where the currency of each country is acceptable in the other, and where bilingual, binational families are so common that a visitor needs a scorecard to keep it all straight." In much this same sense, the Spanish-speaking borderlands constitute a "narrow third country" and, in fact, this term has been applied to them.[31]

To be properly understood, therefore, Mexican immigration should be viewed in the perspective of the North-South geographic flow of the North American continent. This perspective is essential, in fact, to an understanding of the past and the future of Canadian-American and Mexican-American relations. But this perspective is still not as widely accepted as it should be. "Standing upon the border between the United States and Mexico and looking south," as Cecil Robinson has written in his fine study, *With the Ears of Strangers: The Mexican in American Literature* (1963), "an imaginative North American can hardly avoid a feeling of awe at the thought that he is facing a vast extension of territory, embracing all types of climate and terrain and stretching the full distance southward to Cape Hope, in which Indio-Latin America is working out its destiny and pressing upwards toward him, indeed in the Southwest surrounding him. If he is a man of perception, he will recognize here an involvement that the United States cannot abrogate at will. If he is a literary man, he will know in his brain and in his viscera that a paramount task of literature in North and Latin America is to articulate this involvement."

NOTES

1. Stanford University News Service, April 2, 1979.
2. *New York Times*, February 14, 1979.
3. *Washington Post*, March 26, 1978.

4. *New York Times,* June 15, 1979; Henry Reuss, editorial page, *New York Times,* April 22, 1979; Jack Nelson, *Los Angeles Times,* February 3, 1979.

5. *New York Times,* April 9, 1979.

6. Jack Nelson, *Los Angeles Times,* February 3, 1979.

7. *New York Times,* June 22, 1979.

8. *Los Angeles Times,* December 21, 1979.

9. Stanford University News Service, statement of Harry Cross and James Sandos, July 11, 1979.

10. *Los Angeles Times,* November 26, 1978.

11. *Los Angeles Times,* June 15, 1979.

12. See Lester C. Thurow, *Los Angeles Times,* May 15, 1979.

13. *New York Times,* February 18, 1979, and July 2, 1979.

14. See Robert Lindsey, *New York Times,* February 18, 1979.

15. *New York Times,* May 7, 1979.

16. See Albert Camarillo, *Chicanos in a Changing Society: From Mexican Barrios to American Barrios in Santa Barbara and Southern California, 1848 to 1930* (1979).

17. T. R. Fehrenbach, *Lone Star: A History of Texas and Texans* (1968).

18. See Carey McWilliams, *North from Mexico: The Spanish Speaking People of the United States* (1948), pp. 189–93.

19. *The Nation,* December 11, 1967.

20. *The New York Times,* February 14, 1978.

21. See Robert Lindsey, *New York Times,* February 18, 1979.

22. Thomas P. Carter and Robert D. Segura, eds., *Mexican Americans in School: A Decade of Change,* rev. ed. (1978), p. 9.

23. George I. Sanchez, *Concerning Segregation of Spanish-Speaking Children in the Public Schools* (1951).

24. See: *Los Angeles Times: a ten-year retrospective appraisal.*

25. For a general report see Fred E. Crossland, *Minority Access to College* (Ford Foundation, 1971), pp. 19–20. Also see *Los Angeles Times,* June 13, 1979, and Stanford University News Service, May 9, 1979.

26. See the report of the *National Center for Education Statistics,* in *New York Post,* July 26, 1978.

27. See Crossland; see also Lester C. Thurow, *Los Angeles Times,* May 15, 1979.

See *The Report of the President's Task Force on Chicanos and the University of California* (Berkeley, April 1975), which also discusses the existing barriers.

28. *Washington Post,* March 28, 1978.
29. Stanford University News Service, April 2, 1979.
30. Andrew H. Malcolm, *New York Times* March 11, 1979.
31. See Tom Miller, *New York Times,* editorial page, April 4, 1979.

V

The Puerto Ricans

By Joseph P. Fitzpatrick
Fordham University

Puerto Ricans represent a major part of contemporary American migration in the northeastern section of the United States. Although Puerto Ricans have been migrating to the United States since Puerto Rico was annexed to the United States in 1898, large scale migration did not occur until after World War II. Since then there has been a steady stream of Puerto Ricans coming to the continent. In recent years, large numbers have also been returning. The migration, therefore, can best be described as part of the internal migration of the United States, marked by a constant shift of people back and forth. In the process, large numbers remain on the continent. Together with their children who have been born here, they now represent a significant minority. When added to the other Hispanics, they constitute part of the Hispanic minority which is rapidly becoming the largest minority in the United States, surpassing the American blacks.

The Migratory Movement

A 1978 census report on persons of Spanish origin in the United States[1] listed 1,823,000 Puerto Ricans in the United States, an increase of 31 percent over the 1,391,463 reported in 1970. An increasing number of these are second generation Puerto Ricans, born on the mainland of Puerto Rican parents. They numbered 581,376 in 1970, or 42 percent of the total Puerto Rican population. Table 1 presents the Puerto Rican

118

population on the United States mainland from 1910 to 1970. The total population of Puerto Rico was reported as 3.4 million in 1978, meaning that about one third of all Puerto Ricans are living on the mainland.[2]

Table 1
People of Puerto Rican origin in continental United States and New York City, 1910-1970

Generation and year of birth	U.S. total	N.Y.C. total	Percent of U.S. total in N.Y.C.
First and Second			
1910	1,513	554	36.6
1930	52,774	—	—
1940	69,967	61,462	87.8
1950	301,375	245,880	81.6
1960	887,662	612,574	69.0
1970	1,391,463	817,712	54.8
First			
1910	1,513	554	36.6
1930	52,774	—	—
1940	69,967	61,463	87.8
1950	226,110	187,420	82.9
1960	615,384	429,710	69.8
1970	810,087	473,300	58.4
Second			
1950	75,265	58,460	77.7
1960	272,278	182,964	67.2
1970	581,376	344,412	59.2

Source: U.S. Bureau of the Census, *Census of the Population, 1970,* Subject Report PC(2)-1E. *Puerto Ricans in the United States* (Washington, D.C., 1973), table 1; U.S. Bureau of the Census. *Census of the Population, 1970,* Subject Report PC(2)-1D, *Puerto Ricans in the United States, Final Report* (Washington, D.C., 1963), p. viii, table A.

Large scale migration began after World War II. Table 2 gives the data on the migratory movement since 1940. These are not refined statistics. They are arrived at by taking the number of persons who traveled from Puerto Rico to the mainland in a given year, and the number who traveled from the mainland to Puerto Rico. The lower number is subtracted from the higher. This is identified as the net migration either to the United States, or back to Puerto Rico, in a given year. In 1974, for example, 1,661,001 persons traveled from Puerto Rico to the mainland, and 1,630,525 persons traveled from the mainland to Puerto Rico. This gives a net migration to the mainland of 30,476 persons. Table 2 indicates how the net migration fluctuates back and forth. Figures with a minus sign indicate net movement back to Puerto Rico.

Table 2

Net movement of persons from Puerto Rico to the United States or back, selected years 1940-1980

(Minus sign is net movement to Puerto Rico)

1940	1,008
1945	11,003
1950	34,155
1955	31,182
1960	23,742
1965	10,758
1968	−14,249
1970	20,715
1972	−34,015
1973	−20,948
1974	30,476
1977	46,812
1980	49,322

Source: Puerto Rico Planning Board.

These figures are not reliable indicators of migration since there is no way of telling how many of the net travelers in or out are going to stay either in the United States or Puerto

Rico. At best they give an impression of the direction of movement. A more reliable indicator of migration is the data on transfers of school children from mainland schools to schools in Puerto Rico and vice versa. For example, in the 1974–1975 school year, 8,547 children transferred from public schools in Puerto Rico to public schools in New York City; 9,254 transferred from public schools of New York City to schools in Puerto Rico.[3] About 700 more children transferred back to Puerto Rico than transferred up to New York. Since these children are generally moving with parents, the school transfers reflect a sizeable movement back and forth of persons intending to stay. In 1974, more people moved to Puerto Rico from New York, than to New York from Puerto Rico.

Since Puerto Ricans are American citizens, movement between the island and the mainland is unrestricted. No papers are needed. It is no different from taking a bus from New York to New Jersey. This fact distinguishes the Puerto Rican migration from that of other groups coming from foreign lands to the United States. However, Puerto Ricans come from an island where the language and culture are different from that of the mainland. As a result, the experience of travel to the United States involves a change of language and culture not unlike that which faces any immigrant, whether citizen or not.

The Island Background

Puerto Rico is an island in the Caribbean, the easternmost of the Greater Antilles.[4] It is 100 miles long and 35 miles wide. It was discovered by Columbus on his second voyage in November, 1493, and remained a Spanish colony until it was transferred to the United States by the Treaty of Paris in 1898. After a period of military occupation, a series of political arrangements was granted to Puerto Ricans. In 1900 they were given a measure of local government under the Foraker Act; in 1917 they were granted United States citizenship; in 1947 they were given the power to elect their own governor. Their first elected governor was Luis Muñoz Marin, founder of the Popular Democratic Party of Puerto Rico. In 1950, the U.S. Congress passed the

Puerto Rican Federal Relations Act, giving Puerto Ricans the power to draft their own constitution so long as its provisions did not exceed the limitations placed on an incorporated territory of the United States. In other words, the constitution could not provide for independence or statehood. A constitution as a Free Associated State was drafted, passed by the U.S. Congress, accepted by the people of Puerto Rico, and inaugurated on July 24, 1952. This gives Puerto Rico a political status similar to that of a commonwealth. They elect their own Senate and Assembly, and their own governor. They have no representation in the U.S. Congress, nor do Puerto Ricans in Puerto Rico vote for the president. In view of this, they pay no taxes to the federal government. They have an elected resident commissioner in Washington who sits with the House of Representatives. He has voice but no vote. The problem of political status is a point of controversy and tension among Puerto Ricans, whether they should become a state, be granted independence, or continue as a Free Associated State. Nevertheless they are American citizens; they are subject to military draft; and their movement anywhere in the United States is unrestricted.

Causes of the Migration

The migration from Puerto Rico has been largely economic, the search for employment or better economic opportunity. A small number came before World War I. During the war and continuing into the 1920s, they came in larger numbers, settling largely in the Brooklyn Navy Yard section of New York City and spreading to Harlem. By 1930, there were more than 50,000 Puerto Ricans on the mainland, almost all of them in New York City. During the Great Depression and continuing during World War II, very few came. By the end of World War II, the elements of a large scale migration were in place.

First, there had been a rapid increase in the population of Puerto Rico. Birthrates remained high, close to 40 per thousand per year. Due to the advantages of modern hygiene and medicine, deaths declined from 30 per thousand in 1900 to less than 10 per thousand in 1950. The rate of natural increase doubled from 14 per thousand in 1900 to 28 per thousand in 1950. Second, employment was not available for the increasing numbers entering the labor market. Third, a sizeable beachhead of brothers, sisters, and other relatives were already living in New York. Finally, unobstructed movement and cheap transportation were available. Thus the migration increased rapidly in the late 1940s and during the 1950s.

The Puerto Ricans represented the first large-scale airborne migration to the United States. Their experience in this regard has been different from that of earlier immigrants. Travel conditions of earlier immigrants were often hazardous; and the dangerous risks which "boat people" and so-called "illegals" take today to reach the United States are well known. Puerto Ricans have been spared this. Apart from the fear that may attend the first long flight over the ocean, conditions of air travel have been excellent. The trip in the early two engine planes took eight hours, in the four engine propeller planes it was six hours; commercial jets make the trip in three hours and ten minutes. In the late 1940s and early 1950s, plane fare from San Juan to New York was less than $50. The air travel has been impressively safe. The last fatal accident in San Juan–mainland air travel was in 1952.

Location on the Mainland

Table 3 provides the data about the cities with the largest Puerto Rican populations and the increase between 1960 and 1970. New York, for many years, had the largest population of Puerto Ricans. Although it now has only 55 percent of all Puerto Ricans on the mainland, it still has the largest population of Puerto Ricans of any city in the world, almost twice as many as the city of San Juan. For many years the Puerto Rican experience was identified with the experience in New York. During the 1960s and 1970s, there has been a dispersal of the population to other large cities in the nation, and, more recently, to many small cities in the New England and Middle Atlantic states. Characteristics of these cities vary. New York, for example, has experienced a large migration of other Hispanics: Cuban refugees, Dominicans, Central and South Americans. Almost half the Hispanics who married in New York City in 1975 were not Puerto Ricans. In Chicago, Puerto Ricans are an Hispanic minority in the presence of large numbers of persons of Mexican background. In Miami, they are a relatively small minority in an Hispanic population dominated by Cubans. The population in Boston is very mobile and poor; the population of Lorain, Ohio, is very stable: 55 percent of the Puerto Rican families own their own homes, many have good jobs in the steel mills and automobile factories, and few are receiving public welfare.

Table 3

Cities of the United States with 5,000 or More Puerto Ricans, 1960-1970

	1960	1970
New York, N.Y.	612,574	887,119
Chicago, Illinois	32,371	86,277
Philadelphia, Pa.	14,424	40,930
Newark, N.J.	9,698	27,009
Los Angeles, Cal.	6,424	20,500
Miami, Florida	6,547	18,918
Jersey City, N.J.	7,427	19,362
San Francisco, Cal.	—	13,511
Paterson, N.J.	5,123	13,378
Hoboken, N.J.	5,313	10,047
Bridgeport, Conn.	5,084	9,618
Hartford, Conn	—	8,278
Cleveland, Ohio	—	8,135
Boston, Mass.	—	7,747
Washington, D.C.	—	6,732
Passaic, N.J.	—	6,609
Honolulu, Hawaii	—	6,428
Buffalo, N.Y.	—	6,090
Rochester, N.Y.	—	5,916
Milwaukee, Wis.	—	5,889
Lorain, Ohio	—	5,601
Gary, Indiana	—	5,228

Sources: *1960 Census of the United States,* "Puerto Ricans in the United States." PC(2)1D, Table 15, p. 103; and *1970 Census of the United States,* "Persons of Spanish Ancestry." PC(S1)-30. February 1973, Table 2, pp. 2–8.

Age and Socioeconomic Status

Two things must be noted about the Puerto Rican population: it is very youthful and it is very poor. The median age of the nationwide Puerto Rican population in 1976 was 20.4 years in contrast to 29.2 years for the total population of the United States.[5] The significance of this is seen more clearly if only the second generation is considered. The median age of second generation Puerto Ricans in 1970 was 9.3 years of age; in New York State in 1973, it was 9.6 years. In 1970, in New York City, 73 percent of second generation Puerto Ricans were under fifteen years of age. When this youthful population reaches marriageable age, even if they have small families, there will be a compounding effect on the numbers. If present trends continue, the Puerto Rican population will continue to increase substantially in the next twenty years.

It is a very poor population; they are the poorest Hispanics in the United States. Their median family income, nationwide in 1978 was reported as $7,972, more than $3,000 lower than that of the Mexicans, the next poorest group. In 1978, the Census reported 38.8 percent of all Puerto Rican families, nationwide, as below the poverty level.[6] Their poverty is partly related to the poverty level of the Island. Seventy percent of the families in Puerto Rico qualify for food stamps. It is also related on the mainland to the high unemployment rates of Puerto Ricans—11.7 percent in 1978, which in turn is related to their lower levels of education. Poverty strikes mainly among the female-headed households, 28 percent of all Puerto Rican households in the United States in 1978. Fifty-three percent of these female-headed families were below the poverty level in 1970.[7]

Adjustment to the United States

If adjustment to the United States is tested by a person's

staying here, then Puerto Ricans are adjusting to the mainland.[8] Large numbers are staying here. However, a number of factors indicate that their process of adjustment is different from that of earlier immigrant groups; sometimes much easier, at other times more difficult.

New York City

If New York can be taken as an illustration of the Puerto Rican experience on the mainland—since most Puerto Ricans were in that city until recently—the differences in contemporary migration from earlier migration can be recognized. Change has always been a part of life in American cities, but the pace of change in the past generation has been more rapid and extensive than ever before. At many moments in New York City it must be described as convulsive. Furthermore, New York is a completely built-up city; much of its real estate is decrepit and is being replaced on an enormous scale. The displacement of poor populations involves hundreds of thousands of people. Within more recent years, the phenomenon of the burning of the neighborhoods has added an element of danger and terror to the people, largely black and Puerto Rican, who live in the poor neighborhoods. The poor are pushed around more so today than ever before.

The Puerto Ricans have come to New York at the height of the Civil Rights movement and the Black Power movement. As will appear later in the section on "color," the black experience has had a great impact on the Puerto Ricans.

More recently, hundreds of thousands of other Hispanics from Cuba, Santo Domingo, Central and South America have come to New York, creating a problem of "Hispanic" identity in relation to other Hispanics. New York City has lost 600,000 jobs between 1970 and 1980, mostly unskilled and semiskilled jobs through which poor immigrants always worked their way into better paying occupations. It has also lost 800,000 white employees, representing the flight of middle-class whites. Finally, they come to the city when highly developed public welfare programs provide services to the poor such as public housing, medicaid, aid to dependent children, and food stamps which were not available to earlier immigrant groups. No interpretation of the Puerto Rican experience can be adequate without keeping this social context of New York City, or other large northeastern cities, in mind.

Second, no people quite like the Puerto Ricans have ever come before. As indicated above, they were the first large airborne migration to the United States. It is possible for a Puerto Rican to travel from San Juan to New York or back in less time than it took an Irishman to travel from Coney Island to Times Square a century ago. They are the first ones who come as citizens but from a different language and cultural background. They are the first Catholic migrants to come without bringing their own clergy with them. They are different from earlier immigrants, and this makes the process of their adjustment a new and different experience.

The Immigrant Community

The central and most important factor in the adjustment of earlier immigrants to life in the United States was the immigrant community. This was the bridge between the old world and the new, the enclave in a strange world where the stranger was at home; the place where he heard his own language, where his own actions and responses were understood by others and where he understood the reaction of others to himself. It was the little world where the culture of the old country was kept alive as a basis for security and solidarity. It provided the psychosocial satisfaction that every person needs, particularly the stranger as he seeks to find his way in a world where everything is different. The immigrant community was the source of strength from which the immigrant moved with confidence, slowly but surely, into a relationship with the new world. Without it, the danger of social disorganization and psychological collapse is very great. What is called the process of assimilation —always difficult—proceeds most smoothly when the immigrant has the support of a community.[9] "One integrates from a position of strength, not from a position of weakness."

Two things were central to the immigrant community: one was the geographical neighborhood, the place, the ghetto; the other was the parish, the religious congregation. The "little Germany," the "little Dublin," the "little Italy," etc., which have been a familiar feature of American urban life, were really the immigrant communities, the clustering of the newcomers in particular areas of the city where shops and food and smells and manners of behavior were all familiar, where the newcomer was "at home." These were often described by outsiders as dangerous, unfriendly places, marked by poverty, disorganization, and crime. What is understood now, through many of the studies of these neighborhoods, is that, in many cases, they are marked by a high degree of informal social control by the community itself, where people know how to deal with "their own kind" and protect themselves from internal disorder and external attack.[10]

One striking feature of Puerto Rican location in New York is the speed with which they have spread to almost all sections of the city. It is true, there are large concentrations in such areas as East Harlem, known as "The Barrio" (the neighborhood) where "La Marqueta" (the market) along Park Avenue and the commercial life of 116th Street give a decided Puerto Rican character to the area; but it has been much more difficult for Puerto Ricans to cluster in stable, immigrant, or migrant neighborhoods as the early immigrants did. In earlier immigrant periods, new low cost housing in the private sector was available to immigrants. They could move into areas and onto blocks where brothers, sisters, relatives lived. As a result, the immigrant communities formed rapidly as stable, often homogeneous, neighborhoods. Today, the only new housing available to poor people is public housing. Tenant selection is carefully controlled by public policy in this kind of housing. Ideally, a policy of nondiscrimination prevails. The applicant may indicate a preference for one or another housing project; but if space is not available, they must go elsewhere. As a result, Puerto Ricans are more widely scattered, and it is much more difficult for them to achieve the kind of immigrant community that was the major social support for earlier immigrant groups.

A major element in the immigrant community was the parish or the religious congregation. Many of the immigrants to the United States came from a cultural background in which religion played a central role.[11] The one feature of their cultural life which they retained was their religious practice. This took the form of the parish or the congregation. It became the basis for their continuing identity as a people; it was also a physical sign, the church or synagogue, around which the life of the immigrant community crystallized, the symbol of their values and ideals which they brought with them into a new world, and which constituted the continuity of their old world in their new environment. The Catholic Church responded to this need by establishing the national or ethnic parishes, the German parish in the German neighborhood, the Italian parish in the Italian neighborhood, and so forth. For a number of reasons to be explained later, this was not done for the Puerto Ricans. They face the process of adjustment without this source of community strength and stability. Particular aspects of their experience which helped or hindered are described as follows.

Citizenship

The great advantage that Puerto Ricans have over newcomers is the fact that they are citizens. Once they establish residence, they have the right to vote as any other mainland citizen. They can organize politically, nominate candidates, and vote in elections for their own candidates. They do not have to wait for five years to gain citizenship. It comes with them. As citizens they are entitled to all the social security benefits of a citizen. This does not settle all their problems, but it gives them access to an important range of benefits for persons who are at lower socioeconomic levels.

Political Participation

Puerto Ricans in New York have been moving slowly but steadily into the political arena. There has been widespread disappointment about their failure to register and vote in larger numbers. This is more puzzling since politics is a way of life in Puerto Rico; almost everyone votes. The percentage of eligible citizens who vote in Puerto Rico is much higher than among the voting population of the United States. Nevertheless, in New York after the election of 1980, Puerto Ricans had one congressman, two New York State senators, and four New York State assemblymen, one member of the City Council. The mayor of Miami is a Puerto Rican, but this reflects the influence of the Cuban rather than Puerto Rican population. There is a growing awareness of the importance of political influence among the Puerto Ricans. There is some evidence that it is beginning to develop.

Poverty

One of the problems associated with the Puerto Rican migration is the apparent persistence of poverty among them. Some reasons for this have been suggested above. However, there are more aspects to the problem. Some are situational. Puerto Ricans have been coming to the northeast at the time when large numbers of industries are moving to the Sun Belt. New York City has lost 600,000 unskilled and semiskilled jobs since 1970. The move is partly technological: factories in New York are old and outmoded, and modernization is effected more easily by relocating. The move is also prompted by the escalation of fuel costs. These are lower in the south. There is a general population shift to the Sun Belt; industries follow the trend. It leaves Puerto Ricans who live in an area of declining job opportunity, with a high level of unemployment.

There are other unfavorable features to the New York situation. It is predominantly an area of white-collar employment, where at least a high school education is essential to enable a person to qualify. Many of the Puerto Ricans from Puerto Rico do not have that level of education. The anomaly prevails of white-collar jobs with no one to fill them, and thousands of unskilled people who are unemployed. Furthermore, teenage unemployment is unusually high in New York City; the large concentration of Puerto Rican youths in the city leaves them exposed to this condition of unemployment. The dropout rate for Puerto Ricans in the public high schools is well above fifty percent. The dropouts do not have the level of training necessary for white collar employment.

Employment

Table 4 gives the occupational distribution of Puerto Ricans in New York City for 1970. It is characteristic of the Puerto Rican occupational experience generally. A noticeable shift in employment is evident between the first and second generations, from operatives (factory workers, generally semiskilled and unskilled) to white-collar work. There is an increase for men and women in professional and technical occupations; and a particularly large shift among women into clerical jobs. Using occupation as an indicator, there is a considerable shift to higher socioeconomic levels among the second generation over the first. This follows the pattern that was evident among earlier immigrant groups. One thing must be noted in reference to the age of the second generation. They are so young that only a small percentage have reached the age at which full-time employment is allowed. Of all Puerto Rican men in the labor force in 1970, only 13 percent were second generation. Their numbers are still too small to have much impact on the statistical picture of the total Puerto Rican population.

Table 4

Occupational distribution of employed Puerto Ricans, by place of birth, New York City, 1970

Occupation	Born in Puerto Rico	Mainland born
Males, age 16 and over	127,645	19,831
Percent	100.0	100.0
White-collar workers	24.8	41.8
Professional and technical	3.2	7.2
Managers and administrators, including farm	4.4	4.9

Occupation	Born in Puerto Rico	Mainland born
Sales Workers	4.6	7.2
Clerical workers	12.6	22.5
Blue-collar and service workers	75.2	58.1
Craftsmen and foremen	15.4	15.4
Operatives	31.7	20.0
Laborers, including farm	5.7	7.9
Service workers, including household	22.4	14.8
Females, age 16 and over	55,611	13,371
Percent	100.0	100.0
White-collar workers	39.4	76.6
Professional and technical	5.7	8.8
Managers and administrators, including farm	1.6	2.0
Sales workers	3.8	6.1
Clerical workers	28.3	59.7
Blue-collar and service workers	60.6	23.4
Craftsmen and foremen	2.9	1.1
Operatives	44.0	11.0
Laborers, including farm	1.2	.3
Service workers, including household	12.5	11.0

Note: Totals may not add due to rounding.
Source: Decennial Census.
Reproduced from U.S. Department of Labor, Bureau of Labor Statistics, Middle Atlantic Regional Office, *A Socio-Economic Profile of Puerto Rican New Yorkers*, Regional Report 46, July, 1975.

Education

It is the common conviction of Puerto Rican leaders, public officials, and scholars studying the Puerto Rican experience that education is the major problem facing the Puerto Rican community. There are three dimensions to the problem: (1) the low level of schooling of those who come from Puerto Rico: according to the 1970 Census,[12] Puerto Ricans over age 25 on the mainland had a median average of 8.6 years of schooling completed in contrast to 12.1 years for the total U.S. population over 25; (2) the high dropout rate of Puerto Ricans from high school: more than 50 percent drop out during high school in New York City; (3) the small number of Puerto Ricans in college and postgraduate education: only two percent had finished college in contrast to 10 percent of the total United States population, in 1970, 18 percent of the Puerto Rican males eighteen to twenty-four years of age (the college and graduate school age) were still enrolled in school compared with 38 percent of the total United States population.

When the second generation is taken alone, they are much closer to general American educational norms. In 1970, median years of schooling were 11.5 for second generation Puerto Ricans, over the age of 25, almost equal to the national average. In the ages 18 to 24, first generation male enrollment was 13 percent, but 33 percent of the second generation were still in school, close to the national average. In 1972, about 25,000 Puerto Ricans in New York City were enrolled as college students, a substantial advance over previous years. The percentage of students in the City University who were Puerto Rican increased from 4 percent in 1969 to 7.4 percent in 1974. The percentage in the senior colleges increased from 2.9 percent in 1969 to 6.3 percent in 1974.

Despite the evidence of increasing educational achievement in the second generation, the experience of their children in schools is still a major complaint among Puerto Rican parents and community leaders. In New York City, the lowest scores in reading and arithmetic on standardized tests are found in the school districts heavily populated by Puerto Ricans. In the fall of 1973, there were 256,095 Puerto Rican children in the public schools of New York City, about one fourth of the student body. Almost one fifth of these were reported to have moderate to severe language difficulties, but relatively few were receiving any special help. A Report of the U.S. Commission on Civil Rights[13] found serious failures on the part of the schools to respond to the particular needs of Puerto Rican children.

In New York City in 1974, 27 percent of the student body were Puerto Rican; but only 2.5 percent of the teachers were of Hispanic background. The situation was worse in most other cities. The report found other deficiencies in counseling students (language difficulties were often interpreted as a symptom of mental deficiency); testing was often discriminatory; and counseling was inadequate. The absence of Spanish-speaking counselors in a role where verbal communication is critical was very serious.

The decentralization of the school boards of New York City in 1973 was inaugurated with the expectation that this would give control over the schools to parents in the local neighborhoods. However, as of 1981, there is no convincing evidence that this has occurred. A second program, strongly demanded by Puerto Rican parents, is the bilingual program in the schools. This was given initial support by the federal government in the passage of the Bilingual Education Act in January, 1968. This act makes federal funds available in response to proposals voluntarily submitted by schools or educational agencies to provide language training in the schools. Although many proponents of the act wanted bilingual education to be a permanent feature of education as a program to enable the children to maintain a sense of cultural identity while they learned English, it became clear that the U.S. Congress understood it as a transitional program, designed to enable the children to learn English as quickly as possible. However, at a later time, Chinese parents in San Francisco brought a class action suit against the Board of Education there. The court decided that since children were required by law to attend school, if they did not know English well enough to be instructed in that language, they had a civil right to be instructed in a language in which they could learn. This decision was later supported by the Supreme Court in the case of *Lau* v. *Nichols*.

This made bilingual education a matter of law and civil rights. The most celebrated case in this regard is the New York City case where a class action suit was brought by *Aspira*, grass-roots

Puerto Rican educational agency, against the New York City Board of Education. The board accepted a consent decree before the court by which the board agreed to provide bilingual programs for Spanish-speaking children who did not know English well enough to be instructed in that language. The objective of *Aspira* is to win recognition for the programs, not as transitional programs until the students know English, but as programs contributing to the children a sense of respect for their cultural background. At the present time (1981), there are strong efforts in Congress and by federal officials to terminate the bilingual programs.

Aspira is one of the major organizational advocates for Puerto Ricans in the field of education on both the national and local level. It was founded in New York City in the mid-1950s by a young Puerto Rican woman, Antonia Pantoja, and has expanded into an influential, nationwide organization, encouraging Puerto Ricans to advance and excel in education. Miss Pantoja also founded Universidad Boricua (Puerto Rican University), a university without walls chartered to award degrees in association with the Union of Experimental Colleges. It has an affiliate in New York City, also called Universidad Boricua, chartered by the Board of Regents of New York State to grant bachelors degrees.

Other significant achievements are also noted. Professor Frank Bonilla is the prominent director of the Puerto Rican Studies Center at the City University of New York; and Professor Lloyd Rogler Canino holds the distinguished Schweitzer Professorship at Fordham University, where he is director of the nationally recognized Hispanic Research Center.

Color

One of the most serious problems that Puerto Ricans must cope with in the United States is racial prejudice.[14] Puerto Ricans range in color from completely Caucasoid to completely Negroid. This results from the intermingling of the Taino Indians, the inhabitants of Puerto Rico when Columbus discovered the island, the European from Spain, and the blacks who were brought as slaves to Puerto Rico as early as 1511. The offspring of unions of these three peoples are characterized by a wide variety of color. In Puerto Rico, many features such as hair, fingernails, and facial appearance are used to identify a person racially. Three terms, however, are common: *blanco* for white; *de color* for colored; and *trigueño*, which is an intermediary designation, frequently applied to persons who are brown. There is discrimination in Puerto Rico but it expresses itself in very different ways than on the mainland. The preeminent concern in Puerto Rico is class; color is simply one indicator that a person is of a lower class. Among lower class peoples particularly, the social intermingling and intermarriage of persons of different color is quite common. When Puerto Ricans come to the mainland, they meet American color prejudice for the first time. For many of them, they are confronted for the first time with the problem of determining whether they are considered white or black by the American population, or by what color they are going to identify themselves. The autobiography of Piri Thomas, *Down These Mean Streets*, is a vivid expression of the anguish of a young Puerto Rican who cannot determine whether he is white or black.

Puerto Ricans have not only American whites to relate to; they have American blacks. They make a clear distinction between American blacks, whom they call *moreno*, and Puerto Rican blacks, whom they call *de color*. A Puerto Rican black is identified primarily as Puerto Rican and Puerto Ricans relate to him as one of their own. The relationship to American blacks is very different. There is a great deal of fear between them: Puerto Ricans are afraid of blacks, and blacks are afraid of Puerto Ricans.

In a 1959 study of selected New York parishes, it appeared that twenty-five percent of the marriages were between persons whom American citizens would consider persons of different color. If this practice of intermingling of persons of different colors continues, it may be one of the most important contributions Puerto Ricans will bring to the people of the mainland.

Furthermore, the dynamic drive toward integration is confusing to Puerto Ricans. Any social group of Puerto Ricans, particularly any classroom, would ordinarily have Puerto Ricans of all colors. They come as an integrated community, integrated by marriage as well as social custom. Their relationship to the efforts for integration of blacks and whites has left them uncertain what role they should play. Their own life is an example of integration.

Religion

As indicated above, in the experience of earlier immigrants, the parish or religious congregation played a significant role in the adjustment of newcomers to American life. In the form of the parish or congregation, the church or synagogue was the physical symbol of the religious basis of community values, ideals, and solidarity. For the most part, this arrangement was not provided for the Puerto Ricans. The main reason for this was the absence of a native Puerto Rican clergy to come with the migrants. Historically, Puerto Rico, as most of Hispanic America, was served by a foreign clergy, largely from Spain, more recently from the United States. No strong effort was made to develop a native clergy in the Spanish colonies. This left the Puerto Ricans at a disadvantage since it was the native priests, accompanying their immigrant people, who played the major role in the establishment of the national or ethnic parishes. Furthermore, the Puerto Ricans came at a moment in history when the problems of the national parishes were facing the bishops of the United States.

As second and third generations of the immigrants came along, they moved out of the old immigrant community to the suburbs. As a result, there were no congregations left in the old immigrant neighborhoods. In some cases, there would be three or four churches on a block, one Italian, one Polish, one Lithuanian, one Irish, for example and the neighborhood would have become largely black or Puerto Rican. Thus bishops were reluctant to establish new churches for the Puerto Ricans. They sought to train American priests in Spanish and Puerto Rican culture, and create an integrated parish where special services would be provided in Spanish for the Puerto Ricans. As a consequence of social change, some of the old parishes have become Puerto Rican parishes. But the spirit of the old national parish and its role as the basis for community solidarity cannot be achieved very easily in the setting of an integrated parish.

Puerto Ricans come from a culture strongly influenced by Spanish colonial Catholicism. A person considers himself Catholic because he is born into a community that is Catholic, the *Pueblo*, the people of the Lord, not because he registers as a member of a parish and dutifully attends Mass and receives the Sacraments. The great moments of religious practice are the public celebrations, the processions, fiestas, and community celebrations of Holy Week or Christmas in the Plaza. Belief in the power of intercession by saints is very strong: saints are one's friends in a very personal sense. They do favors for one; one honors them in return.

Protestant churches have become established in most cities of the Island; numerous Protestant and Pentecostal churches are among the Puerto Ricans in New York. Small, storefront churches are a common feature of every Puerto Rican neighborhood.[15] Also the practice of spiritualism is common, the effort to communicate with the world of the spirits through the assistance of a medium. This practice can sometimes be helpful, especially to persons who are emotionally troubled.[16] By identifying a person as one troubled by evil spirits, the spiritualists evoke the support of the community for the troubled person and frequently keep the person functional in his or her community. In other circumstances, the practice can be dangerous; the invocation of evil spirits to do harm can be an upsetting experience for Puerto Ricans. *Botanicas*, stores which sell religious articles and all the paraphernalia for folk religious practices—candles, incense, statues, charms, herbs, and potions—are numerous in Puerto Rican neighborhoods. Sometimes there will be three or four on a single block.

The churches have made continued efforts to respond to the religious and spiritual needs of the Puerto Ricans. For many years the New York archdiocese conducted a Center of Inter-cultural Communication in Puerto Rico where hundreds of mainland Americans were trained to minister to the spiritual and social needs of Puerto Rican migrants to the mainland. Nevertheless, the majority of Puerto Ricans on the mainland remain marginal to any religious community.

The Family

The family is the most important institution in any society. As the major influence in the communication of culture to a child and the maintenance of culture in a society, it is the insti-tution most directly affected by the cultural change of migra-tion. Puerto Rican family loyalties tend to be strong; like all Hispanics, family loyalty takes precedence over personal ad-vancement. The role of the father is important; he exercises authority and makes the important decisions for the family. There is also a network of ritual kin called *compadres*, god-parents at baptism, witnesses at a wedding, persons who then become co-parents with the married couple. This relationship is very close, more intimate sometimes than natural kinship, and involving serious reciprocal rights and obligations for personal loyalty, correction, psychological support, and financial assis-tance. Sexual behavior of women, before or after marriage, is carefully restricted. Ideally, the young woman must be brought as a virgin to marriage, and the wife must be faithful to her husband. Much more liberty is granted to the boy or man.

The first problem of migration is the upsetting of traditional family roles. These are changing rapidly in Puerto Rico, but the shock is not as sudden as it is when families come to New York. It is frequently easier for the wife to find employment than the husband, sometimes to earn more. The expectation on the main-land that the wife will play a more decisive role than she played in Puerto Rico creates sudden ambiguities for both. The classic problem of the generations sets in. The children are growing up in a home of Puerto Rican culture, but being taught American culture in the school, and they experience the street culture outside the home. Thus, differences in values, behavior, and life style develop between parents and children. The conflict of generations, so painful for all immigrant groups, strikes the Puerto Ricans sharply. The family begins to reflect the problems of maintaining stability in a mainland environment. Twenty-eight percent of all Puerto Rican families were headed by women in 1970; among second generation Puerto Ricans, it was 25 percent, indicating that this may have become a cultural pattern passed on from one generation to the next. Puerto Rican families are affected, as are all families in the United States, with the increase of teenage pregnancy and out-of-wedlock births. In 1956, of all Puerto Rican births in New York City, eleven percent were out-of-wedlock; in 1980, this had risen to 46 percent. Although sterilization was the most widely used method of birth control in Puerto Rico, abortion appears to be replacing that in New York. In 1978, among Puerto Ricans in New York City, there were 10,378 abortions and 11,733 live births.

The Puerto Rican Family Institute, a city-wide Puerto Rican family agency, conducts a number of programs to assist the Puerto Rican families to retain their strength and stability. Their best known program, a placement prevention program, consists of a staff of trained persons who respond to a family which is seeking to place its child or children in a child-caring institution. By providing supports in the areas of health, education, housing, employment, and family income, the Institute workers have had remarkable success in enabling the families to keep their children at home instead of placing them. Religious programs such as the Movimiento Christiana Familial (Christian Family Movement), the Encuentro Familial (Family Encounter), or the Cursillo, an intensive experience of religious renewal, have had notable success in motivating the families to retain their strength and stability.

The Nuyoricans

A brief word must be added about the "Rican," "Nuyorican," or "Neo-Rican," a member of the second generation of Puerto Ricans, born here of Puerto Rican parents, or brought to the mainland at an early age and raised here. They are described as "hybrid" persons who think and speak both languages but are strangers in both lands. Having been brought up in the poor *barrios*, they have adopted ghetto slang and life styles and are often at odds with the older generation whom they see as passive and submissive, what they call the older and "ay bendito" generation. They have developed the smartness of street life in New York City, a sharpness or "hipness" which enables them to survive in rough and often violent neighborhoods. Some of them were drawn into militant political groups of the 1960s such as the Young Lords and the Real Great Society. Others banded together in violent gangs such as the Ghetto Brothers or the Savage Skulls. They are similar in this, that they are seeking to cope with a difficult environment in their own way, attempting to ameliorate their substandard living conditions, improve their education, and find jobs. They are trying to carve out an identity for themselves as "Nuyoricans." They are generally attracted to political movements for Puerto Rican independence, and third-world revolts against political oppression. They are producing a new literature of the "Nuyoricans"—tough, filled with anger, frustration, and loss of hope. It is marked by a vitality which may break through into a creative hopefulness and promise for the future. Many of them are beginning to excel in the arts, in the Puerto Rican Travelling Theatre and in the Puerto Rican Ballet; in photography such as En Foco, a center for training in photography; and in the graphic arts which are exhibited at the Museo del Barrio, a community-based museum in New York, designed to provide a center for young artists to show their artistic creations, and to make this accessible to the people in the neighborhood. Their music has given New York and other cities a decidedly "Latin beat."

The Emerging Community

Together with the political leadership mentioned earlier, the Puerto Ricans are developing a number of highly respected organizations to advance their interests. The National Puerto Rican Forum, with local chapters in a number of cities, represents the Puerto Ricans on public issues, particularly of a political or business character, and assists the community in job development and business activity. The Puerto Rican Merchants Association is more directly interested in the promotion and protection of small businesses. The Puerto Rican Legal Defense and Education Fund is a prestigious organization, representing the Puerto Ricans through class action suits in the courts to prevent discrimination. The Puerto Rican Family Institute and Aspira have already been mentioned, the latter a very active agency in the area of education. There are organizations of teachers and professional groups, small-town clubs, and local political associations, all of which reflect an aggressive community in the process of moving vigorously into the mainstream of American life.

Return Migration

There are large numbers of Puerto Ricans returning to Puerto Rico, while new ones come to the mainland in the continuous migration described above. In a study done in 1974 at the Social Science Research Center of the University of Puerto Rico,[17] Celia Cintron and Pedro Vales, using 1970 Census data, found that 13 percent of all Puerto Ricans fourteen years of age and older in Puerto Rico in 1970 had been living in the United States in 1965. In the school year 1976–1977, as many as 45,000 children in the public schools of Puerto Rico were reported as having difficulties with the Spanish language. They were probably the return migrants from the mainland. In 1979, the Puerto Rican Family Institute established a branch in Puerto Rico to work with Puerto Rican families who were having problems of adjustment in returning to the Island similar to the problems that original migrants had had in going to New York.

Although the economic factor is important in the return migration (a search for employment, or better employment), other influences have appeared in the return migration: protection of children from the influence of New York City, which parents see as destructive of Puerto Rican values; homesickness, a yearning for the Old World where parents or relatives or friends still live; the effort to avoid the harshness of racial prejudice and discrimination on the mainland; retirement and the desire to pass one's older life "back home"; and the desire to enjoy an environment that is more tranquil and less tense. Return migrants tend to show higher levels of education, occupation, and income than migrants to the mainland. But unemployment rates are high among the returnees, because employment in Puerto Rico is not as available as they think. Returning migrants, particularly the youth, do not share the dominant culture of Puerto Rico. They are, to some extent, strangers in their homeland.

Conclusion

If the political status of Puerto Rico does not change, the continuous movement back and forth will most likely continue. In the meantime, the one third of all Puerto Ricans who are on the mainland represent a large population among whom recent newcomers could find friends, relatives, and Puerto Ricans experienced in American life, to assist them.

There are evidences among the second generation that they may be following the patterns of adjustment similar to those of earlier immigrant groups. Outside of New York City, intermarriage rates are very high with non-Puerto Ricans. They increase noticeably with higher levels of education. Puerto Ricans are slowly developing a network of effective organizations to promote and protect their interests, and their number of elected political officials is slowly increasing. Their lives are complicated by the influx of large populations of other Hispanics, and doubly complicated by the effort to relate to the powerful social movements of American blacks. There are increasing signs of religious vitality and indications that they are seeking to deal with the problems that affect family life.

They are the first Hispanics to come in large numbers to the northeast. They bring with them a new and vigorous culture. If the past is prologue, their Hispanic values and way of life will constitute one more powerful cultural influence to bring new energy and life to the United States.

NOTES

1. U.S. Bureau of the Census, "Persons of Spanish Origin in the United States, 1978," Current Population Reports, Series P–20, no. 328 (advance report) (Washington, D.C.: U.S. Government Printing Office, 1978).

2. Population Reference Bureau, 1978, World Data Sheet (Washington, D.C.: Population Reference Bureau, Inc., 1978).

3. Source: Board of Education, New York City.

4. The best brief history of the island in English is Kol Wagenheim, *Puerto Rican Profile* (New York: Praeger, 1970).

5. U.S. Bureau of the Census.

6. Ibid.

7. U.S. Bureau of the Census, *1970 Census of the Population Characteristics of the Population* (Washington, D.C.: U.S. Government Printing Office, 1970).

8. For details of the adjustment, see Joseph P. Fitzpatrick, *Puerto Rican Americans: The Meaning of Migration to the Mainland* (Englewood Cliffs, N.J.: Prentice-Hall, 1971).

9. See Milton Gordon, *Assimilation in American Life* (New York: Oxford University Press, 1963).

10. See Gerald D. Suttles, *The Social Order of the Slum* (Chicago: University of Chicago Press, 1968).

11. Will Herberg, *Protestant, Catholic, Jew* (Garden City, N.Y.: Doubleday, 1954).

12. U.S. Bureau of the Census, 1970 Census of the Population, *Subject Reports: Puerto Ricans in the United States*, PC (2) 1E, (Washington, D.C.: U.S. Government Printing Office, 1973), Table 4.

13. U.S. Commission on Civil Rights, *Puerto Ricans in the Continental United States: An Uncertain Future* (Washington, D.C.: U.S. Government Printing Office, 1976), pt. 3, "Crisis in Education."

14. Joseph P. Fitzpatrick, "Attitudes of Puerto Ricans toward Color," *American Catholic Sociological Review* 20, no. 3 (1959): 219–33.

15. Renato Poblete and Thomas F. O'Dea, "Anomie and the quest for Community: The Formation of Sects among Puerto Ricans in New York," *American Catholic Sociological Review* 21 (1960): 18–36.

16. Lloyd R. Rogler and August B. Hollinshead, "The Puerto

Rican Spiritualist as Psychiatrist," *American Journal of Sociology* 67 (1961): 17–22.

17. Celia Cintron and Pedro Vales, *Return Migration to Puerto Rico* (Rio Piedras, Puerto Rico: University of Puerto Rico, Social Science Research Center, 1974).

VI

Cuban Immigration to the United States

By Raul Moncarz and Antonio Jorge
Florida International University

Even before the discovery of the New World by Columbus, Cuba was a country with a propensity for forceful displacement of its inhabitants. Specifically, aboriginal Indians were dislodged by the Ciboneyes Indians, who in turn were uprooted by the Tainos, and then by the Caribs. The process has continued ever since, with the peculiarity that from the nineteenth century on, a relatively large number of Cubans have seen the United States as a land of asylum. The motives for this preference could be listed as geographical, political, cultural, and according to some, even ones of dependence.

The history of Cuban immigration to the United States began even before Cuba became a republic, and it continued throughout the republican period.[1] Indeed, coming in exile to the United States has been a firmly established precedent in Cuba's political history. Numerous patriots from Varela to Jose Marti, the foremost figure of Cuban independence, to five chiefs of state, including Batista and Castro, were in exile in this country prior to their return to Cuba and their ascent to historical significance and political power. Even at the time of this writing, a substantial number of political prisoners are being allowed to leave the island as exiles.

In terms of the number of Cubans in the United States, their total number has been calculated to be around one million in 1979, with large increases during the decades of the 1960s and 1970s.[2]

146

The states of the eastern seaboard have attracted almost 85 percent of the Cuban migration. Florida and New Jersey alone claim upward of three fifths of the Cubans in this country. Other states with a significant Cuban population are New York, California, and Illinois. A very interesting aspect about the geographical distribution of Cubans is that they tend to concentrate in metropolitan areas. As an example, 86 percent of Cubans living in Florida are in Miami; 55 percent of those in the State of New Jersey live in Hudson County; 97 percent of those in New York State live in New York City; in California, 79 percent live in the Los Angeles-Long Beach area; in Illinois, 95 percent live in Chicago; and so forth. Nationwide, 98 percent of the Cubans are urban dwellers (compared with 73 percent for the entire United States population).[3]

History of the Migration

Political unrest in Cuba unfolded against a large economic drama. By the middle of the nineteenth century, key sectors of the Cuban economy had become dependent on the North American market.[4] Economic dislocation in the United States impacted directly on Cuba, often with disastrous repercussions. The panic of 1857 in the United States precipitated pressures for higher tariff duties on items manufactured abroad.[5] During the Civil War, moreover, a succession of bills raised the average tariff rate to 40 percent. The effect on the Havana cigar industry was immediate. Fear gripped the manufacturers and many factories ceased operations and went into bankruptcy.[6]

Similarly, almost from its inception, the fate of the cigar industry in the United States was very much linked to developments in Cuba. Repression of Cuban separatists during the Ten Years War (1868–1878) continued, along with the tariff issue, and contributed to the swelling of the exile population in the United States.[7] As war-time conditions in Cuba forced many people to migrate, exile communities were established that eventually would serve as the vanguard for the independence movement.[8] The three major destination points within the United States were New York, Key West, and New Orleans.

The arrival of Cubans in Key West proceeded steadily during that period. By 1870, they numbered approximately 1,100 in that location, as more continued to arrive every week. In December of 1871, the influx intensified as a result of an order by the authorities in Cuba requiring all natives to either enlist in the army or leave the island. By 1873, the Cubans in Key West constituted a majority of the population.[9]

The drive for independence in the 1880s and 1890s displayed several notable features distinguishing it from the previous liberation efforts mounted in 1868, with the city of Tampa playing a very important role. The movement for *Cuba Libre* at the end of the nineteenth century received, on the whole, its major impetus from Cubans residing outside the island.[10]

It seemed that with the establishment of the Cuban Republic in 1902, the periods of exile would have ended for the Cubans. Unfortunately, the years up to 1928 were characterized by a number of difficulties in Cuban political and economic life. These were reinforced by Gerardo Machado's persecutions at the beginning of the 1930s. During this time, Miami became the center of the migration of all sectors of the Cuban population. The immigrant population grew from 1931 onward, as Cuban exiles found a haven in the Miami area.[11]

The coup by Batista in 1952 brought on a new wave of political exiles. Between 1951 and 1959, 10,276 Cubans became naturalized American citizens.[12] However, it was not until the political phenomenon of 1959 that the major flow of Cuban exiles to the United States ensued. With Castro's ascent to power in 1959, and the establishment of a Marxist-Leninist order, one tenth of the Cuban population left the island. Between January 1, 1959, and November of 1979, approximately one million Cubans came to call the United States "home."[13] The magnitude of this wholesale movement of people should be viewed, however, in the perspective of the Cuban population remaining on the island. The population of Cuba was close to six million in 1960, and according to some Cuban sources, amounted to ten million in 1979. In summary, during the period 1960–1979, roughly ten percent of the Cuban people left their homes on the island mainly because of political motives.[14]

At the beginning in 1959, they left on regular commercial airline flights to the United States or to other countries, such as Spain, Mexico, and Costa Rica. Afterward, they departed on special flights and ships provided by private individuals and also by the United States government. At a later point, Cuban political prisoners and others were traded for medicines and political concessions.

Many Cubans have escaped from the island, throughout the years on improvised rafts and boats. These people have faced untold dangers as they came across the Straits of Florida. Hundreds of them never arrived. They died of hunger and thirst, were drowned or were shot by Cuban gunboats or aircraft. Still others have been devoured by man-eating fish.

The Decision to Leave

The Cuban influx into the United States since 1959 has been variously motivated. Fagan, Brody, and O'Leary identified seven major types of motives: (1) temporary imprisonment, (2) fear or threat of imprisonment, (3) harassment and persecution, (4) forcible attempts at integration into the revolution, (5) loss of jobs, possessions, or sources of income, (6) disagreement with governmental action deemed arbitrary, and (7) refusal to accept a Communist regime.[15] Their research was carried out in 1963, and the results obtained only reflect the opinions of the first group of refugees.[16] Balbona has found that compared with a sample taken in 1961, refugees in 1970 cited political divergences or personal security much less frequently as their prime motivation for leaving.[17] They seemed mostly concerned about economic scarcities. Wong has found evidence suggesting that "Cuban migration to the U.S. is not only an entirely political phenomenon, but, rather, that a significant number of the refugees are traditional immigrants who came to the U.S. in search of a higher standard of living."[18]

Another reason not mentioned in the literature refers to the psychological dependence of large sectors of the Cuban population on the United States. It should also be mentioned that the American government sought to discredit the Castro government by pointing to the great number of Cubans leaving the island. And it is obvious that without the help and cooperation of the United States government, the number of refugees would have been smaller.

On a more subjective level, although the Cubans immigrating to the United States have always appreciated the generosity and sympathy of the Americans, they have also tried to retain their customs and traditions. The reason for this attitude is mainly political. The Cuban liberation struggle, both on the island and outside of it, has always emphasized the need to preserve the Cuban identity and culture despite all difficulties and travails.

The average refugee normally tends to integrate well with his host society. He rapidly identifies with his adoptive country and its national interests, willingly engaging in issue-oriented public and political activities. The Cuban refugee feels two allegiances, one to the United States and the other to Cuba. If given a choice, his decision will take place according to what he thinks is better for himself, much in the same manner of any individual who has an alternative.

General Background of the Cubans upon Arrival in the United States after January, 1959

At first, most of the Cubans arriving in the United States did not look upon themselves as refugees, but rather as temporary exiles from a homeland only ninety miles from the Florida coast. As a result, the majority of them decided to reside in Miami.[19] Remaining in Miami, they stayed close to Cuba and could live with their friends and relatives. By being together, they kept alive the hope of an early return to the island.

In Dade County in 1959, the increase in the pool of workers brought about by the Cuban influx resulted in a temporary increase in the overall unemployment and an apparent reduction in nominal wage rates in certain sectors.

Even those Cubans fortunate enough to find employment were frequently unable to put their skills and experience to work. Furthermore, they had no knowledge of job opportunities in the area. Also, their anticipation of an early return to Cuba hampered their employment opportunities. And the desire to remain in Miami was so strong that even professional people preferred to take menial jobs in the area rather than seek elsewhere employment more in keeping with their qualifications.[20]

Prior to the end of 1960, the Cuban government had been lenient in its restrictions on Cubans leaving the island. After that time, however, the Cuban government began confiscating all real and personal property belonging to the Cubans who intended to leave or flee the country. Lack of means of support among Cuban refugees caused a great financial drain on the resources of the local agencies in Miami.[21]

The lack of gainful employment in the Dade County area made public assistance a necessity. At first, local, private, and voluntary agencies and institutions in Miami banded together to assist the refugees. The only governmental assistance received by the Cubans was financed entirely by the federal government and administered by the Florida State Department of Public Welfare under a special agreement. This was provided on the same basis and standards of need applied to other residents of Florida. The maximum amount which a needy refugee family received was $100 per month, and $60 per month was provided for a needy single person not part of a family unit.

Cuban Refugee Center

In December, 1960, the federal government established the Cuban Refugee Emergency Center in Miami, with an allocation of one million dollars from the President's Contingency Fund under the Mutual Security Act, and in 1961 started the Cuban Refugee Program.[22] This program is unique in that it was developed, to the extent possible, through the utilization of the services of existing agencies, the overall responsibility resting with the U.S. Department of Health, Education, and Welfare.

The U.S. Public Health Service provides medical and dental

services for needy refugees through contractural agreements with the Dade County Public Health Service. The U.S. Office of Education supervises the loan program for Cuban students and the refresher courses for Cuban professional people. In addition, the U.S. Office of Education, through the facilities of the Dade County Public School System, supervises programs in Miami related to the education of refugee children as well as English and vocational classes for adults.[23]

At the beginning of the program, the U.S. Department of Labor was asked for help in job placement of refugees in other localities, and the U.S. Department of Agriculture was asked for surplus commodities. While the U.S. Department of Labor participation was transitory, the services of the Department of Agriculture are still being used.

The records of the Cuban Refugee Center do not include the names of all Cuban exiles because it is not required for them to register at the Center when arriving in the United States. Many of the members of the occupations under study have not registered with the Center either because of professional connections with United States firms and individuals or because they arrived prior to the establishment of the Center in 1961 and subsequently did not need or want any help.

Using the Cuban Refugee Center roster of refugees by occupations supplied by the Center, Fagen listed by professional categories the Cubans who registered with the Center from its beginning to March, 1963.[24] Using Fagen's data and Cuban Refugee Center statistics from December 1, 1965, Table 1 lists the number of refugees by professional categories registered with the Center. The number of Cubans coming to the United States between 1963 and 1965 was only around 4,000 because the Cuban government canceled all commercial flights to the United States.

Resettlement

Resettlement encompasses the voluntary resettlement by the Cubans to other parts of the United States from Florida and the efforts directed by the Cuban Refugee Center. Because of

Table 1

OCCUPATIONAL CATEGORIES OF CUBAN REFUGEES, 1961-1969

Occupations	Cuban Refugees	Percentage of Refugees
Professional, semiprofessional, managerial, and executive	31,361	.203
Clerical and sales	35,603	.231
Skilled, semiskilled, and unskilled	29,781	.193
Agriculture and fishing	4,547	.029
Service occupations	4,620	.061

Source: Richard R. Fagen, Resettlement Recap, Issued by the Cuban Refugee Center, Miami, Florida up to February 28, 1969.

friends or relatives in other cities and/or knowledge or hope of better employment opportunities elsewhere, many of the refugees left Florida of their own accord.

The Miami/Dade County area could not begin to support the heavy increase in population or provide adequate employment for all the refugees. Thus, the main thrust of the federal program, with the Cuban Refugee Center in charge, was directed toward resettlement of the refugees in other areas of the state, and even outside of Florida. At the beginning of this program the majority of the refugees refused to leave Miami, still believing they would be able to return relatively soon to a free Cuba.

The Bay of Pigs fiasco in April of 1961, and the October, 1962 missile crisis dramatically changed their hopes for an early return. These events, together with the pressure exerted by the Cuban Refugee Center, made many refugees realize that resettlement in other parts of the United States was the only way to solve their immediate economic problems.

To undertake the important task of resettlement, the federal government turned to four national voluntary agencies, each having had a long experience in the resettlement of refugees: the National Catholic Welfare Conferences, the Church

Table 2

RESETTLEMENT OF CUBAN REFUGEES FROM 1961 TO OCTOBER 30, 1979

Activities by Agencies Since January, 1961	Registered	Resettled
National Catholic Welfare Conference	319,098	191,366
International Rescue Committee	99,303	62,800
Church World Service	54,224	43,829
United HIAS Service	4,492	2,842
Total	477,117	300,837

Source: Cuban Refugee Center, Miami, Florida, October 31, 1979.

World Service, the International Rescue Committee, and the United HIAS Service.[25]

Resettlement was necessary to relieve the burden on Miami as well as to reduce federal expenditures for assistance. The process would enable refugees to become self-supporting, contributing members to our society during their exile; would enable them to retain their skills; and would assist them in the experience of participating in American life. Resettlement was considered to be the most immediate, effective, and economical means of achieving these objectives. As in other welfare programs, the fundamental concern was with the rehabilitation of the recipients. In the case of the Cuban refugee, rehabilitation very frequently took the form of resettlement.

In resettling the Cubans outside of Florida, it was hoped that the jobs they took in other areas would be the same or in related fields as their professions in Cuba. Unfortunately, this was not the case, due in part to the need to get as many of the refugees out of Florida as rapidly as possible. Therefore, only the short-term alternative of moving them out of Florida and finding them any kind of a job at all was achieved.

Several important factors which may have hindered their resettlement and adaptation process were their lack of proficiency in the English language, legal restrictions, unfamiliarity with their new locations, failure to know where to seek job information and guidance, lack of knowledge on the part of both private and public agencies and institutions as to the quality of the individual's educational background and experience, professional and educational restrictions, psychological disorientation due to resettlement and last, but by no means least in importance, age.

When the Cubans came to the United States, the above-mentioned factors mitigated against their professional adaptation; and their necessity to find a *modus vivendi* for themselves and their families caused them to conclude that they were unable to succeed in their original professions. They demonstrated a willingness to accept work requiring less than their highest skills in the hopes that with time they would overcome obstacles impeding their professional adaptation.

Life in the United States

Cubans in the United States are seen as a very diversified group. They are perceived by some as a very successful group. Others see them as a group having faced a number of difficulties while in this country, such as linguistic barriers as well as different social standards, values, and customs.

For the Cuban exiles, the process of creating a new beginning has occurred not amid stable conditions in the host society, but rather in the context of the economic, social, and political turmoil that has characterized the American society during the last twenty years.

The Cubans have witnessed in the short space of the past two decades four economic recessions, double digit inflation, Vietnam, and Watergate.

The organized reception accorded the Cubans since 1959, including concerted community action by diverse local, state, and national groups, and Federal government assistance made available since the 1960 founding of the Cuban Refugee Center, provided an important source of initial support. Other favorable factors include the exiles' prior proximity to and familiarity with the United States, and their cultural-historical affinity with some of the Cubans already in this country.[26]

Rogg's study of the Cuban community of West New York in New Jersey found that although a strong ethnic community may slow acculturation in the short run, with regard to the Cubans, it does not stop it; while on the other hand, it reduces the adjustment problems of refugees.[27] With respect to social class, it seemed that occupational adjustment preceded acculturation for Cubans of lower socioeconomic status, but acculturation appears to precede occupational adjustment among Cubans of higher socioeconomic status.

Portes conceptualized the variables affecting integration within a general reward model, and he tested it in Milwaukee.[28] He interprets his results as suggesting that the same rational individualistic ethic which so strongly influenced the attitudes of the Cuban refugees toward the Revolution, pushing them to leave, is the "key perceptual frame for evaluating the relative attractiveness of their situation in the U.S."[29]

A survey of Cubans in Indianapolis conducted by Prohias found relatively high indexes of acculturation, such as proficiency in English, willingness to learn the language, and proclivity to social interaction.[30] But at the same time, this group was found to be almost completely uninvolved in community organizations with the exception of churches. Carballo studied New Orleans's refugees and found that downward mobility seemed to inhibit acculturation/assimilation at the attitudinal level, although the downwardly mobile, coming from the upper and middle sectors in Cuban society, were best prepared for acculturation in terms of pre-exile exposure and familiarity with the host society.[31]

Lopez Blanco found in Miami that the number of children in the household, occupational level, education prior to arrival, and pre-exile location of residence, were important variables associated with assimilation levels.[32]

Educational Characteristics of the Cuban Population

The Cuban ethnic group, not unlike other immigrant groups and exiles, lay considerable stress on education as a means to promote the social and economic mobility of its members. It is a traditional element in Cuban culture for parents to stimulate the interest and advance the educational attainments of their descendants. In this context, one has to keep in mind that Cuba, as far back as the decade of the fifties, was one of the countries in Latin America with a very high literacy rate.

No doubt, because of the centrality of educational values in the Cuban society, and also because of the emphasis on economic success and material achievement which was very typical not only of the middle class as such but of the upper lower class as well, the Cuban student tends to be achievement oriented and highly competitive in his or her academic behavior.

Regrettably, the educational data in the Dade County School System, as well as that for the state of Florida as a whole, aggregate all Latin nationalities under the generic term, Hispanic. Therefore, valid comparisons as to their educational attainments cannot be made among the various groups comprising the total.

Consequently, one must be extremely careful in the interpretation of figures which lump together highly heterogeneous samples of educational populations. With this *caveat* in mind, some very tentative and general observations may be advanced.

Let us note that about 82 percent of the Hispanic population of Dade County is Cuban or of Cuban origin. About 75 percent of the Cubans in the United States reside in Dade County. And about 85 percent of Cubans living in Florida make their home in Dade.

Keeping the above in mind, it is significant to note that the dropout rate for Hispanic students is only 2.85 percent, which compares favorably with the 4.02 percent rate for non-Hispanic whites.[33] In the same context, it should be pointed out that the enrollment of Hispanics in the Dade County School System has increased more than two and one half times from the close of the sixties to about 1978.

It is equally important to call attention to the following facts. Approximately 51.5 percent of all Cuban persons twenty-five years and older have completed four years of high school or more, compared to 64.1 percent for the total population.[34]

At the other extreme of the scale, 9.5 percent of Cubans in the aforementioned age group had completed less than five years of school, which compares unfavorably with the figure of 3.8 percent for the total population of this country.[35]

The relatively high coefficient for the Cubans in the last group may be explained by a two-fold reason: the increasing influx of refugees from the lower socioeconomic strata after 1965, and the scarcer educational opportunities at their disposal in Cuba relative to those enjoyed in the United States by people in comparable socioeconomic strata.

With respect to those in the first grouping, one should remember that after 1965, the composition of the Cuban population of Cuban birth in the United States has been changing. As already mentioned, the socioeconomic, and by implication the educational, attainments of those arriving since the inauguration of the "Freedom Flights," are lower than those of the earlier arrivals. Therefore, the arithmetic average cited above—51.5 percent—may be quite misleading. Increasingly, we have the case of a bimodal population whose profiles should be considered separately.

All in all, it seems fair to state that, with the passage of time, we shall see Cuban educational indexes increase relative to those for other population segments. As Cuban competitiveness and accent on the merits of formal education assert themselves relative to the first Cuban-American generation, in a social milieu whose educational opportunities and facilities are more abundant than those existing in the society of their fathers, we shall likely see them being taken advantage of.

The end result will be that the educational bimodality referred to previously will disappear. A less skewed curve, resembling more of a normal distribution, will take its place.

Occupational Mobility

Studies in occupational mobility of Cubans started as early as the Cuban migration; thus, there is significant data with which to make valid comparisons.

The University of Miami conducted a survey of Dade County

Cubans in July, 1966, and compared the occupational distribution of Cubans in the United States with their former occupations in Cuba. The comparison (see Table 3) shows what could be termed a truly downward loss of occupational status. The percentage of people in the unskilled labor category had doubled, from 15.9 percent in Cuba to 32.3 percent in Dade County, while the percentage of workers in the professionals, proprietors, technicians, and managers categories had suffered a four-to-one reduction, from 48.2 percent in Cuba to 12.7 percent in the United States.[36]

Table 3

OCCUPATIONS IN DADE COUNTY AND IN CUBA—1966 MIAMI SAMPLE (1)

Occupational Category	In Cuba	In U.S.
Professionals, Proprietors, Technicians, Managers,	48.2%	12.7%
Clerical and Sales	24.3%	27.3%
Skilled Labor	11.6%	17.3%
Unskilled Labor	15.9%	32.3%

(1) University of Miami, 1967, p. 62.

The 1970 census, with its data concerning the employment status and occupation of Spanish-speaking persons in the Miami area (the overwhelming percentage of these being Cuban), can be used as an indicator of the occupational breakdown in Miami as of 1970.[37] It will allow us some rough comparisons with data obtained by the University of Miami in 1966.

If census categories are made comparable to the information available from the 1966 University of Miami survey, it will be observed that there does not seem to be any upward change in mobility between 1966, 1970, and 1974 (data gathered by Raul Moncarz) for Miami Cubans, as seen in Table 4.

Table 4

CUBAN OCCUPATIONS IN MIAMI:
1966, 1970 and 1974

Occupation	1974 (RM) (5)	Miami SMSA 1970 Census (1)	1966 Dade County (4)
Technical Managers and Professionals	13.5%	14.1%	12.7%
Clerical and Sales	24.6%	23.8%	27.3%
Skilled Labor	17.3%	14.5% (2)	17.3%
		3.5% (3)	
Unskilled Labor	44.6%	43.8%	32.3%

(1) U.S. Department of Commerce, *Census Tracts*, Final Report PH(1)–129, Table P–8.
(2) Craftsmen, foremen, and kindred workers.
(3) Transport operatives.
(4) University of Miami, 1967.
(5) Pilot study by the author.

Now let us look in Table 5 at some very interesting data published in 1975, 1977, and 1978 by the U.S. Department of Commerce (in addition to data from the 1970 census), on the employment status and major occupation groups of Cuban males sixteen years old and over. Looking at the data up to 1976, we can see that the figures on employment status by Cuban males have remained relatively the same since the 1970 census. But the data show that the Cuban males in the labor force sixteen years old and over have increased by 15,000 between 1976 and 1978, while the number of professional, technical, and kindred workers increased from 13.4 percent (24,522) to 17 percent (33,588), a very unrealistic figure, even taking into consideration the new professionals licensed under the special legislation passed in the state of Florida in 1973. Furthermore, looking at the category of managers and administrators, their numbers increased from 5.1 percent (9,333) to 13.8 percent (27,324).

Table 5

EMPLOYMENT STATUS AND MAJOR OCCUPATION GROUP OF CUBAN MALES 16 YEARS OLD AND OVER

Employment Status and Occupation	1970	1975	1976	1978
Persons 16 years old and over			237M	259M
Persons in Civilian Labor Force	141M	191M	183M	198M
Percent unemployed		15.1%	12.0%	8.6%
Professional, Technical, and Kindred Workers	12.9%	12.2%	13.4%	17.0%
Managers and Administrators, excluding Farmers	7.4%	9.1%	5.1%	13.8%
Sales Workers	5.5%	3.5%	5.3%	3.4%
Clerical and Kindred Workers	10.7%	12.5%	10.3%	5.6%
Craft and Kindred Workers	18.0%	17.5%	18.0%	16.4%
Operatives, including Transportation	24.2%	24.3%	21.6%	20.3%
Laborers, excluding Farmers	6.1%	2.2%	7.6%	8.6%
Service Workers	14.3%	18.6%	18.6%	14.4%

M = 1,000

If we accept the 1978 figures as accurate, the Cuban community in the United States can be portrayed as bipolar in nature. About 31 percent of the community is composed of two major occupational groups: (a) professional, technical, and kindred workers, and (b) managers and administrators. And over 43 percent of the community is composed of operatives, laborers, and service workers. This unique characteristic would suggest that a number of Cubans have maintained their high employment status, while significant numbers are working in occupations below their capabilities and previous status.

If 1975, 1976, and 1978 census figures are collapsed to make them comparable with our previous information, as seen in Tables 6 and 7, there is no indication of significant upward movement in occupational status at the group level since 1959 in the case of the Cuban community in the United States.

Table 6

CUBAN OCCUPATIONS
IN CUBA VS. IN THE UNITED STATES

Occupational Category	In Cuba	In U.S. 1966	1970	1975	1976	1978
Professionals, Proprietors, Technicians, and Managers	48.2%	12.7%	20.3%	21.3%	18.5%	30.8%
Clerical and Sales	24.3	27.3	16.2	16.0	15.6	9.0
Skilled Labor	11.6	17.3	18.0	17.5	18.0	16.4
Unskilled Labor	15.9	32.3	45.0	45.1	47.8	43.3

An alternative classificatory scheme of occupations held by Cubans in their native country and in Florida in 1970 is presented in the following table.

A *Fortiori*, the above holds true for the Cuban professionals in Florida and, most particularly, in the S.M.S.A. (Standard Metropolitan Statistical Area) of Miami, where most of these professionals reside.

An extensive quotation from a comprehensive study on the subject will serve to clearly illustrate the nature of the obstacles and difficulties experienced by the Cuban professional groups and their concomitant results in terms of imperfect occupational mobility and misallocation of valuable human capital. Other associated consequences of great social and economic import, such as aggravated income maldistribution and a generalized absolute decline in formalized educational levels and social status, are also the result of the discrimination experienced by these professionals.

Professionals

"In addition to unemployment, another problem affecting the S.S.A. in Florida is the problem of underemployment. Most of the previously mentioned causes of unemployment among the Spanish-speaking population are equally causal factors of underemployment. Thus it is that many professionals, tech-

Table 7

U.S. Occupations	Cuban Occupations							
	Craftsmen N=7 3.7%	Ranchers N=8 4.2%	Proprietors & Profess. N=77 40.7%	Sales & Clerical N=46 24.1%	Oper. N=15 7.8%	Service N=25 13.1%	Labor N=9 4.7%	Total N=191 100%
Craftsmen	71.4	—	1.3	—	6.7	4.0	—	4.4
Ranchers	—	—	—	—	—	—	—	0.0
Prop. & Prof.	—	—	9.1	4.3	—	4.0	—	5.3
Sales & Clerical	—	—	15.6	15.2	6.7	4.0	—	12.0
Operatives	28.6	100.0	70.1	69.6	80.0	68.0	66.7	70.0
Services	—	—	—	4.3	—	16.8	11.1	4.0
Laborers	—	—	2.6	2.2	—	4.0	22.2	3.5
Not Available	—	—	1.3	4.3	6.7	—	—	.5

Source: Equal Employment Opportunity Commission, "State and Local Government Information" (EEO–4), 1975, Summary for Florida, pp. 424–26.

nicians, and skilled workers are working in lower income level job categories than their training calls for. The main reasons for this are that they are unable to obtain the proper professional licenses, or that they have not been admitted to a workers' union.

The following table gives us some information about the relative importance of diverse obstacles in hindering the adaptation of some categories of Cuban professionals that participated in the program.

Table 8

Greatest Obstacle in Prof. Adapt.	(1)	(2)	(3)	(4)	(5)	(6)
Language	42%	47%	23%	38%	77%	10%
Age	6	7	—	3	—	8
Health	2	—	—	—	3	—
Other	2	—	6	3	—	13
No difficulty in adapt.	17	—	—	3	6	8
Professional restriction	31	47	71	54	14	61

(1) Physicians; (2) Veterinarians; (3) Optometrists; (4) Pharmacists; (5) Nurses; (6) Lawyers

Source: State of Florida, EEO–4 Report by Salary, Department of Administration, Division of Personnel and Report by Category, p. 1.

From the analysis of the preceding table, it follows that the two greatest obstacles in professional adaptation are language barriers and professional restrictions, depending on the professional group being considered. While 77 percent of nurses stated that language is the greatest obstacle in professional adaption, 61 percent of the lawyers considered 'Professional restrictions' the greatest obstacle to professional adaptation. Although we do not have specific data on architects, only two of 36 passed the examination in December, 1976. 'In spite of the constant increase in population and businesses in Dade County, the proportion of Cuban architects graduated from the University of Havana, Cuba (and practicing in the United

States), tends to decrease.'[38] Language difficulties constitute the most important problem in solving the obstacle of 'Professional restrictions' and also constitute the main cause of failure when taking the licensing examination.

Another problem is the difference between the methods used for examinations in Cuba and those used in the United States, with which most Cuban professionals are not familiar. Specifically in Latin America, university examinations are of the essay type, while in the United States they tend to be based on multiple choice questions.

In 1974, the Florida Legislature (Florida Law 3732), finally took action favoring the Cuban professionals in the state. The law allowed Cuban professionals to take a course in their respective fields and then allowed them to take the board examinations with some exceptions.

Since the inception of the Program in 1970, 970 out of 1,713 (or 57 percent of the examined professionals under the program) have been licensed. The table below shows the number and percentage of professionals passing the exams by professional categories.

Table 9

Professional Category	Started the Course	Drop Outs	Passed	% of Passing
Medicine	641	—	375	59.0%
Pharmacy	416	—	254	61.0
Nursing	217	—	190	88.0
Lawyers	357	40	105	33.0
Dentists	141	19	46	38.0
Totals	1772	59	970	57.0%

Source: Luciano Islas, "Personal Interview About Professional Program," Dade County Office of Latin Affairs, February 7, 1978.

The highest passing percentage was that of the nursing profession (88 percent), followed by pharmacy (61 percent) and medicine (59 percent). The lawyers have a special problem in that there are substantial differences in the legal basis of the

American and Cuban judicial systems. While Cuba's was based on Roman law and the Napoleonic code, the American system is based on common law and precedents. The dentists have a different set of difficulties. The specific requirements of the exam for dentistry make it very expensive, in addition to the fact that dentists must first pass a state level exam, then two national level examinations. Thus, out of 141 dentists who started the course, 19 dropped out, 27 are at 'point zero' (this means that they have not passed any exam), 28 have passed the first part of the national exam, and 21 have passed the national total. Forty-six have obtained the license to practice.

In the case of the podiatrists, though these professionals have twice taken the board exams, not a single one out of 52 has passed to date."[39]

In summary, the evidence gathered so far on occupational mobility seems to indicate a polarization in the occupational structure of Cubans in the United States. Cubans as a group have experienced a very significant loss of occupational status. The above information, though, must not be construed to imply that there have not been individual cases of upward occupational mobility among Cubans in the United States.[40]

Language as a Variable

Language is a basic variable that is of great interest and can be a part of the concept of educational mobility. Many Cubans in Miami feel that a knowledge of English is not necessary to hold their job. This can be explained by the fact that the current total Hispanic population in Dade County, which approximates 600,000 persons, constitutes an economy within an economy, where English is not widely used.[41] In evaluating the meaning of the commonly heard statement that "English is not necessary in their present employment," one has to take into consideration several elements. First, whether such employment carries the same compensation as its American counterpart, and whether in time English will not be required in order for the non-English-speaking Cuban to retain his or her job.

Language is not simply an instrument for social communication. It constitutes one of the most influential cultural elements in shaping the individual's personality. Moreover, inability to express oneself fluently in a given community is immediately associated, in a negative fashion, with the mental capabilities and intellectual skills of a person. As a consequence, people unfamiliar with English in an English-speaking society are, to start with, placed at a considerable disadvantage relative to others in the same community.

There have been a number of programs providing for English education, but the type of training that has been offered and/or is being offered does not seem to fulfill the expectations of the recipients.

Discrimination is another by-product of the language variable. Many people are contemptuous of Cubans because of their enunciation and/or unfamiliar patronymics and will, therefore, not afford them fair or just treatment. Individuals exhibiting these attitudes will hinder the social progress of minorities by denying them the opportunities which would otherwise be open to them. In the typical fashion of circular causative relations in society, such a situation will eventuate in a vicious circle of poverty. It should also be noted that language and surname discrimination is not only leveled at first-generation migrants, but is all too often continued against their descendants, sometimes for generations. Because of discriminatory practices, many Cubans have lost the incentive to continue their quest for economic adaptation in this country; and in many cases, that has proved more of a problem in their total adaptation than unfamiliarity with English.

Age

Cubans as a group are much older than the rest of the population, a fact shown by the University of Miami study in 1966, the Prohias and Casals study of 1972, and the censuses of 1970 and 1978.[42] Specifically, the 1978 census sample survey shows that Cubans have a median age of 36.8, as compared to that of 29.5 for the rest of the United States population.[43]

The age effect (inverse relationship between age and ability to learn a language) also hinders the learning of the English language, which together with the impression that English is not necessary, creates or is helping to create a marginal group within the society.[44]

In view of the foregoing, a few comments can be made with respect to educational mobility as follows: (1) There has been downward educational mobility by the Cubans in the United States when compared to their educational level and experience in Cuba. (2) Even though there have been a number of programs designed to teach English to various segments of the Cuban population, there still seems to be an insurmountable language barrier for some. Also, an inverse relationship has been found to exist between age and the ability to learn English.

Income

A pilot survey conducted in 1974 in Miami showed incomes for Cuban immigrants below the United States median average ($10,285).[45] This figure is approximate, because it shows the individual income of the respondents rather than family income.

The low income earned by a large segment of the sample tends to indicate significant income differentials within the Cuban community. This serves to attest that generalizations about Cuban success stories are not always valid.

According to the 1970 population census, the median family income for blacks in Dade County, Florida, was $5,983; for Spanish-speakers $8,091; and for non-Latin whites $10,562; with an overall county median of $9,245.[46] In a statistical sense, the source of this income differential, which Poston and Alvarez (1973) have referred to as the "cost" of ethnicity or minority status, should be obvious.[47] Cubans and white males differ in the primary determinants of income—employment and earnings.

It is important to keep in mind that there is no single socio-economic status for any group. There are well-to-do, educated Spanish-speaking people, and very poor, uneducated non-Latin whites. Thus, the average and median information is used to describe the central tendency of each group, although a wide range of conditions exists on either side of the averages.

An interesting sociocultural aspect to be noted in this context is the economic role played by Cuban women and children. By generating gainful income of their own, they tend to increase the median household income of the Cuban family, more so relatively speaking than is the case with their counterparts in other population groups.[48]

Theory Explaining Results on Income Differentials

Reason suggests that the impact of employment discrimination will vary among occupations. Becker (1957) specified three sources of discrimination—that originating with employers, with fellow employees, and finally, that attributable to consumers.[49] This suggests that the intensity of employment discrimination will be influenced by various job characteristics, such as, among others, the amount of direct contact with consumers or fellow employees, the social status attached to the job, and the opportunity for self-employment. According to Becker's theory, employment discrimination against Cubans should be most intense in occupations that involve considerable contact with consumers and white employees. Furthermore, the "etiquette of supervisory relationships" referred to by Siegel (1965) suggests that Cuban workers will be denied access to higher-paying managerial positions involving supervision over white thus compelling them to engage in small-scale retail activities.[50] Similarly, the "crowding" hypothesis of Bergman (1971) implies that the more desirable jobs will be closed to males of Spanish origin.[51]

To estimate the intensity of differential earnings discrimination within major occupations, Long calculated a Cuban/white earnings ratio adjusted for age, education, and region factors which strongly influence money earnings.[52] The results of the study were that the relative earnings of Cuban males were much lower than those of white Americans when adjusted for these variables. This indicates the existence of two independent earning functions, one for Cubans and another one for white

Americans. The former is such that Cubans receive a lower payoff than white Americans do for the same educational level, given the same geographical locations and age intervals. One of several explanations for the lower payoffs is the high level of unemployment and underemployment among Cuban professionals.

These findings have important implications for the prospect of earnings equality between Cubans and white males. They suggest that the effects of past discriminatory practices in both employment and the acquisition of human capital continue to reduce the earning power of Cuban males in the labor force. In summary, the empirical findings suggest that employment discrimination has contributed to the relative inferior economic status of Cubans in the United States.

The evidence gathered in this study seems to indicate that upward educational and occupational mobility have been minimal. In terms of educational mobility, the study shows that the loss of potential human capital has been very significant. It is noteworthy that even though the Cuban exodus has now lasted for over 20 years (starting in 1959), there is still very little success in terms of the preservation and/or enhancement of the group's human capital.

From an occupational viewpoint, if the latest (1978) census figures are taken as representative of the Cuban occupational structure, the existence of a bipolar population is apparent. This means that 31 percent of the Cubans have achieved higher occupational status, such as that of professionals, technicians, managers, and administrators, while over 43 percent are part of the lower strata of the occupational categories, consisting of operatives, laborers, and service workers. The findings also suggest that Cuban males working in the United States have experienced employment discrimination, which has adversely affected both their earnings and employment. Furthermore, relative to white males of similar age, educational attainment, and regional location, males of Cuban origin are more likely to hold jobs as operatives, laborers, and service workers—occupations usually characterized by low pay.

The overstating of personal achievements has been to the detriment of the larger group of Cubans who have been unable to -use their education and experience, and who face the tremendous task of emulating a success that in this country has not been theirs, and as time goes by, becomes more elusive.

Conclusions

The Cuban exile in the United States has been characterized throughout the years as exhibiting very nationalistic traits and not being easily assimilable. The historical antecedent of this attitude is rooted in the fact that, since the nineteenth century, Cubans in the United States have always been engaged in struggles to free Cuba from one form of oppression or another. To attain this goal, activist refugee and émigré communities have always constituted a prominent factor in the Cuban historical experience. Because of its proximity to the Island, the state of Florida has become a traditional gathering point for dissatisfied Cubans seeking to influence the political situation in their homeland.

Coexisting with a strong cultural identity and nationalistic drive is the typical Cuban élan. This has manifested itself in a strong drive and close affinity for social and economic success. The competitiveness of the group and its achievement orientation have been repeatedly noted by those who have come in contact with it. In some respects, it has become by now more than commonplace, a cliché in the description of the behavior ascribed to Cubans. Nonetheless, as far as observed behavior goes, particularly in the marketplace, it is not devoid of a considerable measure of truth.

Practically no Cuban exiles returned to the Island until a new turn of events took place in November of 1978. In that month, the Cuban government decided to allow these exiles to visit with their families; and a number of them have made brief visits to the Island for that purpose. In light of this, it would seem that the motivating forces actuating Cubans in the United States to visit their native country are of a humanitarian and familial nature.

In summary, the Cuban exiles in the United States have long constituted a singular group with traditions and peculiar circumstances of their own. Their long-preserved concern for the affairs of the motherland, perhaps reinforced by its geographical proximity and the historical, political, and economic relations between the two countries, have molded Cuban exiles into a different breed of migrants: one that is never able to entirely turn its back on the past—a romantic type of exiled individual who goes on dreaming of a future *Patria* and lives on idealized visions of a *Cuba Libre*.

NOTES

1. Rosa M. Abella, "The Cultural Presence of the Cuban Exile in Miami," in *The Hispanic Presence in Florida*, (1976), pp. 133–40.

2. Hispanic Commission of Florida, 1979, Annual Report, p. 12.

3. Javier Miyares, "Cuban-Americans—Who are They?", *NCCA News*, July, 1978, p. 2.

4. Luis A. Perez, Jr., "Cubans in Tampa: From Exiles to Immigrants, 1892–1901." *Florida Historical Quarterly* 57 no. 2 (1978): 129.

5. Julio LeRiverend, *Historia Economica de Cuba* (Havana, 1965).

6. G. E. Poyo, "Key West and the Cuban Ten Years War," *Florida Historical Quarterly* 57 (January, 1979): 289.

7. Martin Duarte Hurtado, "La Lucha de los Tabaqueros en Tampa y Callo Hueso," *Granma*, January 2, 1967.

8. *New Orleans Daily Picayune*, February 19, 1869.

9. U.S. Census Office, Ninth Census of the U.S., 1870, microfilm population schedule, Monroe County, Florida, *Tallahassee Weekly Floridian*, December 12, 1871.

10. Juan E. Casasus, *La Emigracion Cubana y la Independencia de la Patria* (Havana, 1953).

11. Abella, "The Hispanic Presence in Florida," p. 137.

12. R. Prohias and L. Casal, *The Cuban Minority in the U.S.* (Boca Raton: Florida Atlantic University Press, 1973), p. 229.

13. Ruben D. Rumbaut and Ruben G. Rumbaut, "The Family in Exile: Cuban Expatriates in the United States," *American Journal of Psychiatry* 133, no. 4 (April, 1976): 395.

14. Ibid.

15. Richard R. Fagen, R. A. Brody, and Thomas J. O'Leary, *Cubans in Exile* (Stanford, 1968), pp. 4–5, 73, 93.

16. L. Casals and A. Hernandez, "Cubans in the U.S.," *Cuban Studies* 5 (July, 1975): 26.

17. Manuel Balbona, "Causal Factors in the Cuban Exodus," 78th Annual Convention of the American Psychological Association, Florida, September, 1970.

18. Francisco R. Wong, "Political Orientations and Participation of Cuban Migrants—A Preliminary Analysis," unpublished paper presented at the *Annual Meeting American Political Science Association* (New Orleans, 1973).

19. John Thomas, "Cuban Refugees in the United States," *The International Migration Review* 1 (Spring, 1967): 48.

20. Raul Moncarz, *A Study of the Effect of Environmental Change on Human Capital Among Selected Skilled Cubans*, (U.S. Department of Commerce, 1970), p. 22.

21. Thomas, "Cuban Refugees in the United States," p. 47.

22. Ibid., pp. 47–48.

23. Ibid., pp. 48–57.

24. Fagen, *Cubans in Exile*, p. 19.

25. John Thomas, "U.S.A. As a Country of First Asylum," *International Migration* 3, no. 1 (1965): 11.

26. Rumbaut, "The Family in Exile: Cuban Expatriates in the United States," p. 396.

27. E. M. Rogg, *The Assimilation of Cuban Exiles: The Role of Community and Class* (Aberdeen Press, 1974).

28. A. Portes, "Dilemmas of a Golden Exile: Integration of Cuban Refugee Families in Milwaukee," *American Sociological Review* 34 (1969): 505–18.

29. Ibid., pp. 514–17.

30. Rafael J. Prohias, *The Cuban Exile Community in Indianapolis: A Study in Accommodation* (Bloomington: Indiana University, 1967).

31. Manuel Carballo, "A Socio-Psychological Study of Acculturation/Assimilation: Cubans in New Orleans" Ph.D. diss., Tulane University, 1970).

32. Marino Lopez Blanco, *A Study of Attitudes of Cuban Refugees in the Miami Area* (Miami: Barry College, 1968).

33. Hispanic Commission of Florida, 1978, Annual Report, p. 35.

34. See R. Moncarz, *Commissions Report* (1978), p. 235.

35. Ibid.

36. *The Cuban Migration 1959–1966 and Its Impact on Miami, Dade County, Florida* (University of Miami, Center for Advanced International Studies, 1967).

37. U.S. Department of Commerce, *Census Tracts*, Final Report, PH (1)–129, Table P–8.

38. The quote inserted in the text is from a research project conducted by Mr. Mariano Sole under the supervision of Dr. Raul Moncarz. The study is based on the methodology developed by Professor Moncarz for his doctoral dissertation on the Cuban professionals in the United States. Mr. Sole's study appears in the First Annual Report of the Commission on the Spanish Speaking Populace of Florida, published in 1977.

39. Ibid.

40. R. Moncarz, "The Golden Cage: Cubans in Miami," *International Migration*, no. 3 (1978), pp. 160–197.

41. *Commission on Spanish-Speaking Populace in Florida*, p. 80.

42. *The Cuban Migration 1959–1966 and Its Impact on Miami*, 1967; R. Prohias and L. Casals, *The Cuban Minority in the U.S.*, p. 70; *Population Characteristics*, U.S. Department of Commerce, Bureau of the Census, March, 1978.

43. *Population Characteristics*, U.S. Department of Commerce, Bureau of the Census, March, 1978.

44. Andres Hernandez, ed., *The Cuban Minority in the U.S.: Final Report on Need Identification and Program Evaluation* (Washington, D. C.: Cuban National Planning Council, 1974), p. 17.

45. Ibid., p. 23.

46. *Profile of the Latin Population in the Metropolitan Dade County Area* (Office of the County Manager, 1976), p. 20.

47. D. L. Poston and D. Alvarez, "On the Cost of Being a Mexican American," *Social Science Quarterly* 53 (March, 1973): 695–709.

48. *Manpower Report of the President* (U.S. Department of Labor, 1973), p. 98.

49. G. Becker, *The Economics of Discrimination* (Chicago: University of Chicago Press, 1957).

50. P. M. Siegel, "On the Cost of Being a Negro," *Sociological Inquiry* 35 (1965): 44.

51. B. R. Bergmann, "The Effect of White Incomes on Discrimi-

nation in Employment," *Journal of Political Economy* 79 (March/April, 1971): 297.

52. J. F. Long, "Productivity, Employment Discrimination and the Relative Economic Status of Spanish Origin Males," *Social Science Quarterly* 58, no. 3 (Fall, 1977): 47.

VII

Canadian Immigration to the United States

By T. J. Samuel

*Strategic Policy and Planning Division of the
Department of Employment and Immigration
of the Canadian Government*

Since the settlement of North America, there has been constant and continuous movement of people to the north and south of the 49th parallel that separates Canada and the United States. This "mingling of the Canadian and American peoples"[1] or "the spilling of great waves of men and women into each other's territories"[2] between the two countries, which for many decades have shared the most undefended border between any two sovereign nations in the world, has been a unique phenomenon. The volume and direction of this migration varied, as did the composition and geographic destinations of the migrants themselves. "So natural has been this interplay of population in the North American scene that it constitutes what is perhaps the largest single reciprocity in international migration in history . . . ,"[3] observed Marcus Lee Hansen.

In this essay (the views of which are personal and should not be attributed to any organization with which the author is currently associated), immigration of Canadians into the United States will be examined with special focus on the postwar period, the composition and destination of these migrants, their motivation for migration, adaptation to the American life, and the return migration of some of these immigrants. Immigrants from Canada to the United States consisted of native-born and naturalized Canadians, immigrants in Canada from other countries,

176

and a sprinkling of students and visitors in Canada who later moved south.

In the nineteenth and early twentieth centuries, many immigrants to North America had "failed to differentiate between the United States and Canada once they had decided to go to America."[4] Many who came to Canada as immigrants later moved to the United States as the following account shows: ". . . of the total number of immigrants arriving at Quebec in Montreal in 1856, forty-one percent went to the United States . . . practically all of the Norwegians, one half of the Germans and Irish and one half of the English and Scottish settled in the latter country. In 1856, out of 72,251 immigrants entering Canada, 37,034 went to the United States."[5] It was observed a century later that "little cognizance has been taken of the fact that many so-called Canadian immigrants have been immigrants from other parts of the world who have used Canada as a stop-over point for a few years on their way to the United States."[6]

At the beginning of the twentieth century, 1.6 percent of the American population was Canadian-born. That corresponded to a quarter of the Canadian population at that time. Between 1900 and 1940 the number of Canadian-born in the United States population exceeded one million (see Table 1).

Table 1

Canadian Born in the U.S., 1900-1940

Year	Canadian-born (million)
1900	1.17
1910	1.20
1920	1.12
1930	1.28
1940	1.04

In 1930, the number of Canadians in the United States reached the highest number ever, representing 1.1 percent of the entire U.S. population and 9.1 percent of the country's foreign-born population. This represented one eighth of the Canadian population in 1930 over the previous years. If they had remained in Canada, Canada's population in that year would have been about 15 million or 50 percent higher.

If one looks at the population exchanges between Canada and the United States, there were very few years when there was a net gain for Canada. The years 1896–1914 was one such period, as have been the years since 1968.

For the first time in this century, the number of Canadian-born in the United States fell below one million in 1950. It declined again in 1960 to 0.95 million and in 1970 to 0.81 million. Table 2 and Chart 1 show the immigration from Canada for the period 1940-1977, as well as the Canadian-born segment of the movement.

Table 2

Immigration From Canada, 1940-1977

Year*	Number of Immigrants Whose Country of Last Permanent Residence (CLPR) is Canada	Who are Canadian-born	Proportion of Canadian-born to CLPR
1940	10,806	8,303	76.8
1941	11,280	8,428	74.7
1942	10,450	8,519	81.5
1943	9,571	7,235	75.6
1944	9,821	7,023	71.5
1945	11,079	8,866	80.0
1946	20,434	18,627	91.2
1947	23,467	20,983	89.4
1948	24,788	21,794	87.9
1949	24,516	20,798	84.8
1950	21,885	18,043	82.4
1951	25,880	20,809	80.4
1952	33,354	28,141	84.4
1953	36,283	28,967	79.8
1954	34,873	27,055	77.6
1955	32,435	23,091	71.2

* Year ended June 30

Number of Immigrants

Year*	Whose Country of Last Permanent Residence (CLPR) is Canada	Who are Canadian-born	Proportion of Canadian-born to CLPR
1956	42,363	29,533	69.7
1957	46,354	33,203	71.6
1958	45,143	30,055	66.6
1959	34,599	23,082	66.7
1960	46,668	30,990	66.4
1961	47,470	32,038	67.5
1962	44,272	30,377	68.6
1963	50,509	36,003	71.3
1964	51,114	38,074	74.5
1965	50,035	38,327	76.6
1966	37,273	28,358	76.1
1967	34,768	23,442	67.4
1968	41,716	27,662	66.3
1969	29,303	18,582	63.4
1970	26,850	13,804	51.4
1971	22,709	13,128	57.8
1972	18,592	10,776	57.9
1973	14,800	8,951	60.5
1974	12,301	7,654	62.2
1975	11,215	7,308	65.2
1976	17,826	7,638	42.8
1977	29,844	12,688	42.5

* Year ended June 30

Source: U.S. Dept. of Justice, Annual Report of Immigration and Naturalization Service, 1940–1978.

After World War II, there was a sudden increase in the immigration from Canada. The number of immigrants doubled from about 10,000 a year in the early forties to over 20,000 in the late forties. In the spring of 1946, *Time*, the U.S. newsmagazine, reported that Canadians were "besieging American consular offices from Halifax to Vancouver in greater number than any time since 1921."[7] The reasons given were: removal of wartime restrictions on labor permits to leave the country, easing of exchange restrictions on taking money out of Canada, increased availability of urban employment in the United States vis-à-vis

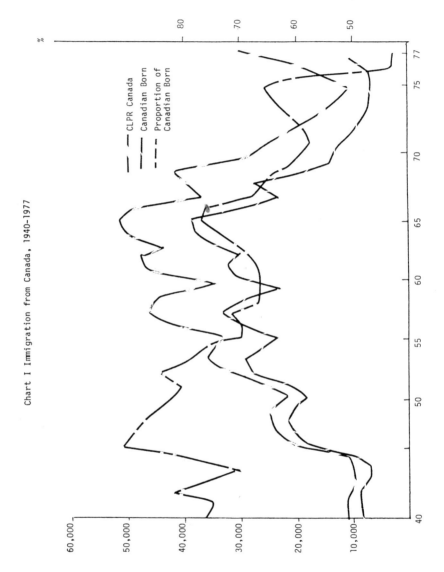

Chart I Immigration from Canada, 1940-1977

Canada, the continuation of wage controls in Canada, the higher wages of American industry, and better economic prospects of the United States. Canadian brides of American servicemen added to the flow. The number of Canadian-born among the immigrants remained between 75 percent and 90 percent.

On April 1, 1950, there were 994,562 Canadian-born in the United States (i.e., about ten percent of all foreign-born in the United States). The estimate of the persons who were landed immigrants or naturalized citizens in Canada and who migrated to the United States later was about one fifth of the number of Canadian-born in the United States, yielding a total of about 1.2 million persons whose former country of residence was Can-

Table 3

Destination of Canadian-born Immigrants in the U.S.

States	Percentage of Canadian-born White Population by State of Residence	Percentage of Canadian-born Immigrants by Intended Destination	
	1950	1956–69	1970–75
Massachusetts	19.4	8.9	5.9
Michigan	14.3	7.1	6.6
New York	11.9	10.0	12.0
California	11.1	24.2	12.3
Maine	5.5	3.6	4.4
Washington	4.8	4.3	4.2
New Hampshire	3.5	1.7	1.8
Connecticut	3.1	2.8	3.0
Illinois	2.9	3.4	4.3
Rhode Island	2.5	0.5	—
Ohio	2.1	2.4	2.5
Florida	1.5	5.6	1.0
Total	83.2	74.5	58.0

Source: Dominion Bureau of Statistics, *The Canadian-Born in the United States*, Ottawa, p. 7; U.S. Dept. of Justice, Annual Report of Immigration and Naturalization Service, 1956–1976.

ada. By 1950, the number of French-Canadians in the U.S. had declined to a quarter of the total Canadian-born as compared to one third in 1930. Canadians of non-English, non-French origin have shown an increase since the 1950s.

Regarding their destinations in their new country, as seen in Table 3, in 1950 about half the Canadian-born population had settled in three states—Massachusetts, Michigan, and New York. The Sun Belt states, such as California and Florida, contained only one tenth of the white Canadian-born population in the United States in 1950. The vast majority of the French-Canadian immigrants were located in the northeastern and New England states.

Twelve American states each had over one percent of the Canadian-born white population in 1950 and a total of over 83 percent of the Canadian-born white population residing in the United States, according to the census. The same states, however, received only three quarters of the Canadian-born immigrants in the late fifties and through the sixties. And this dropped to 58 percent in the 1970–1975 period.

During the quarter century since 1950, almost half the Canadian-born immigrants went to the six states—Massachusetts, Michigan, New York, California, Maine, and Washington—where the highest percentages of Canadian-born people were found. However, between 1970 and 1975, states such as New Jersey, Pennsylvania, and Texas together received one out of every ten Canadian-born immigrants.

During the 1950s, immigration from Canada remained in the range of 22,000 to 46,000 annually. The proportion of Canadian-born among them, however, declined steadily from four fifths to two thirds. As seen in Table 4, over a quarter of those immigrants in the labor force were professional and technical workers. In absolute numbers about 30,000 of them immigrated to the United States during the period 1951–1960. The next most important group, occupationally, was clerical workers followed by craftsmen, foremen, and similar workers. These immigrants formed significant parts of several occupational groups in Canada. For example, during the years 1950 to 1960, a number

Table 4

Occupational Distribution of Canadian-born Immigrants to U.S.A., 1955-1977

	Canadian-born Immigrants During					
	1951–60		1961–70		1971–77	
Occupational Groupings	Number	Pct.	Number	Pct.	Number	Pct.
1. Professional, technical, and kindred workers	29,452	25.5	58,664	28.2	20,432	41.6
2. Managers, officials, etc.	6,611	5.7	10,495	5.0	5,674	11.5
3. Clerical and kindred workers	26,956	23.4	34,991	16.7	5,618	11.4
4. Sales workers	6,971	6.0	10,272	4.9	1,721	3.5
5. Craftsmen, foremen, and kindred workers	16,141	14.1	37,940	18.2	5,301	10.8
6. Operators and kindred workers	11,277	9.8	20,530	9.8	3,547	7.2
7. Service workers	7,509	6.5	19,098	9.1	4,577	9.3
8. Farm laborers and other laborers	8,447	7.3	16,146	7.7	2,258	4.6
9. Others	2,002	1.7	865	0.4	69	0.1
10. Total	115,366	100.0	209,001	100.0	49,197	100.0

Sources: U.S. Department of Justice, Annual Reports of Immigration and Naturalization Service, 1955–1978.

equivalent to 12 percent of all mining engineers counted in the 1951 Canadian census immigrated to America. For physicians and surgeons and metallurgical engineers this was 14 percent, for electrical engineers 15 percent, for architects 17 percent, for mechanical and aeronautical engineers 19 percent, and for graduate nurses a hefty 37 percent.[8]

During the sixties, in the years 1963, 1964, and 1965, Canadians crossing the 49th parallel reached its peak in this century—over 50,000 immigrating each year. The proportion of Canadian-born among them remained in the range of two thirds to three quarters of the total movement. During the sixties, as it was during the previous decade, Canada's "brain drain" to her southern neighbor became a live issue in popular periodicals and in the Canadian Parliament. The proportion of professional and technical workers from Canada comprised 28 percent of the Canadian immigrants whose occupations were known. However, in 1962 and 1963, half of the scientists and engineers who crossed the border into the United States as immigrants were not born in Canada. There was some decrease in the percentage of clerical and sales workers, but the opposite was true of service workers.

It appeared possible that the trend of immigration from Canada might have continued but for the 1965 changes in the American immigration regulations which affected immigration from Canada for the first time. Numerical limitations imposed by the provisions of the Immigration Act of 1965 (which came into force in July, 1968), curtailed the immigration of Canadian-born. In 1969, their level of immigration was less than half of the 1965 level.

The new regulations governing immigration established a system of priorities based on skills and on the needs of the American labor market. While some groups, such as professionals with advanced degrees as well as those in designated occupations, received virtually automatic certification, many occupations which immigrants wanted to enter needed labor certification. Canadian immigrants came within the Western hemisphere quota of 120,000. This quota, however, was effectively reduced by something like 40,000 for several years, since the Cuban refugees already living in the United States and seeking permanent status were to be subtracted from this quota.

Potential immigrants intending to enter unskilled occupations could not receive labor certification and were discouraged unless they successfully applied under one of the other preferences (such as brothers, sisters, etc.). There were no country limitations for the Western hemisphere. The rule that applied was first come first served.

According to the American census, in 1970 there were 0.81 million Canadian-born in the country; one out of every 12 was foreign-born. If those who used Canada as a stepping stone to the United States are included, there were no less than one million Canadians who lived in the United States in 1970. In the same year, the Americans of Canadian or mixed parentage numbered 2.2 million.

As far as the composition of Canadians in the United States was concerned, there were more women than men. For every hundred men, there were 140 women. This ratio was even more marked for the 65 and over age group. However, this was not a phenomenon restricted to that age group. In the prime 20 to 24 age group, there were three Canadian-born women in the United States for every two such men. The median age of Canadian-born in the United States in 1970 was 50.8, the women being older than the men by an average of two years. Two thirds of the Canadian-born were in the working age group 20 to 64.

Regarding their geographic distribution in 1970, the northeastern states had the largest number of Canadians followed by the western states, the New England states, and the Pacific states. In five of the New England states, Canadians were the largest single group among those of foreign stock.

During the period 1970–1975, the immigration from Canada contracted by sixty percent from 27,000 to 11,000 per year. This was also true of the Canadian-born whose proportion as seen in Table 2 reached its lowest point in 1970, at 51 percent. By 1977, however, immigration from Canada rose again to 29,844.

Occupationally, as seen in Table 4, during the 1971–1977 period, the professional and technical workers among the Canadian-born reached their highest level in the century—42 percent, compared to 26 percent in 1951–1960. The same was true of managers and officials as well, whose proportion doubled compared to the two preceding decades. Clerical workers, craftsmen, foremen, and sales workers declined significantly in numbers, though service workers did not show this decline.

During the 1970–1975 period, two states, New York and California, attracted a quarter of all Canadian-born immigrants. Immigrants from Canada usually settled in urban and industrial centers in the border states of Maine, Massachusetts, New Hampshire, New York, Vermont, Pennsylvania, Ohio, Michigan, Minnesota, Illinois, North Dakota, Montana, Idaho, and Connecticut as well as in the other states of New England. Often the French-Canadians formed significant minorities in some New England states, including Connecticut and Rhode Island. Evidence also indicates that Canadians are increasingly taking retirement in the Sun Belt states of Florida and California. These states also offer better economic prospects apart from warm climates. Between 1940 and 1970, the number of Canadian-born increased in Florida from 9,368 to 43,816 and in California from 95,741 to 153,725.[9]

The question has often been asked: "Why do people move?" Traditionally, the reasons for moving have been examined within the framework of the push and pull theory which says that populations are generally static and that it requires a positive push or pull to overcome inertia and encourage migration.

Often it is not easy to distinguish what precisely are the causes determining the push or the pull. It is even more difficult to measure the relative strength of push or pull factors in causing a person to move from one geographic location to another. These push and/or pull forces will have varying degrees of strength depending upon the time, the individual, his/her environment, and the evaluation of prospective changes.

Push factors differ from country to country. Restricting the discussion to developed countries, broadly speaking, "the causes of push lie in many cases in the general setting of a socio-economic environment which may be considered as hostile to the work of professionals in general and to research efforts in particular. . . . The lack of economic and technological strategies on the national, industrial and individual firm's level . . . does not yet allow specialized efforts in this direction, or . . . the social structure may be the strong impeding factor preventing economic and technological progress from taking place."[10]

According to a study that compared the push factors for migration from Canada and Britain, Canadians generally expressed less dissatisfaction with conditions at home and little dissatisfaction for their government compared to those from Britain.[11] Only less than a quarter of Canadians cited "dissatisfaction with home conditions."

Pull factors, on the other hand, are identified with favorable conditions of employment and higher levels of income in the country of immigration. A sudden growth of hugh research projects, such as special programs financed by the government, creates an increased demand for particular skills, such as those of engineers and scientists. Similarly advancing technology also may result in greater need for specific skills, the price for which would rise, thus exercising a pull on potential immigrants. The rising income differentials, better promotional opportunities, better research facilities, better working environment, and warmer climates would act as pull forces.

Brinley Thomas once stated, adapting Samuel Johnson: "The noblest prospect which a Canadian ever sees is the high road that leads him to the United States."[12] A study that anaylzed the immigration of Canadians to south of the border since 1947 found that "the relative availability of employment in Canada and the United States, and the income differential of the two, account for most of the outflow from Canada to the United States."[13]

The magnetic pull of the United States for Canadians is attributed to economic factors, the perception of opportunities in the United States, a better climate, cultural similarity with Canada, nearness of friends and relatives, and the desire by some for travel and adventure.

Differentials in economic opportunity in various countries

have been a major determinant in the rate and direction of migration. The term economic opportunity, however, docs not lend itself to a precise definition. Broadly speaking, it is considered to be associated with the degree of optimism of the prospective migrant, often governed by current and comparative levels of economic growth. To the prospective immigrant, it means largely the ease with which employment can be found and the level of income which can be expected.

A survey of Canadian immigrants in the United States in the seventies asked the reasons why they had decided to migrate. The immigrants were free to give more than one reason. Over half of them mentioned opportunities for a "better job" and another half wanted to improve "future prospects." Over one third mentioned "better living conditions," and two out of five cited American family ties or friends.[14]

An available measure of the relative levels of economic opportunity in the two countries can be found in the concept of per capita national product. In 1965, Canada's per capital gross national product was only 76 percent of the United States gross national product. Such disparities have often meant greater economic opportunity in the latter and therefore have acted as a pull force.

Similarly during the postwar period, American real wages on a per capita basis have been above Canadian wages. Such differences have been more conspicuous in professional occupations. Evidence indicates that the incomes of professionals rose faster in the United States than in Canada (e.g., the differential in starting salaries paid to newly graduated engineers in the United States compared to the salaries in Canada were 14.6 percent higher in 1953, 17.2 percent in 1956, 22.5 percent in 1958, and 31.3 percent in 1960).[15]

Undoubtedly higher salaries were a necessary incentive for many Canadians to move south, but not necessarily a sufficient one. As John Kenneth Galbraith, a prominent former Canadian, said: "one insults the business executive and scientist by suggesting that his principal motivation is the pay he receives."[16]

Apart from average earnings being higher in the United

States, its wealth, stage of industrial development, and larger population offer greater opportunities, as well as better jobs at the top levels of employment. This was particularly true of scientific and technical occupations, especially during the period when the United States outer space research program was being actively pursued.

A Canadian committee that examined the problem of "brain drain" from Canada to the United States said that "establishment of new and well-endowed centers of excellence both in universities and in industry . . . able to offer a highly intellectual atmosphere" in America has been one of the main causes of immigration of scientists and technologists.[17] This conclusion is supported by the views of the following individuals.

A young Ph.D. immigrant from Canada said: "I had to come if I wanted to grow as a scientist. The leading people in my field are here, and the kind of vigorous, exciting research no Canadian firm can offer is going on in the labs of the U.S.A. I naively thought I could come back when the scientific scene at home had improved, but I doubt now that it will—certainly not until I am an old, old man."[18]

Another Ph.D. said: "I didn't come here because I was bitterly unhappy with opportunities at home, but because I was stimulated by an offer to assist the most eminent man in my field on an important project financed by a huge foundation. . . . It was the freedom, the almost unlimited funds available for research, and the feeling that I can get something really important done."[19]

Hare Gobind Khorana, an immigrant to Canada from India, who won a Nobel Prize in organic chemistry in 1968, took four top Ph.D.'s with him when he migrated south. Dr. Khorana emphasizes that he did not make the move for extra money. If anything, he said, he ended up a little worse off as a result of the change. He commented:

There are many advantages in working in the U.S. The climate of research is undoubtedly more congenial in the better U.S. institutions, and I think there is no denying that the facilities are superior. . . . If you put ten scientists in ten separate laboratories in different universities or companies, you may get no results at all, but when you put ten good men in one laboratory, then things begin to hum.[20]

According to a study, much the same view has been expressed by Canadian medical scientists in the United States. The study says: "The multitude of interrelated factors which attract basic medical scientists to the United States can be summed up in the word 'opportunity.' Opportunity for rapid career advancement, opportunity to take on added responsibility, to test one's ideas with enlightened and stimulating colleagues, to reach for a goal, and in some cases simply to work."[21]

The comparative availability of research funds in the two countries adds weight to this argument. In 1963, the total Medical Research Council grant for facilities in 12 Canadian universities was $4.8 million compared to the National Institute of Health grant of $900 million to 78 American universities. On a population basis, Canada's grant should have been about $100 million.

A former Canadian, a Harvard law graduate, and special legal advisor to a White House trade representative claimed: ". . . it's difficult to imagine too many areas where the challenges would be as great as they are here, and by extension, people who love complexity and problems are going to head for the places where they can deal with these problems. A gross national product at something like a trillion dollars a year, a population of 200 million people and an American corporate team that controls millions and millions of dollars of foreign investment, all obviously give range to international, commercial and legal problems that just don't exist in Canada. . . . I'll put it this way. It took me between 30 and 60 seconds to accept the offer to teach at Harvard. And it took me between 30 and 60 seconds to accept this job at the White House. These were not hard decisions."[22]

Observed John F. Kennedy, in his book, A Nation of Immigrants: "Canadians do not leave Canada for trivial reasons. They do not leave for political, religious, or individual liberty. All of these they have in Canada in as great measure as they can possibly have them in any other country in the world. *Industrial opportunity* is the American lodestone that has attracted to the United States millions of emigrants. . . . When Canada can offer to the world industrial opportunities the equal of those to be found in the United States, there will not be blizzards enough, nor zero temperatures enough, from Halifax to Vancouver, to drive Canadians over the line, or induce them to renounce the country of their birth, in favor of a citizenship which, however good it may be, is in no way superior, in 'Life, Liberty and the Pursuit of Happiness,' to the citizenship to which they were born."[23]

Another factor which induces Canadians to move south is the desire on the part of many to get away from the rigorous climate. Commented a Canadian surgeon in California: "I came to California because there were more opportunities in my surgical speciality and better facilities to work with. Then the warmer climate made the idea that much more attractive."[24]

Migration to pleasant climates is an attractive proposition to many. And there is, at times, a "trade off" between good climate and more money. To what extent one is prepared to sacrifice one for the other depends on the individual. With the recent increase of recreation-based, rather than resource-based, employment opportunities, however, the sacrifice of money is becoming less important. It is also likely that people who have achieved their goals of saving and investment may decide to retire to "sun and sand." This type of movement from Canada to the United States is likely to be more or less a one-way traffic and will likely increase in the future. An early indication of this is seen from the number of Canadian-born residents in the Pacific area of the United States in the 1970 census which stood at 20 percent higher than the number recorded for the same area in the 1950 census.

The geographic proximity of the two countries and the similarities in cultural, educational, and standard of living aspects facilitates migration between the two countries. Since most of Canada's population are within one hundred miles of the American border, many Canadians travel south and become familiar with the opportunities available. Many Canadian nurses, an important occupational group among immigrants, migrate for "adventure and new experiences."[25]

Canadian immigrants to the United States do not face any problems of culture shock often faced by those who come from cultures so different from that of North America. Many of these immigrants were molded by the mass media dominated by, and school textbooks published in, the United States. Their initial impressions in the United States, therefore, do not contain any major elements of surprise. They know more or less what to expect. They are aware that the pace of life is a bit faster south of the border and that meritocracy rules along with democracy. "I love the dynamism of this country," said a Boston realtor from Montreal. "There is just more of meritocracy here, willingness to recognize talent, and guts."[26] The integration of Canadians occurs faster and better than it does for other immigrants in the United States. Observed a Canadian immigrant, "Almost as soon as Canadians get down here they vanish without a trace. You have to be involved in a pretty unusual conversation to hear from any American that his father came out of the North."[27]

Canadians in the United States were not too amused when they realized that while they were familiar with the names of most of the American states, "Americans would look vague at the mention of Saskatchewan or Nova Scotia. Canadians are as familiar with *Time* or *Reader's Digest* as Americans, but few Americans had ever heard of *Maclean's*—Canada's national magazine—except as a toothpaste!"[28] According to Kenneth Lines, "Coming to the United States, the young Canadian often felt like the private school student who suddenly found himself surrounded by the equalitarian banalities of a large state university."[29]

Though immigrants in the United States initially earn less than the native-born, after ten to fifteen years they attain earning levels that surpass the native-born.[30] Canadian-born immigrants earned more than most other immigrants. According to the 1970 United States census, those of Canadian origin had a medium family income of $10,794, slightly more than the average for people of all foreign stock. Canadian professional, technical, and related workers in the United States in 1969 had a per capita income next only to that of Swedish immigrants. A Canadian professional earned more than a British, German, or Japanese immigrant.[31] "Canadians were recognized as better educated than any foreign nationals as a group and superior to home products in many specialized fields of training such as nursing, medicine and engineering."[32]

Historically, Canadians in the United States have shown a greater degree of reluctance to give up their allegiance to Canada in order to acquire American citizenship. It has been observed that the Canadian-born in the United States naturalize "not to the same extent as British, Germans and Scandinavians."[33] In 1950, 71.3 percent of Canadian-born in the United States were citizens. This declined to 63.4 percent in 1970.

In order to obtain the relationship between the number of Canadian-born immigrants and the number becoming naturalized in the United States, one has to compare these figures after allowing for a time lag of five years, since a five-year period of residence is necessary before naturalization. During the years 1955 to 1959, the number of Canadian-born who became naturalized in the United States corresponded to 50 percent of the number who entered in the period 1950–1954. These percentages, after allowing for a time lag of five years, were 32 percent for the Canadian-born who came in 1955–1959, 20 percent for those who immigrated in 1960–1964, and 17 percent for those who came in the years 1965–1969.[34] These figures indicate that there is an increasing degree of reluctance on the part of Canadian-born immigrants in the United States to give up their Canadian citizenship.

Nevertheless, apart from contributing to the growth of American population, Canadian immigrants have acquitted themselves creditably in various walks of life which they entered upon in the United States. Mention should be made of areas such as business, academic life, scientific life, and the entertainment world. It is well known that industrialist Cyrus Eaton as well as economist Professor John Kenneth Galbraith were born in Canada. In the scientific world in 1961, of the 151 foreign-born members of the National Academy of Sciences, 17 were born or trained in Canada.[35] From Canada have come two of the Nobel Prize winners in chemistry: Dr. Hare Gobind Khorana in 1968 and Dr. William Gianque in 1949. The list of scientists includes Dr. Frances Kelsey of the U.S. Food and Drug Administration, who kept thalidomide[36] out of circulation in the United States.

Apart from the Canadian-born, there were many scientists who were immigrants in Canada before moving south. For example in 1962–1963, 50 percent of the scientists and engineers who migrated to the United States from Canada were foreign-born (1157 out of 2316).[37] During the 1957–1961 period Canadian scientists and engineers migrating to the United States was equivalent to 29.8 percent of those who received their first degrees in science and engineering in Canada.[38] In 1962 and 1963, Canada supplied about one quarter of the scientists and engineers the United States received from abroad.[39]

There were many Canadians who entered the American entertainment world and achieved remarkable success. A number of Hollywood writers, directors, dancers, and actors came from Canada. Among them are Walter Pigeon, Mary Pickford, Glenn Ford, Rich Little, Norma Shearer, Raymond Burr, Ron Clark, Allan Blye, and Saul Ilson. The list is extensive and proves that many Canadians are on their way to stardom in their neighboring country.

The migration of professionals between Canada and the United States has always been a two-way affair. If attention is focused on a number of numerically significant professional groups, during the period 1962–1970, the exchange of these professionals resulted in a net loss to Canada in many occupations (see Table 5).

Table 5

Migration of Selected Groups of Professionals between the United States and Canada, 1962-1970

	From U.S. to Canada	From Canada to U.S.	Excess to U.S.
Physicians, surgeons	2,479	3,199	720
Professional nurses	1,816	11,243	9,427
Dentists	129	117	—12
Architects	163	457	294
Professional engineers	2,579	8,543	5,964
Teachers	12,542	6,866	—5,576

Source: St. John Jones, *The Exchange of Population Between the United States of America and Canada in the 1960's*, (Ottawa: n.p., n.d.) p. 18.

As the above table demonstrates, Canada had a net loss in most occupations except teaching and dentistry. However, this loss was only with reference to the United States. During the same period, Canada was receiving immigrants from other parts of the world and Canada's loss due to migration to the United States was only 37 percent of the physicians and surgeons received, 45 percent of the professional nurses, 41 percent of the professional engineers, and 15 percent of the teachers.[40]

Canadians have always been concerned about the "brain drain" aspect of the movement from Canada to the United States. It is not difficult, though, to agree with the view of Professor Harry Johnson (another prominent Canadian economist who lived in the United States) that overall, "Canada has enjoyed a 'brain tap' on the rest of the world; it has not suffered from a 'brain drain.' If one wants to think in terms of 'brain drain,' Canada has provided the drains rather than the brains for the rest of the world."[41]

Not all Canadian immigrants who move south with the intention of settling in the country adjacent to their own stick to their decisions. Many decide to return to Canada for a variety of reasons. Some realize that distant pastures only looked greener; for many, the spirit of adventure and the urge for new experiences wear out after a while; some miss their friends and relatives back in Canada; and a few do not feel they can achieve the goals they had set for themselves. There are many professionals and scientists who feel that the working conditions in their field of endeavor have changed for the better in Canada and decide to return to take advantage of them. The social and political conditions (explosive race situation, high crime rate in certain cities, the Vietnam War, etc.) may have prompted many Canadians to return. A few might have taken the decision to migrate rather lightly, unlike many immigrants from far off lands who make total and unrecoverable commitments to America since they have placed vast distance and centuries of traditions behind them.

Return migration to the countries from which people came is an experience for some migrants from all countries, though the rates may vary from country to country and from time to time. If the migration stream has been significant, the counterstream will also be significant. Moreover, if the migration is caused more by push forces than by pull forces, the rate of return migration is likely to be lower (e.g., few of the Irish who fled the famine in the nineteenth century returned to Ireland).

The extent of return migration of Canadians had been underestimated for some time. Recent studies have attempted to correct this.[42] During the period January 1, 1955, to April 1, 1960, a total of 150,662 Canadian-born, who were in Canada in 1955, migrated to the United States. On the United States census day of April 1, 1960, however, only 94,527 of them were counted. After allowing for a certain number of deaths, the number of Canadian-born should have been 146,727. This yields the figure 52,200 as the number of Canadian-born in United States returning to Canada or remigrating to another country during the period shown. The rate of return migration works out to be 34.6 percent of the Canadian-born immigrants who came to the United States during the period.

The rate of return migration was found to be higher for the professionals, and almost half of the professionals who came to the United States during the above period were not counted in the 1960 census. It is unlikely that deaths, retirements, and remigrations claimed a large number of them.

Canadian immigrants to the United Statees have been a significant segment of the total number of international migrants America has received in the past. Apart from the numbers, the quality of such migrants who came from Canada (whether born in Canada or outside) has been quite high as judged from their qualifications and the contributions they have made to the United States economy and society.

NOTES

1. Marcus Lee Hansen, *The Mingling of the Canadian and American Peoples* (New Haven: Yale University Press, 1940).

2. Ibid., p. 9.

3. Ibid., p. 5.

4. Ibid., p. 254.

5. Paul W. Gates, "Official Encouragement to Immigration by the Provinces of Canada," *Canadian Historical Review* (March, 1934), p. 27.

6. Donald J. Bogue, *The Population of the United States* (Glencoe, Ill.: Free Press, 1959), p. 349.

7. "Southward Treck," *Time*, April 1, 1946, p. 38.

8. Canada Department of Labour, *The Migration of Professional Workers into and out of Canada, 1946–1960* (Ottawa, 1961), p. 30.

9. Kenneth Lines, *British and Canadian Immigration to the United States since 1920* (San Francisco: R. & E. Research Associates, 1978), p. 63.

10. K. Weiermair, "Economic Implications of the International Migration of High Level Manpower" (n.p., n.d.) p. 5.

11. Lines, p. 92.

12. Psacharopoulos, "On Some Positive Aspects of the Economics of the Brain Drain," *Minerva* 9 (April, 1971): 239.

13. Harold George Allan Hanes, "A Study of Canadian Emigration to the United States, 1947–1967" (M.A. thesis, Kingston University, 1968), p. 56.

14. Lines, p. 92.

15. Canada Department of Labour, p. 25.

16. John Kenneth Galbraith, *The Affluent Society* (Boston: Houghton Mifflin, 1958), p. 175.

17. Committee on Manpower Resources for Science and Technology, Ottawa, p. 70.

18. *Macleans,* July 20, 1963.

19. Lines, p. 84.

20. Lenora Leonard Bertin, "How we can stop our brain drain," *Canadian Weekly,* May 9, 1964.

21. C. de Hesse, and D. G. Fish, "Canadian-Trained Medical Scientists View Canadian Academia from their American Laboratories," *Canadian Medical Association Journal,* November 5, 1966, p. 2.

22. Lines, p. 38.

23. John F. Kennedy, *A Nation of Immigrants* (New York: Harper and Row, 1964), p. 279.

24. Lines, p. 94.

25. *Macleans,* July 20, 1963.

26. *Macleans,* "Expatriates Without Tears," November 1922, p. 40.

27. Lines, p. 84.

28. Ibid.

29. Ibid.

30. Barry R. Chiswick, "The Effect of Americanization on the Earnings of Foreign-born Men," *Journal of Political Economy* 86, no. 5 (1978): 520.

31. Psacharopoulos, p. 239.

32. Lines, p. 84.

33. Dominion Bureau of Statistics, *The Canadian-Born in the United States* (Ottawa, 1956), p. 18.

34. U.S. Department of Justice, *Annual Reports of Immigration and Naturalization Service, 1950–1975.*

35. National Science Foundation, *Scientific Manpower from Abroad* (Washington), p. 16.

36. A tranquilizer believed to be responsible for the birth of thousands of deformed babies in Europe.

37. Herbert G. Grubel and Anthony Scott, *The Brain Drain: Determinants, Measurement and Welfare Effects* (Waterloo, Ontario: Wilfrid Laurier University Press, 1977), p. 77.

38. Herbert G. Grubel and Anthony Scott, "The Immigration of Scientists and Engineers to the United States, 1949–61," *Journal of Political Economy* 74, no. 4 (August, 1966): 372.

39. National Science Foundation, *Reviews of Data on Science Resources* (Washington, July, 1965), p. 6.

40. St. John Jones, "The Exchange of Population Between the United States of America and Canada in the 1960s," (n.p., n.d.), p. 18.

41. Harry G. Johnson, "The Economics of the 'Brain Drain': The Canadian Case," *Minerva* no. 3, (Spring, 1965).

42. T. J. Samuel, *The Migration of Canadian-Born Between Canada and the United States, 1955–1968* (Ottawa: Queen's Printer, 1969), p. 5.

VIII

Contemporary Black Immigration to the United States

By O. C. Wortham
Atlanta Magazine

Definition of the Black Immigrant

One of the major obstacles in conducting research on ethnic or racial relations in the United States is the extremely irrational manner in which various terms are created and adopted to describe individuals and groups from a wide variety of gene pools and cultures.

In 1908 the United States Immigration Service began using the term "Africans, black" to cover all persons of supposed Negro extraction. In doing so, this country was one of the few nations in the world that analyzed its international migration on the basis of race.[1] The problem with this type of classification was that few of the Negro immigrants who came to the United States from 1908 to 1932 (when the United States began to report by nationality instead of race) were either Africans or black.

According to statistics available from 1916 to 1932 from the Bureau of Immigration of the Department of Labor, of the 74,891 "African, black" aliens admitted to the United States by "Area of Last Residence," only 1,609 (or 2.14 percent) were *not* from the West Indies, Central America, South America, British North America, or Portugal.[2] Therefore, even if all of the remaining 1,609 were from Africa this would be less than three percent of the total so classified.

200

The term "black," as used in this country, did not mean the same thing to the immigrants who were assigned the term. Prior to coming here, they may have been colored, Negro, mulatto, or black. Mixed people in the West Indies are considered "colored." "Negro" to a Latin means a full-blooded black! As Gunnar Myrdal pointed out in his famous work on race in America, people having a known trace of black ancestry, no matter how far removed, are defined as black.[3] This does not always hold true, however, for we all are aware that many countless thousands of Americans of part-African ancestry are *not* classified as "blacks" or "Negroes" (such as some Puerto Ricans, Mexican-Americans, American Indians, Cubans, or Louisiana Creoles).

From 1900 to 1920 the United States Census separately identified "blacks" and "mulattoes." After 1920, one either was or was not black, and black ancestry was considered dominant; and persons of Indian-Negro or white-Negro or other mixed ancestry were simply defined as blacks.

Special Research Problems

Since 1932, because of government budgetary limitations, specialized statistics by race have not been available. The immigration statistics that now are reported by the Immigration and Naturalization Office are reported by nationalities and country of birth, rather than race. Therefore, although it is known that a large number of individuals immigrating from the British West Indies are of African descent, they will be reported in the official statistics and annual reports as "West Indians." True statistical data on the Negro or black immigrant is almost non-existent. This is true for at least two reasons: (1) prior to 1932 the term "African, black" was so inclusive that it included many thousands who had never been considered "black" before, until they were so identified by our Immigration officials; (2) after 1932, as noted above, no statistics were kept by race by the United States government. If they were kept, they are not reported to the public through the reports of the Immigration and Naturalization Department.[4] Because of this lack of primary data, it is difficult, if not impossible, to find reliable information on the social characteristics of the foreign-born black population regarding such areas as intermarriage and institutional forms. Very little also has been written about the cultural characteristics of the black immigrant.[5]

Background to Migratory Movements

The United States, like many countries during the nineteenth century and the first half of the twentieth century, had a very strict policy with regard to immigration quotas for those of other than European descent. The logic used to legitimatize these racist restrictive policies was that non-Europeans were so different in life style, culture, mores, and even ethical systems that they would be a source of continued interracial problems, and "biologically unassimilable" in the United States "Melting Pot."[6]

An example of this type of thinking was given by Maurice R. Davie in his 1936 book on immigration, *World Immigration.* "Experience shows that the yellow, brown, and black races are unassimilable, at any rate by us, and the United States would only be inviting trouble and adding to her already large and serious race problems by admitting members of such races. This exclusion is indispensable to the welfare of the United States."[7]

At that time, just prior to World War II, it was estimated that "... the present foreign-born Negro population numbers approximately 100,000 persons, and is larger than the number of foreign-born Japanese, or Chinese,... than all other groups of foreign-born colored peoples in the United States combined."[8]

Prior to a revision of the United States immigration policies in 1965, when President Lyndon B. Johnson signed into law Public Law 89–236, the United States policy was governed by the National Origins Quota Acts of 1920 and 1924. Under these laws, from 1920 to 1967 (the first full year in which the act of October 3, 1965, went into effect), it was stated that the "Annual quota of any quota area shall be 1/6th of 1% of the number of inhabitants in the United States attributable to national origin."[9] In practice, this means that only 122 Africans were allowed into the United States in 1924![10]

The Western hemisphere was not considered a "quota area" under this law. This explains the relatively large number of West Indians and Latin Americans who have immigrated to the United States during the first half of this century. Changes were made in this policy, however, by the McCarran-Walter Immigration Act of 1952, which put a ceiling on immigrants from the Western hemisphere of 120,000, and a maximum from any one country of 20,000 per year. In theory, this was supposed to limit the number of immigrants coming from nonquota areas. One serious flaw in this plan was that there were individuals who were allowed to move to the United States for temporary employment with the United States Department of Agriculture, refugees, and United States citizens from Puerto Rico, the Canal Zone, and the Virgin Islands. These were considered "Insular Dependencies" of the United States. In 1967, however, an amendment was added to the 1965 law which limited immigrants from the Canal Zone to 20,000 per year.[11]

Other countries in the Western hemisphere also had immigration policies to limit the number of people of color. In 1918, Venezuela excluded Negro immigrants entirely. El Salvador in 1923 barred Negroes officially in their constitution. Honduras adopted a similar policy at the same time. Both of these latter countries justified their actions by saying that foreign Negroes competed with their own natives for employment in the banana industry.[12] In 1928, Panama established a quota of "five persons yearly of Chinese, Syrian, Turks and Negroes."[13] Guatemala after 1944 decided to "forbid Negroes and Gypsies and persons of the Mongolian Race."[14] And Brazil in the same year stated that "It preferred that only white persons should be admitted as immigrants."[15] Also, contrary to some mistaken beliefs, Canada did not exactly offer open arms to its fellow citizens of the British Empire from the West Indies. Although there is no official policy, it is well known that Canada does not encourage any immigration from these islands.[16]

As stated earlier in this essay, prior to 1967 immigration from Africa was limited by the National Origins Act. Those "Africans" who did come came mainly from Egypt (or the United Arab Republic). Most of these were not black Africans but Arabs. Some immigrants also came from Morocco and South Africa. Between 1916 and 1932 there were less than 1,609 Negro immigrants from Africa to the United States.[17] During this period, 74,891 Negroes immigrated legally from the West Indies, 5,403 from Central America, 2,276 from South America, 3,892 from British North America, and 5,082 from Portugal, mainly the Azores and Cape Verde.[18] Thus, 75 percent of the Negro immigrants during this period came from the West Indies.

Reasons for Leaving Homelands

Since the turn of the century, millions of citizens from the developing nations have looked outside their country for increased opportunities for employment and personal freedom. With depressed economies due to European and American exploitation and domination, most of the citizens in countries in the Western hemisphere looked to the United States as a refuge because of our policy prior to 1952 of not restricting immigrants from nonquota countries. Other countries in the hemisphere either had laws limiting Negro immigrants or had informal policies to forbid them in various ways. The majority of the population in the Caribbean is considered "colored." The following are racial ("colored") percentages of people on the major islands prior to World War II:[19]

Bahamas	77% of	62,679 =	48,262
Barbados	90% of	180,055 =	162,049
Bermuda	59% of	29,896 =	17,638
Cuba	33% of	4,011,088 =	1,323,659
Grenada	79% of	78,662 =	62,111
Guadeloupe	80% of	267,407 =	213,925
Haiti	99% of	2,650,000 =	2,623,500
Jamaica	95% of	1,090,269 =	1,035,755
Leeward Islands	80% of	132,973 =	106,378

Martinique	80% of	234,695 =	187,756
Puerto Rico	30% of	1,623,814 =	487,144
St. Lucia	79% of	62,000 =	48,980
St. Vincent	92.9% of	47,961 =	44,555
Santo Domingo	97% of	1,478,121 =	1,433,777
Trinidad	62% of	425,572 =	263,854
Virgin Islands	95% of	22,012 =	20,911
TOTAL	65% of	12,349,243 =	8,027,007

As these figures show, it is clear that there were a large number of people of color in the Caribbean who, along with their fellow noncolored citizens, might be seeking admittance into the United States, legally or illegally.

From this writer's investigations, it appears that the largest number of illegal black immigrants since 1945 have come from Haiti. It is estimated that over 100,000 Haitians have fled to the United States during the past forty years.[20] These figures cannot be verified; it is an area requiring further research.

Blacks have immigrated in large numbers from the West Indies to countries other than the United States. We are well aware of the influx into England during the last twenty years and the attempts of the British to limit such immigration. Canada has also seen a sharp increase of British subjects from the West Indies, India, and other former British colonies. It is ironic that the United States is presently experiencing its greatest addition of "foreign-born blacks" from one of its present "colonies," Puerto Rico. Although black Puerto Ricans do not consider themselves "black" or "Negro," and they are not considered by immigration officials as "Immigrants," blacks from Puerto Rico presently constitute the largest influx of blacks onto the United States mainland. Therefore, when the experiences of foreign-born blacks are discussed in the body of this essay, it must be remembered that many of their experiences are identical to those of black Puerto Ricans.

It is important to note also that although dark, Mexicans and Mexican-Americans do not consider themselves black or Negro. Prior to 1932, however, when racial data was kept by the Immigration authorities, a small percentage of Mexican immigrants were identified as "African, black." As an example, in 1920, 3,123 Mexicans were labeled "African, black." In 1930, 915 of the 641,000 Mexicans admitted that year were also identified as "African, black."[21]

Reasons for Migrating to the United States

The reasons for black immigrants to come to the United States are similar to the reasons of most immigrants who come to this country. Relatively, there is greater economic opportunity and there is greater social freedom. Education of the young is also a primary factor. Another motivation is the "Open Door Policy" the United States has had for countries in the Western hemisphere prior to 1952.

President Kennedy led a tough battle against Congress to abolish the National Quotas Act. He did not succeed, but his administration laid the groundwork for President Johnson's success in 1965.

Under the 1965 Immigration Act, there are three major groups of immigrants. The first are "Special Immigrants," who are principally natives of the Western hemisphere countries and their immediate relatives. The "immediate relatives" constitute the second group, and this includes spouses, children, and parents of United States citizens. The third group consists of relatives of United States citizens with specific skills or those desired in needed occupations.[22]

In keeping with the spirit of the worldwide quotas set by the McCarran-Walter Immigration Act of 1952, there is a ceiling of 170,000 from the Eastern hemisphere, and 120,000 from the Western hemisphere. The 20,000 per country limit was retained.

At times, however, special consideration has been given to some countries. Mexico had 45,163 legal immigrants in 1966, and Canada had 28,358.[23] Cuba, because of its revolution in 1967–1968, had 33,321 immigrants in 1967, and 99,312 in 1968. Cuba also was allowed to surpass its quota in 1971 with 21,611; in 1972 with 20,045; in 1973 with 24,147; in 1975 with 25,955; and in 1976 with 29,233. From Mexico, 70,141 immigrated in 1973, and 71,586 in 1974.[24]

The vast majority of the Cuban immigrants were not black. The bulk of those who left Cuba because of political reasons were from the professional and upper classes. Although Cuba is approximately 33 percent "colored," its class structure is similar to most developing nations; therefore, the vast majority of the professionals, government workers, and business class consisted of Caucasians and those of Spanish ancestry.[25] This would be true also of the 168,648 individuals listed under the Cuban quota as "refugees" from 1946 to 1972. Only 392 people from all the other West Indian islands were listed as "refugees" during this same period.[26]

Another interesting category of immigrants are aliens who are admitted to the United States for temporary periods and classified as "nonimmigrants." This category covers students and workers.

In 1967, 3,668,836 individuals filed alien address reports with the Immigration and Naturalization Office. Of these, 3,210,788 were listed as permanent aliens, and 458,068 were listed as students and workers. In this last subgroup, 63,370 were students, and 394,698 workers.[27] Black students and workers, although not officially "immigrants" to the United States, are also subject to a reception similar to the black immigrant who has established legal residence in this country. Often, the public makes no differentiation between immigrants and non-immigrants. All are considered "foreigners." As with the black Puerto Rican or Mexican, because of racism and conflicts with the native black population, the experiences of nonimmigrant black workers and students are of special interest.

A significant number of the workers admitted to the United States from 1943 to 1972 came from the British West Indies. These were in addition to the hundreds of thousands who immigrated, legally and illegally, during this period. The Mc-Carran-Walter Immigration Act of 1952, which put a ceiling of 20,000 per nation in the Western hemisphere, did affect the flow of immigrants from all of the Caribbean, except Cuba. It drastically reduced the number of immigrants from Jamaica and some other predominantly black islands. Not affected, however, were the number of West Indians who were admitted for "temporary employment" with the United States Department of Agriculture. Assuming that this group of agricultural workers was at least racially representative of the islands from which they came, it can be estimated that over 75 percent of these workers were black. To give the reader an overview of this migration during a period of great historical significance, the official United States figures of British West Indian workers admitted to the United States for agricultural work from 1943 to 1972 are reproduced below.[28]

Assuming that *at least* 75 percent of these 225,908 agricultural workers were black, this would be 169,431 individuals. In all probability, since agricultural workers are drawn from the poorest classes and since the poorest classes in the British West Indies were almost entirely of African descent, the percentage of workers in this group who were black is probably closer to 100 percent.

Year	Workers	Year	Workers	Year	Workers
1943	13,526	1953	7,741	1963	11,930
1944	19,622	1954	4,704	1964	14,361
1945	19,391	1955	6,616	1965	10,917
1946	13,771	1956	7,563	1966	11,194
1947	3,722	1957	8,171	1967	13,578
1948	3,671	1958	7,441	1968	10,723
1949	2,765	1959	8,772	1969	13,530
1950	6,225	1960	9,820	1970	15,470
1951	9,040	1961	10,315	1971	12,143
1952	7,910	1962	12,928	1972	11,419
				TOTAL	308,979

Problems of Social Adjustment

The black immigrant experience in the United States is one of unique adjustment, because being black in America itself requires an abnormal amount of mental and spiritual strength. The United States is still one of the few countries on earth that has a rigid caste system based upon race. Because of this fact, it is also one of the few nations in the world where social distance is primarily determined by a person's perceived race or ethnicity.[29]

For those who cannot accept the above statement, let us review the definitions for the terms "caste" and "class." A caste is a social rank that may be lost but not gained.[30] Blacks in the United States are discouraged from intermarriage. The lowest class of white is still considered superior to a black of the highest class. An upper-class black is always lower in status than a lower-class white (at least by the lower-class white).[31] Caste is not determined by cultural features but by biological ones—color, hair, form, etc.[32]

Classes, on the other hand, are a loose form of social grouping which share some implied common interests.[33] There is an automatic exclusion from certain activities in America purely because of a person's "race."

Another unique problem of black immigrants to the United States is the adjustment that must be made in leaving communities where they were a part of a numerical *majority* to become a part of the numerical and social *minority*. From the moment persons of color set foot in America and are labeled "Negro" or "black," they realize that they are in a lower status group and they are expected to act accordingly. There is also the rapid recognition that their new lower status is not due to their nationality, but that they are now members of a rigidly defined color-caste system, in other words at the bottom rung of a racist society.

In addition to the racism that is prevalent throughout the new culture, there are other special problems when one comes from a less complex rural background to a major modern city.

The black from the West Indies usually represents a serious threat to the native-American black. This threat to the existing order of black adjustment to the social order is the basis for significant *intraracial conflict* between foreign-born and native-born blacks.

Unknown to many whites, the native-born black generally gives rise to the creation and formulation of stereotypes, myths, and ideologies to maintain some kind of superiority over the immigrant of color. Also, native-born blacks tend to lump all black immigrants together into one category. This helps to make the black immigrant problem more than just racial. With the intraracial conflict, the problem of the black immigrant becomes one of a difficult process of social absorption and assimilation into the common culture.

Cultural Differences of Immigrants

Some detail must be given at this point to make clear the differences among black immigrants, and the significant differences in social background between the native-born and foreign-born blacks.

For consistency, the term "people-of-color" should be used instead of "black." "Black" is a political term that has been forced upon our vocabulary by politically conscious persons of African descent during the mid-sixties. It is not a universal term, and it does not have a common meaning in the countries from which the immigrants came, or even in the United States. Africans do not call themselves "blacks." West Indians do not call themselves "blacks." Latin Americans and South Americans of partially African descent do not call themselves "blacks." None of the above call themselves "Negro" either. It appears that another of Gunnar Myrdal's insights still holds true. Speaking of the striking asymmetry of racial definitions in America, he noted that it was the whites who set the standards defining who was "Negro" and who was not. Regardless of the announcements of some civil rights leaders, it appears as if the whites are still setting the standards defining for us today who, or what, is a "black."

The above discourse is relevant because in the Caribbean (the primary source of our "black" immigrants), European customs have combined with racial mixtures to produce a more flexible physical and social type than is found in the United States.[34]

Races voluntarily keep apart in most of the West Indies. In this way, there is no overall race problem as there is in the United States. As mentioned previously, mixed people in the Caribbean are considered "colored." They form a separate social caste, superior to the unmixed black, but lower than the white population.[35] One problem caused by the existence of this middle caste is that it tends to fracture race solidarity among those who are of African ancestry.[36]

Among the French-speaking immigrants from Haiti, Guadeloupe, Martinique, and French West Africa, culture is more important than race, and the French language and culture are the most impressive in the world.[37] They prefer to be with those who speak French and respect French culture. Also, most of the French-speaking immigrants are likely to be Roman Catholic.

From Portugal, a sizable number of immigrants of color have migrated to the United States. Most are from the Azores and Cape Verde. Immigrants from the Azores consider themselves white and superior to the Cape Verde immigrants, whom they consider Negroes. When they move to the United States, mainly to New Bedford, Massachusetts, and the shipbuilding industry, there is no social mingling between the two groups. The Cape Verde immigrants, who were mainly considered "African, black" before 1932, have little social contact with the native-born blacks in the area. The native-born blacks consider themselves superior to all Portuguese.[38]

The intense rivalry that exists between inhabitants of the various islands of the Caribbean is not well known to most Americans, white or black. The British told the Barbadians and Jamaicans that they were superior to Cubans and Puerto Ricans because they were of purer African descent and not mixed with Indians or whites. English education was also accepted as the finest in the world by the rising colored and black middle class. The British motivation for teaching each island group to hate or fear the other was used to prevent West Indians from coming together to form unions.[39]

The Assimilation Process

It is not very difficult to locate large pockets of black immigrants in the United States. Like most newcomers to a strange land, individuals and families tend to move to areas where they have friends and relatives. Large groups of foreign-born blacks are concentrated in parts of New York City, Massachusetts, and Florida. It has been estimated that up to 90 pecent of the foreign-born blacks are located in these areas.[40]

The black immigrant entering the United States enters in the dual role of a Negro (or black) and an immigrant. Although their visibility is low in the black community, if one speaks Spanish, French, or Portuguese, they usually move into their own language groups. Externally, the physical characteristics are the same. It is usually the differences in mores, life style, religion, and culture that force the black immigrant into a form of isolation.

As with all immigrants, the chief factor for consideration is the transfer of the individual from one social group to another. With the black immigrant, this acculturation involves a change in nationality, status, possibly a new language, and the necessary personal adjustments involved in settling in a new land. The black immigrants find that they must adjust in at least three ways: (1) new nationality, (2) adjustment to the social role played by their racial group, and (3) continual intraracial conflict with the native-born black population.

Also, when these immigrants became "Negroes," or "blacks," they underwent a complete change of status. They became a part of a minority group here and their entire mode of living, their relationship with the government, their ideas of liberty, and all traditions were vastly different.[41] By becoming part of a socially restricted population, the immigrants soon realized that they would not be accepted fully into the dominant white society. Once the black immigrants overcame the shock of racial discrimination, as practiced in this country during the past forty years, they then had to adjust to the unique world of problems that exists within the black community in the United States.

Because of a history of rejection and segregation, the blacks in America have been forced to set up a separate class structure and social hierarchy. This also happened in the West Indies and in other places around the world. Moreover, after 1945, "... the black class structure started to take on some of the characteristics of the white class structure."[42] The black middle class in America is greatly influenced by trivial divisions and subdivisions of social rank. "Negroes are not just Negroes to each other. Cutting across their social relationships are myriads of status lines that make for important distinctions within the group."[43] Some of these subclass and subcaste distinctions are skin color, hair texture, facial features, and place of birth. It is this last category, "place of birth," that becomes a source of friction between the native-born and the foreign-born black.

The black immigrant has been called "Monkey Chaser," "Garvite," "Spic," or just "A West Indian," by the native-born blacks. Black immigrants have been forced to become "... a minority within a minority."

The techniques used by native-born blacks to maintain status and to restrict and suppress the black immigrant do not deviate significantly from the tactics employed by other groups.[44] The ironic part of this tragic situation is that the native-born black usually has some kind of amused feeling of superiority over the black immigrant, when in reality the immigrant is usually better educated, better trained, more highly motivated, has a high degree of pride in his culture, dignity, a sense of history and family, and is less inclined to accept any degree of second-class treatment or opportunity. Like most immigrants, they came here for the opportunity to make more money and to increase their standard of living.

Most of the middle class black immigrants suffered a sharp decrease in social status when they moved into the black ghettos on the East Coast. They realize, though, that their loss of status is temporary, and they inwardly feel vastly superior to the native-born blacks.

The ex-peasant immigrants, who might be farm workers or unskilled laborers, are better off economically in America than ·

in their native land; but most suffer from an inferiority complex upon their arrival, and they tend to withdraw and remain invisible. These feelings of superiority and inferiority are an important part of the adjustment of black immigrants.[45]

It is illogical to generalize about the experiences of black immigrants in the United States. "It is difficult to speak of a uniform black experience when the black population can be meaningfully stratified into groups whose members range from those who are affluent to those who are impoverished."[46] Many black immigrants, however, are self-conscious of their values, sensitive to criticism, and uncertain of themselves.

The major difference between the adjustment period of a black immigrant and the adjustment period of a non-black immigrant lies in the changes that one must often go through to fit into the patterns of social role as one becomes a "Negro," or "black." Thus the new immigrant undergoes a reorganization of status and life style, adjusting to not only an interracial situation, but an intraracial situation as well.

In some respects, the immigrant from the Western hemisphere has an advantage over an immigrant from Europe. Besides the language, the Western-oriented black is more familiar with many of the customs, mores, and idiosyncrasies of Americans. This is of great help in seeking employment, and it helps to break down barriers in many informal settings.

Spanish-speaking and Portuguese-speaking black immigrants deserve special attention because their problems are even more complex and frustrating. They have come from a culture, or a family, where the color of a person's skin has not been important among people of the same socioeconomic class. In Puerto Rico, however, clubs and social functions of the higher classes have historically been reserved for whites only. The majority of the business, political, and military leaders in most countries where there is a sizable white population have been white. The color-caste system that exists in the United States is generally the rule in most countries in the world today.

In the United States, the problem is still more complex, because there is a division within classes along racial or ethnic lines. This is what is upsetting to the Latin from a country where there is interracial mixing among the lower classes. By becoming a "Negro" or a "black" in America, they are accepting an inferior caste which creates a degree of social isolation and limits their personal development by preventing them from achieving their desired goals and objectives socially, politically, and economically.

Often Africans, Puerto Ricans, Mexicans, Portuguese, or "Hispanics" will go to great lengths to make clear that they are not "Negroes." The language, if other than English, is retained and spoken frequently so that everyone knows that they are not native-born blacks. If English is their countries' tongue, the British accent is retained to let all know again that they are not American-born blacks. Experience has shown them that there are distinct advantages in not becoming identified with the American-born black.

Many employers prefer to hire "West Indians" over American Negroes because they believe they are more dependable, better workers, better educated, and most important, cheaper. When the immigrants first arrive in this country, they will work for lower wages than the average American worker. For this reason, foreign blacks have often been used as strikebreakers and scabs to prevent unions from organizing in many industries. Over 65,000 West Indians were imported into Panama to build the Panama Canal. After it was completed, they were pushed out of the Canal Zone and left to congregate into ghettos in the cities of Panama. While the population within the Canal Zone went on to develop a life style and standard of living which is one of the highest in the world, the slums in Panama have grown to be major centers of poverty and crime.[47]

The Black Immigrants' Contributions

It is a well-documented fact that black immigrants and their descendants have played a major part in the advancement of blacks in the United States. They have helped to broaden the social vision of the native-black group, and they have been some of the strongest fighters against injustice and discrimination. Presently, in New York City, most of the black leadership in private industry and the government are blacks with West Indian backgrounds.

A major difference between a West Indian black and an American black is the great sense of pride and dignity the West Indian usually has in his or her land and culture. For the American black, this sense of pride is usually absent because of the legacy of slavery. American blacks are forced to skip over the past three hundred years and identify with kingdoms and civilizations in West Africa hundreds and thousands of years ago.

The West Indian family unit is usually a more closely knit, male-dominated family that is held together by close family ties and responsibilities. This pride in one's country and in one's family produces a type of internal discipline and direction which leads to a great emphasis on education and personal advancement. This kind of generalization can also be made about other cultural and ethnic groups—the Chinese, Japanese, Jews, Armenians, Greeks, Koreans, and East Indians.

As intermarriage increases between native-born blacks and foreign-born blacks, the intraracial conflict between the two groups will be of less significance. Increased educational and social opportunities are producing a class of highly educated persons of partially African descent whose life styles, aspirations, and goals are similar to the more educated foreign-born Negro.

Reasons For Returning to Homeland

Most black immigrants only return to their native lands for visits or to pick up relatives to bring back to the United States.

During the 1920s and 1930s, there was a movement of blacks to Africa. The height of this emigration movement was in 1933 when 1,058 blacks departed from the United States. All of them did not go to Africa, however, as a significant number migrated to Europe. During the entire period from 1925 to 1930, more blacks left the United States than entered it.[48]

As many West Indian islands and African nations have achieved independence, there has been a very slight movement of some former nationals back to help build a new nation.[49] Students who were studying here on educational visas are mainly those who return to help run the new countries. Many of these students are forced to return by conditions set before they left their former country of residence, especially if the country is providing major financial aid to the student and his family. Others must return because of pressures put directly upon relatives still living in their native land.[50] Given a free choice, it appears that most foreign students upon the completion of their education prefer to remain in the United States because of the higher degree of personal freedom, and the higher incomes and higher standard of living in this nation.

The racism that still exists in the United States is a minor problem compared to the problems involved in living in some of the developing nations. Relations between the native-born black and the foreign-born black are improving. The major factor here is the attitude of the foreign-born. As long as they do not attempt to project an attitude of superiority over American blacks, there is a good chance that the two groups will intermix and work together to improve the condition of blacks in America. It has been stated that the foreign-born black ". . . sometimes steps on the heels of the native Negro, . . . but both groups hear the same drummer and are aligning in a common cause."[51]

NOTES

1. S. M. Dumasi and C. B. Keely, *Whom Have We Welcomed?* (Staten Island, New York: Center for Migration Studies, 1975), p. 10.

2. Ira DeAugustine Reid, *The Negro Immigrant* (New York: Columbia University Press, 1939), p. 239.

3. Gunnar Myrdal, *The American Dilemma* (New York: Harper & Row, 1962), pp. 113–15.

4. Reid, p. 12.

5. Ibid.

6. Maurice R. Davie, *World Immigration* (New York: Macmillan, 1936), p. 368.

7. Ibid.
8. Reid, p. 11.
9. "Report of the Commissioner of Immigration and Naturalization, 1967," p. 6.
10. Reid, p. 34.
11. "Report of the Commissioner," p. 8.
12. Thomas C. Wheeler, ed. *The Immigrant Experience* (Baltimore: Penguin Books, 1971), p. 34.
13. Ibid.
14. Ibid.
15. Ibid.
16. Ibid.
17. Reid, p. 239.
18. Ibid.
19. Monroe N. Work, ed. *The Negro Year Book* (Tuskeegee, Ala.: Negro Year Book Pub. Co., 1937), p. 238.
20. From personal interviews with Haitian refugees.
21. "Report of the Commissioner of Immigration and the Secretary of Labor, U.S. Department of Immigration, 1937," p. 6.
22. "Report of the Commissioner . . . , 1967."
23. Ibid., p. 59.
24. "Report of the Commissioner of Immigration and Naturalization, Department of Justice, 1975," p. 65.
25. Reid.
26. "Report of the Commissioner . . . , 1975." p. 36.
27. Ibid.
28. Dumasi, p. 41.
29. Numerous studies measuring "Social Distance" in the United States.
30. Gunnar Myrdal.
31. Lloyd W. Warner, "Formal Education and the Social Structure," *Journal of Educational Sociology* 9, no. 9 (May, 1936): 236.
32. Ibid.
33. Ibid.
34. Reid, p. 37.
35. U. G. Weatherly, "The West Indies as a Sociological Laboratory," *American Journal of Sociology* 29, no. 3 (November, 1923): 39.
36. Ibid.
37. Ibid.

38. Reid, p. 200.

39. Weatherly, p. 41.

40. Reid, p. 314.

41. Ibid., p. 30.

42. William Julius Wilson, *The Declining Significance of Race* (Chicago: University of Chicago Press, 1978), p. 13.

43. John Dollard, *Caste and Class in a Southern Town* (New Haven: Yale University Press, 1937), p. 15.

44. Reid, p. 31.

45. Ibid., p. 71.

46. Wilson, p. 200.

47. Reid, p. 181.

48. Ibid., p. 201.

49. Conversations by author with numerous foreign students.

50. Ibid.

51. Reid, p. 221.

IX

America's Arabs

By Philip M. Kayal

Seton Hall University

Middle Easterners have been coming to the United States for over a century, and since they are Arabic-speaking they are often considered as being of the "Arab race." While it is not uncommon for nationality groups to be identified in terms of their language and culture, it is inaccurate to do so for Middle Easterners, because they do in fact belong to a variety of nations, races, and religions which are Arabic-speaking, but who are in fact not Arab in race. The modern "pan-Arab" movement has encouraged the idea that there is a unified Arab "race" which is a sociopolitical, economic, and cultural reality. This recent attempt at creating an international Arab consciousness and identity, however, is a sporadic and futile enterprise, because it challenges more traditional modes of thinking as well as newly derived national identities such as Syrian, Lebanese, Egyptian, Jordanian, Palestinian, etc.

Because "Arab" is a culture and not a race or nationality, it is very difficult and confusing to describe clearly the Arab migration to the United States. It would be more accurate to speak of immigration from the Arab East. However, if we use the term "Arab" to mean a person who speaks Arabic and either participates in or identifies with the Arab culture of the Middle East, then we can consider Middle Eastern Americans as members of a sociocultural group of "Arab" origin. It is these people of many nationalities and races and their descendants in this

220

country whom I have chosen to call Arab and upon whom this discussion will focus.

Arab-Americans coming from the Middle East arrived here without national identities. Actually, they came from the cities and towns of Greater Syria which was itself only a Turkish province until the end of World War I. Hence, there were immigrants from Beirut, Damascus, Aleppo, Homs, etc., and not immigrants from Syria, Lebanon, Jordan, or Palestine. National entities did not exist at the time of the migration, and given the importance of religion in the life of the Middle East, the inhabitants of the region had not yet learned to identify themselves in national and/or broad or geographic terms. They were used to identifying each other in religious terms and began to find out about racial and cultural identities after they got here.

Many of the early immigrants were Moslem, but the vast majority were Eastern-rite Christians from the Melkite, Maronite, or Syriac rite of the Roman Catholic church or Antiochians from the Eastern Orthodox church. At the same time that there are about 9,000,000 Arab Christians, there are hundreds of millions of Moslems who are not Arab. It is a common error to assume that all Moslems are Arab in race, culture, and language. The Moslems of Iran are Persians and those of Syria are Semites. The Moslems of Lebanon can be considered to be Phoenicians like their Christian counterparts and those of Pakistan are Indo-Aryan in culture and history.

In order to gain a foothold in the Middle East, the French unfortunately taught the Christian Arabs that they would never be treated or accepted as Arabs even though their history, thought, and way of life was and is as indigenous and authentically Arab as that of any other Middle Eastern peoples. They introduced the idea that Arab meant Moslem, and when the Moslem-Turkish oppression came upon them, the Christian Arabs used this as undeniable evidence of inherent Islamic hostility. They did not realize that their Moslem, Arab neighbors were also suffering under the Turks and that the Ottomans were oppressing them because they were "bad citizens," and not because they were Christians *per se*. The Christian Arabs were not only bargaining with the French and English to defeat the Turks, but were using the Western imperialists to gain more economic and political power which in turn antagonized their Moslem compatriots whose nationalism was beginning to transcend mere sectarian interests.

The Ottomans likewise capitalized on the divisions present among the Christians by encouraging each religious group or rite to think of itself as a separate nation or "millet" under the leadership of its own "patriarch" or religious leader. The Christian Arabs began to identify themselves as distinctive nations competing with each other for favors from the Turks and/or Westerners. Indeed, they actually began to see themselves as Westerners, and therefore, somewhat distinct from their Arab neighbors. In truth, their Christianity was both Eastern and Arab and was in fact sacrificed and altered for the sake of economic gain and prosperity.[1]

After 1850, when the Turkish oppression was intensified, the Christians began to seek a better life elsewhere. To avoid conscription into the Turkish army and unreasonable taxation, they started to come to America in ever-increasing numbers. Being traders, they had always scattered themselves throughout the known world. Some historians even suggest that they both influenced Columbus's trip to the New World and that some were actually members of his crew.[2] Isolated Arabs were in the country before the Civil War, and small communities of immigrants began to develop in Philadelphia and St. Louis by the time of the mass migrations from Syria between 1880 and 1924. Eventually, Brooklyn, New York, and Detroit, Michigan, emerged as the largest and most significant Arab colonies in the country.

Generally, these immigrants came in search of a better life. Typhoid, disease, pestilence, and warfare with the Druse population on Mt. Lebanon had made life intolerable for them. With the arrival of "generous" American missionaries (whose "give-away programs" literally overwhelmed the Syrians), they began to learn about the New World and to seek refuge here in ever-increasing numbers. The opening of the Suez Canal had also undermined the Syrian silk industry and thousands of Christians were forced to emigrate—first to Egypt—and then to North and South America. All we can be certain of at this time is that the Christians dominated this stage of the migration. "Fear of losing their religion," according to Abdo A. Elkholy, "in the Christian, missionary-minded New World delayed the emigration of the Arab Moslems to America by twenty-five years, until the start of the twentieth century."[3] This migration did not become significant, however, until after World War II.

At first, American immigration officials did not know how to identify these Middle Easterners and often listed them as "Turks" because they came with Turkish passports. Hence, Greeks, Armenians, and Syrians were considered Turkish nationals in the early census reports. Ironically, the immigrants from Syria thought of themselves primarily in religious terms, that is, as Melkites, Maronites, or Antiochian Orthodox, and the sworn enemies of the Turkish government. They spoke Arabic and identified each other as "wlad Arab" or "the children of Arabs," but since they possessed no Arab consciousness or even secular, national identities, they passed into American society as either Catholic ethnics or members of the Eastern Orthodox church.

This first wave of Arab immigrants, then, had distinctive characteristics which differentiate them from the new wave of immigrants arriving here in the last twenty-five years. Before the enactment of the restrictive immigration code of 1924, these Arabs were basically the Christian entrepreneurs from Mt. Lebanon and the large cities and towns of Syria. Morroe Berger tells us that, in terms of their values, they "arrived here in the middle-class."[4] However, they were also poverty stricken and demoralized refugees whose Arab sense of pride, dignity, and industry caused them to avoid anything that would bring discredit upon themselves, their kin, or compatriots in general. That they had limited social identities which rarely extended beyond their relatives, religion, and town of origin, and which may have hindered both their political development and sense of responsibility, was a factor that may actually have helped them to succeed economically as they could only depend on their immediate families for assistance. Hence, survival and success became a family obligation and a matter of great concern.

It would be an understatement to say that these early Arab immigrants have been successfully assimilated. Because of their work habits, frugality, and values, they quickly evolved from peddlers of notions and clothing to become successful manufacturers and distributors of dry goods. In every city in the northeast where they settled, there are millionaire families whose fortunes were made by the immigrants themselves and not by their children as often is the case in American society.[5] The disgrace of failing to succeed was enough to inspire them to accumulate capital and live respectably as American citizens, but their desire to assimilate or even acculturate without disappearing as a distinctive group was undermined by their economic success which left them undistinguishable from other successful Americans. This affected considerably their communal and social life. Being Syrian-Americans made them no different from being middle-class Americans. Hence, they learned English quickly, and Arabic as a second language was rarely successfully taught to their offspring. Indeed, the language is dead among third and fourth generation Syrian-Americans, and the cultural content being preserved is no greater than food, music, and dance. These latter items are enjoyable pastimes acceptable in private settings and reserved for family reunions, weddings, and other festive occasions.

Because they lacked institutional completeness (i.e., they could not recreate a totally integrated communal life), and because their numbers were small (by 1914, there were only about 125,000 "Syrians" here), they assimilated rapidly. Indeed, they wanted to be American and by the second generation, their out-marriage rate was over 50 percent, and their children had entered every occupation and profession open to middle-class Americans.[6] Their assimilation was facilitated by the general lack of conflict with American values and institutions. The only area of significant difficulty was the religious. This conflict affected the quality of communal life they were to experience and their own consciousness about being "Arab."

When they arrived from Syria, these immigrants were divided by patriarchal family lineages, religion, and hometown affiliation. They had to learn to transcend these boundaries in order to survive as an American ethno-interest group. The American Catholic church, which was dominated by the assimilationist Irish, taught the Catholics among them that they were not good Americans until they gave up their ethnicity and assimilated. Ironically, the Syrians migrated here precisely because they thought that this was a multiethnic society and not a melting-pot leading to sociocultural oblivion. To make matters worse, they were forced to view their Orthodox "cousins" as "schismatics" with whom they should limit social intercourse. This had both a negative and positive effect on their communal life. While it divided the community, it spared the Orthodox the total dissociation from the Arab world that seems to characterize so many of the Maronite Catholic Syrians (now called Lebanese). Because they share the same Byzantine Christian tradition as the Orthodox, the Melkites continuously associated with the Orthodox and have been able (against enormous pressures) to consistently identify themselves as Arab in origin and commitment. Consequently, an integrated and politically astute Arab-American community has not emerged until the present.

In order to find an acceptable identity in a pluralistic society, the Syrians transformed their cultural heritage rather than give it up completely. The churches of the Catholic Syrians became "Latinized" (which they confused with "Americanization") at the same time that they joined with their Orthodox compatriots over purely social and cultural issues such as intermarriage—something they all feared would decimate the community. They created a refined Arab-American culture which they kept to themselves and used as an excuse to cross traditional boundaries. Publicly, they were Americans, but privately they were Syrian-Lebanese. It took the 1967 war between the "Arab" nations and Israel to change this complacent, ambivalent, and easygoing ethnic group into a conscientious American interest group. Without realizing it, they had so fully entered the American middle class as individuals that any attempt to maintain an Arab distinctiveness would be romantic at best and, of necessity, either halfhearted or useless. Had they had a strong collective consciousness and had they entered into the American mainstream as a group or people (rather than as isolated individuals), it would be considerably more difficult to generate the pervasive negative feeling against Arabs that is so characteristic of the American mass media. Nevertheless, by the 1950s there was little more than cuisine and religious practices which distinguished them from other Americans—and these distinctions were generally acceptable to the American public, since everyone could enjoy these traditions.

Just as the second and third generation of Syrians in America were settling into stable and relatively affluent communities, the so-called "Israeli-Arab" controversy erupted with full vigor on the American sociopolitical scene. The Syrian-Americans were again being forced to examine their history, identity, and relationship to one another and their homeland. Up until then, their major identity problem was over the question of their nationality (i.e., should they be known as Syrians or Lebanese?). Many Syrians were in fact "Lebanese"-Americans. The fact that the nation of Lebanon did not exist until after World War II did not deter many Syrians from reinterpreting their roots and ancestry. They emerged as Lebanese-Americans because it suited their interests to be identified as descendants of a progressive and Western-oriented nation rather than "belligerent, anti-Semitic, and socialist Syrians."

However, because both the Syrians and Lebanese shared the same history as Christian Arabs, and since they belonged to the same institutions, a complete dissolution of the community was avoided. Henceforth, all references, clubs, and organizations of the community would be called Syrian-Lebanese. Ironically, the old-timers resisted this the most because the Lebanese were always considered "mountain-folk" (peasants) and not to be identified with and/or imitated. The rise of Lebanon as a capitalist pseudo-democracy changed this, and it actually became more prestigious for most Syrian-Americans to be called Lebanese rather than Syrian—a half century after the immigration from Syria ended.

The peace and relationship between the two communities was seriously threatened by recent developments in the Middle East and the establishment of the Zionist state of Israel which wreaked havoc on the sociocultural life of the Arab world. Other factors affecting the Arab-American community are the images of the Arab created by the biased American press both before and after the June, 1967, war, and the Lebanese "civil" war which has reached crisis proportions in the last four years. Obviously, the erroneous definition of that conflict as religious in origin has affected the solidarity of the Arab-American community.

Most Lebanese Christians both abroad and here are in fact members of an ethno-religious group known as Maronite Catholics, while most Syrian Christians belong to the international Melkite Catholic rite or Antiochian Orthodox tradition. The displacement of thousands of Christian (Melkites and Orthodox) and Moslem Palestinians from their homeland into Syria, Lebanon, and Jordan only accentuated the differences and tensions among all these communities. In accepting the Palestinian refugees, Lebanon left itself open to Israeli attacks which recently have caused the total dissolution of the legitimate authority of the central Lebanese government. It is only the presence of the Syrian army which keeps Israel from dominating the whole country. Unfortunately, many people see the Syrian military as a potentially imperialistic force ultimately serving and protecting Syria's interest while also solidifying the position of leftist Christian and Moslem Lebanese.

For the time being, suffice it to say that Israel has forced Lebanon to disassociate itself from the "Arab cause" in order to survive as a "neutral" nation. The Lebanese Phalangist party has suddenly become the mouthpiece for that nation (in opposition to the legitimate central government) and has opted for the Israeli definition of the situation. As a consequence, Lebanon cannot decide if it is an Arab nation at war with Israel (or at least one which should defend itself against Israeli aggression) or a Christian nation suffering because of the Palestinian (Moslem) presence. In truth, Lebanon is an "Arab" nation and its Christianity in no way interferes with its pan-Arabism.[7] Nor should the civil war be defined as one between religious groupings when it is a complex economic and political upheaval.[8]

The major factor, however, affecting Arab-American communal life is, of course, the presence of the new immigrants from the Middle East. They are arriving here better educated and informed, more articulate about sociopolitical issues, and very proud of their Arab heritage. This later immigration began around 1945 with immigrants who were vastly different from their predecessor. To begin with, they came from Palestine, Jordan, Yemen, and Egypt. Elkholy estimates that almost 30,000 Arab intellectuals left these countries (as well as Syria and Iraq) for America since late 1967 alone. Before that, another 70,000 had already entered. These newcomers were mostly professionals and well-educated (many of them in American schools and universities), and a substantial majority of them were Moslems.[9]

Because they are multilingual, their mobility is virtually unrestricted and they are employed as university professors, school teachers, engineers, technicians, physicians, and scientists. Some, like Farouk El-Baz, an Egyptian-born geologist who helped plan the Apollo moon landing, have already achieved national prominence.

Like their Syrian predecessors, almost all of these immigrants have elected to stay in the United States. Once children are born and businesses or professions established, returning to the old country (where opportunity and mobility are restricted by archaic feudal codes) becomes highly unlikely. The early settlers were living so well and the return trip was so tedious that the "return-migration" so characteristic of other groups never materialized among them. After the eligibility for citizenship was established at the turn of the century (they were deemed unacceptable aliens because they were thought to be "Negroids"), they became American citizens in ever increasing numbers. The newer Arab immigrants have also begun to identify themselves as Americans, and they see a long-term future here for themselves and their children. America has again proved to be the land of opportunity, and the absence of "returnees" among them confirms the feeling that they are being accepted as desirable citizens and feel comfortable in their new surroundings.

This "brain-drain" has negatively affected the intellectual life of these Arab countries. On the other hand, the positive effects they have on the Arab-American community cannot be underestimated. The beginning of a positive self-identification as Arabs among the American Syrian-Lebanese has been heightened by the presence of these proud and informed professionals. This factor, plus the political leverage that oil has given the OPEC nations, and Arab military advances during the October War of 1973, have restored a sense of pride, significance, and accomplishment among Arabs everywhere. The traditional stereotypes, no longer tenable, were finally put to rest.

Whether an Arab nationalism truly exists is debatable. What is certain is a trend among them to identify themselves as Arabs. In this country, having a common language and culture might mean that Arab-Americans will finally emerge as an integrated ethno-interest group. Just as many Syrians transcended their historically limiting identities and then redefined themselves as Lebanese, so too can a common heritage hopefully transcend and unite all of the following Arab-American communities and groups with one another: the older immigrants from Syria/ Lebanon, including those few misinformed or uninformed Maronite clergy and laity who think of themselves as Phoenicians; the Coptic Christian and Moslem/Egyptian community; the Palestinian, Jordanian, Yemenite, Iraqui (Moslem and Chaldean) refugees, students, and professionals; and other isolated Middle Eastern groups such as the "Syriac-Arameans" and Circassians. These groups, together with the American-born Syrian/Lebanese would create a new American ethnic group of over 1,000,000 people.[10]

However, there are differences between the first and second wave of immigrants, the old-timers and their American-born offspring, and the informed and misinformed members of the community. This can be seen in their relation to Arab culture

and history and their reactions to recent sociopolitical developments in their homeland, necessitated by the establishment of
the state of Israel in 1948, which resulted in the displacement
of approximately 2,000,000 Palestinians. (How else could room
be made for European and American Jewish settlers?) With no
place to go, many came to America and began laying the ground
for a Palestinian national consciousness and ideology to defend
their rights and interests. They were helped here by the exodus
of Egyptian intellectuals who were frustrated in their attempts
to democratize their own country's political and economic institutions after the revolution of 1952.

It is no easy task for the newly arrived to convince the Syrian-
Lebanese of the merits of Arab nationalism. Having learned
their history from the French, they are suspicious of "Arabness"
as such and usually prefer to keep their ethnicity and origins to
themselves. According to Morroe Berger, "although Arab nationalism has already emerged as a strong ideology in the Middle
East, it has not yet penetrated the largely Christian groups here
who still remember their inferior status under the Moslem Turks
and their uneasy relations with the Moslems in general."[11]

Ironically, since Zionist ideology has consistently presented
the conflict in the Middle East as a Jewish-Arab encounter, the
American Syrian-Lebanese consequently have no choice but to
argue their position from within this framework. Zionism, therefore, is generating a pan-Arab consciousness! To be heard, the
Syrian-Lebanese must identify themselves as Arabs or at least
speak as Arabs even though the issue is between Palestinians
and Zionist Israelis. In fact, Arab-Americans themselves have
continually differentiated between the Israeli state as representative of a political ideology and Jews as members of a revered
and respected religious faith. As the Arabs have achieved greater
unity in their position against both Israel and its Western
supporters, and as they have become increasingly angered over
the stereotype that they are Jew-haters and primitive people,
their American cousins have become more willing to identify
positively with the Palestinian cause. Evidence of this possibility
was first noted in 1958 by Berger:

The Syrian community in America, by now composed mainly of the second and third generations for whom the "old squabbles" were not so important, began to think more of Arab independence of the West, the removal of the remains of Western domination in the now independent states of Lebanon and Syria, and the support of the Arabs as a whole against Zionism. Moreover, such attitudes, Syrians felt, were in accord with traditional American anti-colonial policy (at least outside of Latin America). The United States, indeed, supported England against France in favoring independence for Lebanon and Syria during World War II.[12]

Older Arab-Americans can thus be brought into the conflict on the side of the Palestinians precisely because many of these refugees are, in fact, Christians. Indeed, Christian Arab-Americans are worried about the fate of Christianity in the Holy Land. Since the Six-Day War in June of 1967, the Christians of the Holy Land now number fewer than 90,000, and those remaining in Israel prefer to leave for countries where religion or race has less influence on ordinary life. Israel's forays into Lebanon and Syria also arouse them in regard to the concept of national identity. Indeed, the third and now fourth generation Arab-Americans (numbering perhaps 800,000) are learning about the Middle East from the newly arrived Arab intellectuals. They are also assimilated Americans whose "return to ethnicity" means identifying with Arab culture with pride and understanding. They are learning to argue the Arab point of view from their position as concerned American citizens who realize that the prejudiced American approach favoring Israel is detrimental to world peace, international justice, and now international finance. Only the older leadership of the American Lebanese/Maronite community in this country resists completely identifying with the Arab cause. Many of these French and/or Western-oriented immigrants actually see the situation from the Israeli perspective, because they do not have any vocabulary to analyze the situation except that which was prevalent some seventy-five years ago when they emigrated. Fortunately, their children and grandchildren as well as the legitimate Lebanese government and the Maronite hierarchy in Lebanon are more cognizant of

CONTEMPORARY AMERICAN IMMIGRATION

232

the truth. For example, all the Christian hierarchs and patriarchs in Lebanon issued a heady denouncement of Zionism in 1971 because of Israel's intention to change the status of the city of Jerusalem which is also sacred to Christians and Moslems. Their publicly circulated statement was vigorously supported by all American Arabs regardless of religion or nationality.[13]

To Christian Arabs, Palestine (and more specifically, Jerusalem) was not only the cradle of civilization but also the source of life, since God was made "man" there. Christian civilization, which they call "The Civilization," grew there, and the events of the 1960s represent to them a complete and radical distortion of its human and spiritual significance. This is the consciousness which pervades the thinking and feeling of Arab-Americans— not as barbarians, but as "People of the Book!" By definition, to be Christians, Arabs feel Zionism must be condemned, and this task of educating the American public has fallen to the Christian Arab-Americans. Christian Arabs in America uniformly support the recent United Nations declaration that Zionism in its present form is synonymous with racism.[14]

My interpretation of the evidence supports the sociological observation that events in the old country affect the sociopolitical life of American ethnic groups. As a result of their leaders' remarks, all the Eastern Christian religious groups of Arab extraction in the United States have adopted resolutions on the Middle East. The most outspoken of them is the Antiochian (Syrian) Orthodox church, which went on record urging the then United Nations Secretary General U-Thant to convene the Security Council to scrutinize breaches in the 1967 General Assembly resolution on Israel.

The resolution in question protested the annexation of the Arab section of Jerusalem by Israel, an annexation they feel was forced in unilateral defiance of world opinion and moral law. Arab-Americans especially condemned the recent physical changes made in East Jerusalem by Israeli occupation forces. These changes were allegedly made arbitrarily and without regard for the wishes of the indigenous inhabitants or for their legal and spiritual rights.

In June of 1972, Dr. Frank Maria, chairman of the department of Near East and Arab refugee problems of the Antiochian Orthodox Christian church in America, appeared before the Executive Committee of the National Council of Churches to present the Christian Arab perspective on the Middle East crisis. His concern was over the reluctance of the American Christian establishment to tackle the controversy head on:

At stake in the Middle East . . . for American Christians are: the future of Christianity, the relationship between the three great monotheistic religions (Judaism, Christianity, and Islam), the geopolitical interests of the United States, the integrity of the United States as a democracy and as a Christian nation, the peace of the world and possibly even the survival of mankind.[15]

After Israel's shooting down of a Libyan airliner in 1973, she was condemned by Syrian Eastern Christian clerics in many cities in the United States. The most unified action to take place among the American Syrian-Lebanese, however, was in response to the bombing of the Lebanese consulate in Los Angeles. Claiming to represent some 60,000 Arab-Americans living in Southern California, every Moslem and Syrian Christian leader living there sent telegrams indicating their shock and dismay to Mayor Samuel Yorty, the district attorney, and the chief of police.

Other examples of the newly emerging attitude of Arabic-speaking Americans can be found in the official position of the National Association of Federated Syrian-Lebanese American Clubs. Combining a statement of loyalty to the United States with support for the position of the Arab League on the Palestinian question, the association points out that it is an American organization devoted to the best interests of all the American people. Because its members are of Arab descent, Berger feels that "it can and has served as an effective link between America and the Arab World. . . . However . . . it has not and does not interfere in the internal affairs of these Middle Eastern nations."[16] The Association refers to the responsibility of American citizens to make their views known on foreign policy: "Because its membership has close cultural ties and intimate knowledge of the Arab World, the National Association has a special responsibility to make recommendations regarding foreign policy in the Middle East." Guiding itself "solely by the dictates of the genuine interest of all the American people," the association urges the United States to insist upon the implementation of all the United Nations resolutions on the Palestinian question as a means of bringing "peace and justice" to the area.[17]

It is this writer's thesis that Americanization, education, and the need to respond to the mass media's negative depiction of them has led Arab-Americans to an awakening of their political consciousness. In fact, the American-born have more in common with the educated new arrivals than with their own parents or grandparents, since they are willing to shed the old limitations of rite, religion, and nationality and to identify themselves as Arabs. For these reasons, the Arab-American community was able to bring pressure to bear on the censure of President Jimmy Carter's aide, Paul Rand Dixon, who called consumer advocate Ralph Nader a "dirty Arab" in one of his news conferences. On the other hand, the community could not help congressional candidate George Corey of San Mateo County, California, win a seat in Congress when his Democratic opponent for the nomination accused the American-born Corey of being an "Arab" candidate supported by the PLO. Ironically, Corey was supported by Governor Brown, and the racism generated by Holsinger, his Jewish opponent, ended in defeat for both of them. When county residents were given the facts and learned the truth by and through Arab-American press releases, they refused to elect the racist who introduced the ethnic variable in the first place, electing instead the Republican candidate.

Fortunately, other Arab-Americans have been able to enter the American political scene with less difficulty. Witness the startling success of former Senator James Abourezk of South Dakota in bringing attention to the crisis in the political and economic life of Lebanon, and the effects that special presidential aide William J. Baroody, Jr. and Assistant Secretary of State Philip Habib have had in the shaping of American Middle

East foreign policy. Further evidence of this tendency to act as a unified American interest group can be seen in the membership roles of both the Association of Arab-American University Graduates and the National Association of Arab-Americans. While these two organizations differ in objectives, both draw their membership from the widely dispersed and diversified Arab-American population.

The former organization has attracted leading Arab-American scholars to its ranks, and its membership is open to all American citizens of Arab ancestry and to "anyone interested in Arab society and culture and in fostering understanding between Arabs and Americans." Significantly, a substantial proportion of its one thousand members are children of the original Christian Syrian-Lebanese settlers. Interestingly, the AAUG is a professional and academic endeavor that demands an intellectual understanding and commitment to the Arab cause. This is probably why it can attract the American-born Arabs who are, after all, so Americanized that they could not relate to the Middle East situation in any way other than as interested and concerned Americans. This is quite an accomplishment considering the particular and localized histories of most Middle Easterners!

To bring together newly arrived Moslem Arabs with the older Americanized Christian Arabs required that they all be identified as "wlad Arab" (children of the Arab East). This was actually facilitated by Israel's attacks on Lebanon. Previously, there was a tendency for Arabs to bury their heads after each defeat by Israel, but this has changed drastically as of late. What the disparate Arab-American communities seem to share, notes the *New York Times*, "is a sense of being aggrieved. All deny, at least to strangers, being anti-Jewish, but all complain that the Arab side of the Mideast conflict is unfairly presented here."[18]

Most Arab-Americans feel that the Palestinians among them and in the Middle East are desperate and alone in their battle for autonomy and recognition. More importantly, the Lebanese feel that their country is being penalized for simply sheltering the refugees. "They are [in Lebanon] because they got thrown out of their country. Our Lebanese now feel they've been let down. They felt the United States wouldn't let Lebanon get into the war. Now they're afraid because the invasions by the Israelis seem to negate this."[19]

As a result, a group of concerned Americans of Arab heritage met in Washington to discuss the United States' posture toward the Middle East, and Lebanon in particular. It was determined that a lack of political action on the part of Americans of Arab descent was very evident. Since that time, discussions with officials of various American government agencies, including the Departments of State and Defense, and the National Security Council at the White House, have not only verified this deficiency, but reiterated the need for a national body.

The National Association of Arab-Americans (NAAA) was incorporated in April, 1972, to fill this gap. One of the prime objectives of the NAAA is to provide moral, financial, and political support to those Americans of Arab heritage who seek political or public office, regardless of party affiliation. Another objective is to seek a more "balanced" United States policy in the Middle East. Members of the association have met with and maintain a continuous dialogue with senior officials throughout our govrenment. The founder of the organization, Maronite attorney Richard C. Shadyac of Washington, notes that "we do not seek the destruction of Israel, but we believe there should be an evenhanded policy in the Middle East. The energy [oil] problem and trade deficit are of prime concern to Americans and we feel the U.S. now is not acting in its best interests."[20]

Conclusion

What we now have in the United States is a diversity of Arab people who are in different states of assimilation and affluence. Americans are not in the habit of differentiating between the peoples of the Arab world and tend to stereotype them all negatively. Since they do share so much in common, however, it has actually become advantageous, both politically and socially, to accept the term "Arab" as a descriptive category and sign of differentiation. Thus, the exigencies of life in America and the

X

Australian Immigration to the United States: From Under the Southern Cross to "The Great Experiment"

By Dennis Laurence Cuddy

Today the population of the United States is over 220 million, and from 1820 to 1976 nearly 50 million immigrants have entered this nation's borders. Migration to this country from Australia, which Herman Melville in *Moby Dick* called "that other great America on the other side of the sphere," and New Zealand reached a total of 133,299 from 1861 to 1976, with anywhere from roughly 60 to 90 percent coming from Australia during any given year (Table 1).[1] Thus, though Australians have made a significant contribution to American life, it is clear that they form a very small percentage (approximately .2 percent) of the total number of migrants who have arrived in the United States.

Early contacts between the two nations began when whalers and sealers visited both Sydney and San Francisco.[2] Because the continent under the Southern Cross was initially settled by convicts in 1788 when England could no longer use America as a repository for those who had crowded British gaols, one might reach the immediate conclusion that the first Australian migrants to the United States were undesirables. In that regard, however, one would do well to remember that nearly 100 years before the antipodean continent was settled by members of the white race, "lewd, disorderly and lawless persons" were transported to the American colonies from England.[3]

240

---

need to find an acceptable and functional identity has forced Arab-Americans to band together to protect their interests and to inform Americans of the complexities of the economics, politics, and social organization of their homelands.

Previously, most of their energies went into building religious institutions such as churches and mosques which they used to sustain their culture and identities. Now that they are successfully established in American society, they are eager to bring their heritage to the attention of the American public, who, at one time, abused them for being "ethnic" or different. Indeed, they are different, but it is this difference which the Arab-Americans now feel should be stressed rather than disparaged, for they are proud of their traditions. After all, they are family people who like to express themselves enthusiastically through poetry, song, and dance. They are hard workers and successful entrepreneurs. They have been characterized as frugal, industrious immigrants with solidly middle-class aspirations, traditions, and moral consciences.

Generally speaking, most Arabs are self-disciplined and honorable people who believe in God, on Whom they feel dependent. They are hospitable, dignified, and very aware of their obligations to one another. William Cole wrote of the Syrians among them in the 1920s:

Pride of race, a high degree of native intelligence, an individualism which retards cooperative effort and often passes into factionalism, shrewdness and cleverness in business, devotion to the institutions of this country, imaginativeness, religious loyalty, love of domestic life, courtesy, and hospitality, eagerness for education, fondness for music and poetry, temperance in the men and chastity in the women, self-respect and self-reliance . . . such are some of the more obvious traits of the Syrians.[21]

If this was true of the Syrians, it was also true for all Arab people. Honor, pride, and dignity had to be maintained by all family members so as not to "blacken the family name." Life was to be enjoyed and experienced as social. Hence, socializing would take place in the homes of relatives and friends and not in lonely, impersonal public settings. Crime was virtually non-existent in the group because of the social pressures exercised by the family and church. These were the same forces which kept the Syrians, and now all American Arabs, off the public dole. This is the heritage Arab-Americans want to pass on to their children and to which other Americans can turn for inspiration and/or hope.

Arab-Americans are tired of being the victims of the "new racism" which blames them and their contemporaries for the suffering of the Jews, when, in fact, they have sheltered the world's persecuted (Armenians, Circassins, Jews, and others) for centuries. Previously, they could not articulate their feelings about their past and their present role in American society, and they always feared total absorption into the dominant society which did little to encourage their distinctiveness either socio-culturally or religiously. Now they are beginning to realize that America is really *not* a "melting pot" and that they have a right to maintain their own way of life. While the purity of their ethnic and religious heritage is less than ideal, their ethnicity is alive in the subtle and covert ways of acting and feeling which only an astute observer of their behavior would notice. Externally, they are indistinguishable from their American neighbors, but their reaction to American sociopolitical issues (like the place of older people in the life of the community) is traditional and highly exemplary. Arab-Americans, then, form an ethnic group because they recognize in each other values and behaviors with which they identify and which they know originated in the Arab world.

NOTES

1. This question was definitely resolved in Melkite Patriarch Maximos V, "Christians and Arab Nationalism," *Sophia* 9, no. 2 (February–March, 1979).

2. See Beverlee Turner Mehdi, *The Arabs in America: 1492–1977* (Dobbs Ferry, N.Y.: Oceana Publications, 1978).

3. Abso A. Elkholy, "The Arab-American Family," in *Ethnic*

Families in America, ed. C. Mindel and R. Habenstein (New Elsevier Press, 1976).

4. Morroe Berger, "America's Syrian Community." *Comm* 25, no. 4 (April, 1958): 316.

5. See Philip and Joseph Kayal, *The Syrian-Lebanese In Am* (Boston: Twayne Publishers, 1975), chap. 5.

6. Kayal, chap. 11.

7. Elaine Hagopian, "Lebanon and the Arab Question," in *Lebanon*, ed. E. Hagopian and S. Farsoun, Special Report n (Detroit: Association of Arab-American University Graduates, gust, 1978).

8. Fouad Moughrabi and Naseer Aruri, *Lebanon: Crisis Challenge In The Arab World*, Special Report no. 1 (Detroit: ciation of Arab-American University Graduates, January, 1977.)

9. Abdo A. Elkholy, "The Arab-Americans: Nationalism Traditional Preservations," in *The Arab-Americans*, ed. E. Hago and A. Paden (Wilmette, Ill.: Medina University Press, 1969), 11–17.

10. Philip M. Kayal, "Problems in Classification: Estimating Arab-American Population," *Migration Today* 2, no. 5 (Septem 1974): 3.

11. Berger, p. 317.

12. Ibid.

13. "Christian Religious Leaders of Syria Appeal to Christian C science," *Action* 3, no. 2 (June 26, 1971): 2.

14. Ibid. A Christian interpretation of the concept "Zionism" also given in this article.

15. "American Christians and the Holy Land," *Action* 4, no. (June 12, 1972): 2.

16. Berger, p. 318.

17. Ibid.

18. *New York Times*, October 7, 1972, pt. 2, p. 1.

19. Ibid.

20. "U.S. Arabs Rap Policy on Mideast," *Christian Science Mo itor*, May 12, 1973, p. 6.

21. William I. Cele, *Immigrant Races in Massachusetts* (Bostor Massachusetts Department of Education, 1921), p. 4.

Although there is little doubt that a few convicts from Australia did disembark in San Francisco, official statistics indicate that the first Australian, a male, immigrated to the United States in 1839.[4] It would not be until ten years later and the discovery of gold in California, though, that a large number of Australians followed him. At that time, Edward Hammond Hargraves, who would return to Australia in 1850 and discover gold "Down Under," came to California along with many others; San Francisco was inhabited by the infamous Aussies known as the "Sydney Ducks" and the even more notorious "Derwent Ducks" (the Derwent River runs through Hobart, Tasmania), both of which were comprised of criminal elements.[5]

Table 1

Immigration to the United States from Australia and New Zealand*

Periods	Number of Immigrants
1861–1870	36
1871–1880	9,886
1881–1890	7,017
1891–1900	2,740
1901–1910	11,975
1911–1920	12,348
1921–1930	8,299
1931–1940	2,231
1941–1950	13,805
1951–1960	11,506
1961–1970	19,562
1971	2,357
1972	2,550
1973	2,466
1974	1,978
1975	1,804
1976	2,133
1976 (July–Sept. 30)	606
1977 (Sept. 30, 1976–Sept. 30, 1977)	2,544

* Yearly totals are from July through June. Figures prior to 1906

(country whence alien came); 1906 and after (country of last perma-
nent residence).
Source: United States Immigration and Naturalization Service
Annual Reports.

During the latter half of the nineteenth century, between 500
and 1,000 migrants departed Australia and New Zealand for the
United States and Canada each year. Australian immigration
to America decreased, however, in the 1890s with only 87 making
the trip in 1896.[6] Most settled in California while some chose
New York; few decided to make "Dixie" their new home; and
those who did come to the United States during the 1890s
brought with them the "Australian (secret) ballot," which was
adopted by the American government.

Although many Australians who came to the United States
during the latter half of the nineteenth century had considerable
financial resources, "ordinary Aussies" came to America in
search of work. They came through the port of San Francisco
and noted the inferiority of the streets, public buildings, parks,
and institutions, but superiority of the trams and hotels in comparison to Melbourne's, for example. Los Angeles was described
as just "a rather sleepy little community only beginning to stir
itself."[7] The variety of migrants from Australia at this time is
perhaps its most notable aspect. Around the year 1900, outlaw
Frank Gardiner immigrated to the United States after his release
from jail; yet during roughly the same period, Alfred Deakin,
who would later be prime minister of Australia, also spent some
time in America.[8] The latter noted rather astutely at the time
that the residents of Chicago and New York looked "busy"
rather than "happy," an opinion shared by many Australians
nearly one hundred years later.[9]

Shortly after the turn of the century, other notable immigrants
came to the United States, including Stella Maria Sarah Miles
Franklin (known as "Miles Franklin") who was one of Australia's
best-known novelists, and Henry Braddon who would become
the first Australian trade commissioner to the United States. By
the end of World War I, when the "roaring twenties" were about
to begin, approximately 10,000 Australians were living in Amer-

ica.[10] During that decade, they brought with them the "Australian crawl" swimming stroke to their new land; and for those who "Went East," the "polygamous Salt Lake City" was a favorite stop.[11] For some of the immigrants, the United States had gained the reputation of a "decadent" nation; and upon embarking for America in 1926, J. B. Murray was "admonished by a tearful elderly lady not to start taking those 'terrible drugs' when he arrived in that 'awful country.'" She was also amazed that he would even consider going to a land where "he might be murdered within minutes after his arrival."[12]

Other Aussies noted the "frenzied state" of the stock market and automobile traffic in the United States at the end of the 1920s, and with the onset of the Great Depression, immigration again declined during the 1930s.[13] Still, there were positive aspects about America during this decade. For instance, two Tasmanians, Errol Flynn and Merle Oberon, were starring in motion pictures throughout the United States. By the beginning of World War II, there were 15,000 Australians living in America.[14]

During the war, 500,000 United States servicemen either were stationed in or visited the continent in the Southwest Pacific; and in 1944, Australian "war brides" (eventually 15,000) began arriving in their husbands' homeland.[15] On July 10, 1944, *Life* magazine ran an article on the "mini invasion" telling that the Aussie wives "often found the bread too sweet and the butter too salty." One bride noted that skirts were shorter and meat higher than in Australia; and she further advised women still in the country which she had left "that clothes were much less expensive in America and 'plastic shoes, which are more lovelier [*sic*] than leather ones, are unrationed.'"[16]

Since the end of World War II, Australian immigration to the United States has increased significantly, with females outnumbering males, especially in the 20 to 29 years of age category (Tables 2–4). As newcomers to the United States, the migrants could perhaps view American society somewhat more objectively than native Americans; and some judged the decade of the 1950s as a rather passive time of "reacting rather than acting."[17]

They also noted that for all of the talk about "freedom," it seemed that there was a definite lack of freedom for black Americans.

To Australians in the United States during the late 1950s, America gave the appearance of becoming a "now" society where in the words of one Aussie, "Gross materialism rubs shoulders with simple virtue."[18] Yet, Americans were perceived to be creative and adaptive; and an Australian journalist living in the United States at the time wrote: "The civilized man of yesterday had two countries—his own and France. Today his second country is not France, but America."[19]

Table 2

Australian (By Birth) Immigration to the United States, 1951 to 1977*

Period	Number of Immigrants
1951	274
1952	276
1953	333
1954	451
1955	333
1956	429
1957	519
1958	715
1959	646
1960	671
1961	625
1962	552
1963	677
1964	679
1965	757
1966	858
1967	1,247
1968	1,319
1969	1,384
1970	1,714
1971	1,400
1972	1,551
1973	1,400

Period	Number of Immigrants
1974	1,236
1975	1,116
1976	1,366
1976 (July–Sept. 30)	394
1977 (Sept. 30, 1976–Sept. 30, 1977)	1,389

* Year ends June 30.
Source: United States Immigration and Naturalization Annual Reports.

With the decade of the 1960s came an ambivalent view of the United States on the part of many Australians living here. They noted the apparent inferior quality of manufactured items, the fear of nuclear war, and increasing racial unrest.[20] Seeing the violence associated with integration in the early 1960s, many became more accepting of their own nation's "White Australia" policy. Journalist Stewart Cockburn wrote on October 26, 1962: "One of the effects of the [race] riots on me personally is to compel me at least to eat my words on White Australia. I've always found the policy distasteful, . . . [but] I accept now that human nature being what it is, a serious color problem will inevitably promote trouble."[21]

From 1964 to 1970 the number of Australians entering the United States as migrants increased sharply; but it was still a period of unease in America. Sir Howard Beale, Australian ambassador to the United States from 1958 to 1964, noted during each of his ten return visits to America from 1964 to 1969 that there was a growing "national malaise."[22] There was a sense of perpetual crisis in the country; and, according to John Hammond Moore in *Australians in America 1876–1976*, some of the migrants wondered, as did perhaps a few Americans, whether the United States was "really a land of freedom or a fragmented nation where freedom has become in fact anarchy."[23]

The answer to this ponderance for a significant number of migrants was that the social unrest they witnessed in America in the latter part of the 1960s was simply a passing phase. In that regard, Australian Sam Lipski wrote an article in 1970 entitled "America Has *Not* Been Cancelled," in which he indicated

Table 3
Australian (By Birth) Male Immigration to the United States (By Age), 1960 to 1977*

Period	Age Under 5	5-9	10-19	20-29	30-39	40-49	50-59	60-69	70-79	80+	Total
1960	59	63	20	44	59	10	11	6	3	0	275
1961	48	37	18	57	54	14	8	6	1	0	243
1962	29	26	25	37	50	17	6	2	2	0	194
1963	55	58	28	52	65	22	7	7	0	1	295
1964	69	41	24	39	61	13	7	3	2	0	259
1965	63	47	30	39	55	19	6	2	4	2	267
1966	62	63	42	69	66	22	6	5	0	0	335
1967	114	80	56	97	126	33	9	3	5	3	526
1968	102	88	55	121	112	37	11	1	1	0	528
1969	98	90	52	91	109	43	8	3	1	0	495
1970	118	83	70	154	134	43	12	5	2	0	621
1971	77	83	71	145	110	31	11	2	0	0	530
1972	99	104	57	128	130	31	15	9	3	2	578
1973	88	72	53	154	102	35	12	3	1	1	521
1974	51	60	56	154	95	28	13	0	4	0	461
1975	58	63	46	148	117	29	7	6	4	0	478
1976	63	66	82	167	134	43	15	7	3	0	580
1976 (July–Sept. 30)	22	28	19	53	34	14	9	4	0	0	183
1977 (9/30/'76–9/30/'77)	58	77	63	180	155	43	14	6	8	1	605
TOTAL	1,323	1,229	867	1929	1768	527	187	80	44	10	7,974

Source: United States Immigration and Naturalization Service Annual Reports.

* Year ends June 30.

Table 4.
Australian (By Birth) Female Immigration to the United States (By Age), 1960 to 1977*

Period Age	Under 5	5–9	10–19	20–29	30–39	40–49	50–59	60–69	70–79	80+	Not re-ported	Total
1960	61	57	26	130	68	22	11	15	5	0	1	396
1961	54	52	26	124	75	21	7	16	7	0	0	382
1962	44	36	35	127	65	23	12	7	9	0	0	358
1963	57	40	42	133	60	23	11	10	6	0	0	382
1964	64	41	34	159	69	29	9	8	6	1	0	420
1965	68	43	47	201	66	34	11	9	11	0	0	490
1966	68	37	59	204	88	36	14	12	4	1	0	523
1967	86	73	71	294	110	40	24	13	9	1	0	721
1968	96	79	71	338	135	41	15	11	5	0	0	791
1969	87	90	87	400	141	49	21	8	4	2	0	889
1970	94	106	124	525	145	56	19	12	10	2	0	1093
1971	77	48	89	445	126	43	25	7	7	3	0	870
1972	80	89	90	493	141	40	24	10	6	0	0	973
1973	79	58	89	437	135	46	22	8	4	1	0	879
1974	68	65	73	362	129	36	19	12	4	7	0	775
1975	45	56	82	268	125	21	17	11	9	4	0	638
1976	48	73	80	329	165	47	21	14	6	3	0	786
1976 (7–9/30)	14	22	26	79	43	13	7	7	0	0	0	211
1977 (9/30/'76–9/30/'77)	53	67	105	305	165	36	24	18	9	2	0	784
Total	1,243	1,132	1,256	5,353	2,051	656	313	208	121	27	1	12,361

* Year ends June 30.   Source: United States Immigration and Naturalization Service Annual Reports.

that "change and on-going revolution are very American products and always have been."[24]

Thus, by the early 1970s, 24,000 Aussies could be found living in the United States (38,000 if one includes the second generation), again predominantly in California, and many bringing with them considerable business and "know-how."[25] Australian National Industries bought a majority interest in a major Louisiana equipment company; Davis Consolidated Industries of Australia together with a German company purchased the giant Wilson Foods Corporation; Concrete Industries (Monier) Limited built thirteen plants in the United States; Australia's Lend Lease Corporation recently bought a $11.3 million (Australian) shopping center in Savannah, Georgia; and in February, 1979, Wormald International took over the American company Ansul, the specialist fire extinguisher group, for $50 million (Australian).

There are also many examples of experience and expertise being brought to the United States during this same period. One Sydney firm supplied the eight 170-ton "Kangaroo" cranes used to construct the two 110-story buildings of the World Trade Center in New York City; a Melbourne company developed an American National Standards Institute "COBOL" compiler for the world's largest-selling minicomputer; Australia has assisted the American National Metric Council in preparing for the use of the metric system in the United States; and the popular TraveLodge motel chain in western American states is controlled by the TraveLodge firm in Australia.[26]

America has witnessed a simultaneous increasing interest in things Australian during the decade of the 1970s. Films like *Walkabout*, television programs like *Skippy*, and Australian beer, wine, and beef (steaks used by the Bonanza chain) have been well-received. In addition, the Chair of Australian Studies was inaugurated at Harvard University in 1976; the 1978 autumn season on Broadway opened with the Australian play, *Players*; and in October, 1978, the city of Grand Rapids, Michigan, celebrated "Australia Month" with films, speeches, and exhibits.

Table 5
Australian (By Birth) Immigration to the United States (By Occupation), 1960 to 1977*

Period / Occupation	1	2	3	4	5	6	7	8	9	10	11	12	13
1960	99	12	7	50	24	8	3	1	0	12	4	451	671
1961	116	22	11	43	28	9	1	2	0	9	2	382	625
1962	103	7	12	54	15	7	5	1	0	14	1	333	552
1963	138	11	10	57	14	4	2	1	1	8	5	426	677
1964	130	8	12	54	10	3	1	0	1	10	0	450	679
1965	129	14	8	77	11	5	2	0	1	14	5	491	757
1966	197	19	12	67	6	7	1	0	1	8	6	534	858
1967	306	31	11	96	22	9	2	0	1	10	8	751	1,247
1968	307	26	16	117	34	9	4	0	0	14	9	783	1,319
1969	300	31	8	151	27	4	3	0	0	22	7	831	1,384
1970	381	26	24	201	33	16	7	4	2	25	13	982	1,714
1971	339	46	15	157	32	17	4	1	1	39	30	719	1,400
1972	354	51	17	150	27	12	4	1	2	29	10	894	1,551
1973	324	55	21	149	30	16	9	0	2	26	8	760	1,400
1974	304	40	16	122	23	9	5	1	2	36	11	667	1,236
1975	275	58	12	105	26	12	5	0	3	29	8	583	1,116
1976	344	70	28	112	34	10	14	0	1	25	14	714	1,366
1977 (Sept. 30, 1976–Sept. 30, 1977)	309	106	34	108	42	15	8	2	2	22	13	728	1,389
Total	4,455	633	274	1,870	438	172	80	14	20	352	154	11,479	19,941

(1) Professional, Technical and Kindred Workers. (2) Managers and Administrators (except Farmers). (3) Sales Workers. (4) Clerical and Kindred Workers. (5) Craftsmen and Kindred Workers. (6) Operatives. (7) Laborers (except Farm). (8) Farmers and Farm Managers. (9) Farm Laborers and Farm Foremen. (10) Service Workers (except Private Household). (11) Private Household Workers. (12) Housewives, Children and others with no occupation reported. (13) Total.

*Year ends June 30

Source: United States Immigration and Naturalization Service Annual Reports.

Concerning the types of immigrants who have joined us in the United States in the recent past, they have come from all walks of life and from various pursuits (Table 5). From employees of Australian banks operating in this country to university students and chairpersons of university departments, the migrants have made their mark upon American life; and some have even received national acclaim. In addition to actors such as Rod Taylor and athletes like Evonne Goolagong in tennis and Jan Stephenson in golf, a number of immigrants have developed distinct reputations in various fields of music. These would include Diana Trask in country music, Joan Sutherland of operatic fame, as well as Andy Gibb and the BeeGees, Olivia Newton-John, and Helen Reddy in the field of popular music—the latter is now an American citizen and has remarked that the United States is "the best country in the world." Other Australian notables now living in America are Jill Conway, president of the prestigious Smith College; Rupert Murdoch, publishing magnate who bought the *New York Post*; and Patrick Oliphant, nationally popular political cartoonist.

With regard to the motivations of immigrants who have settled in the United States over the past several decades, they have been obtained via research into relevant secondary sources and through personal interviews by this writer with Australians who have come to America since the 1950s. A general rule which one might follow in examining the immigration of Australians (or any other people for that matter) during any given period is that any preponderance of negatively perceived conditions in Australia coupled simultaneously with positively perceived conditions in the United States, or vice versa, would tend to cause immigration to increase or decrease respectively.

Although Australians have not tended as much as other nationals to emigrate from their native land because of discontent or desperation, there have been several motivational "push factors," which have caused some of them to choose to live elsewhere. In a brief essay such as this, however, there is only space to mention a number of the more important factors:

government ineffectiveness and interference, antiquated ideas and methods in business, overpowerful labor unions and too many strikes, as well as extremely high income taxes. According to migrant and physician Alan Baird, who came to the United States with his family, "I was bloody tired of going cap in hand to the bank each April Fool's day for a loan to pay income tax."[27] Additional push factors include the high cost of living in Australia; a spouse's parent's or offspring desire to make a change; the continent's isolated geographical position; and a desire for travel and adventure or the chance to live in a colder climate.

Concerning "pull factors," or why the migrants would choose the United States instead of some other country, such as England, for example, there are a variety of reasons. For younger Australians, travel and adventure are important motives, and many of them feel "Los Angeles would be 'the' place to go."[28] In general, however, it seems that economic reasons are an important consideration, because many Australians are inclined to think that there are better economic and employment opportunities to be found in America. They come seeking greater material satisfaction via higher salaries offered here for the same type of work which they performed in the nation from which they departed.

Other factors pulling these migrants to the United States include a job assignment here with an Australian firm or subsidiary, the opportunity to attend an American school or university, or the desire to be with relatives already living here. Still others come to marry an American or because an American to whom they are already married wants to return to his or her homeland, while some have their own personal reasons for immigrating which do not apply to any other Australian migrants.

Why many more do not migrate is in large part due to both the distance and expense as well as the strong family ties among Australians; and although there may be one "triggering event" which causes any individual to feel that emigration is necessary or desirable, there is often more than one reason needed (unless it is life- or freedom-threatening) to compel emigration.

In the case of Australians, as with other migrants, one must also ask what they really know about the United States and Americans, for much of their knowledge is based upon Hollywood films and television portrayals of the United States as a land of riches and exciting pleasures.

Upon arriving in the United States, there is initially no real "culture shock" for most Australians. Obviously, there is a period of adjustment, but they do not have to contend with many of the problems with which other migrant groups, many of whom do not even speak English, must contend. Thus Aussies, who tend to be rather adaptable people, adjust to American life quite easily. This is not difficult to understand, as the United States and Australia have shared certain historical parallels and have basically the same common language. In his 1884 work, *Tour in America*, Australian Thomas Kirkland Dow wrote: "... the man who has lived for a lengthened period in the Australian colonies has experienced a kind of conversion and a probationary period which fit him for falling easily into American ways, and enable him to see much that is admirable where those who do not possess this inward light see nothing but unmeaning strangeness."[29]

Probably it is the physical aspects of the United States and American life which the migrants notice at first. They find a cooler climate, that the sun traverses the southern sky, and that the evening stars are different (no Southern Cross). Today, they also note larger cars and highways than those to which they were accustomed in their homeland; and they must learn to drive on the right-hand side of the road. Geographically, the United States has greater variety as there is nothing in Australia equivalent to the Grand Canyon or the Mississippi River, for example; and although the nation under the Southern Cross contains large cities and very small towns, cities of a moderate size are a rarity.

The immigrants notice additional differences in language, sports, and other areas. Depending upon where they travel, they find various Americans will speak with different accents; and they find that there are differences in the uses of certain words (e.g., the American word "cookie" is a "biscuit" in Australia; and the word "diaper" here is a "napkin" there). In sports, they note that American football is different from "Aussie Rules" football, and that baseball is played in the United States to a far greater extent than in Australia where cricket enjoys greater popularity. Other areas which the migrants notice initially are the wider use of central heating and air conditioning, and the greater availability of nighttime and weekend shopping as well as greater personalized service (e.g., water served automatically with meals in restaurants, and windshields wiped at service stations) than they experienced in the country from which they departed.

Concerning the American people, although Australia is also an immigrant nation, new arrivals from the antipodean continent to the United States almost immediately notice the larger nonwhite American population compared to the nonwhite population of their homeland. In Australia, the Aborigines (who are actually a fourth race, distinct by blood-type from the other three major races) are almost equivalent in number to the American Indians; but the vast majority of Aborigines are not found in urban settings, where most Australians live. Thus, when an individual from a population of 14,248,500 (the total for Australia as of June 30, 1978) comes to a country in which there are approximately 30 million blacks, it is truly a new experience. Probably the American people and the complexity and diversity of American life are what interest most of the immigrants, at least at first.[30]

Friendliness is also a quality which the migrants are quick to note regarding Americans, but they soon begin to question whether the ready friendliness exhibited by many Americans is actually superficial, like that of a welcoming host or hostess simply trying to give the newcomer a favorable first impression.[31] In his work, "Letter from Seattle," published in 1958, Australian Kenneth E. Read, now chairman of the Department of Anthropology at the University of Washington, wrote that the immediate impression an Australian receives in the United States is that Americans are affable, "until it occurs to you that the white smile, the easy manners are weapons in the arsenal of salesmanship."[32] Though most of the migrants eventually conclude that many Americans are genuinely friendly, this is not always the case. Ray Polkinghorne, for instance, an Adelaide (capital of South Australia) newspaperman was told in no uncertain terms by a San Francisco cab driver that it was customary to tip cabbies generously. Polkinghorne concluded in the *Advertiser*, November 30, 1978: "I think the message was that I would be emptied out onto [the] . . . street, unless I paid up."[33] Unfortunately, he was not alone among Australians in the United States to comment on incidents like this.

After an initial period in which the new arrivals become acquainted with the United States and its inhabitants, statistics reveal that most Australians settle in California or New York.[34] They do not often settle in small towns, and because of their independence, they do not tend to form "Australian communities" in this country.

With respect to the interaction among the new settlers and their hosts and hostesses, Americans generally like the migrants and their "Aussie accents." The Australians themselves tend to act here as one might expect them to act, in a sometimes rough but friendly and democratic manner; and they have very definite opinions about Americans in general.[35] Americans are judged as thinking they are at the center of the world and the best in everything. They are also considered by many of the immigrants as being spoiled, for as this writer indicated in *The Yanks are Coming: American Immigration to Australia*, "latter 20th century American culture is one which has bathed its citizens in comfort to such a degree that it has spoiled its society to a considerable extent."[36]

To the Australian immigrant in the United States, Americans today also seem to be obsessed with change, dissatisfied with traditions and values generally held to be constant. No longer are words such as "good" or "fine" sufficient to describe a pleasant occurrence or feeling; it is now necessary to say "fantastic" or some other superlative to describe even the most common experience. The migrants find that they have settled into a fast-paced, high-pressured life style, which allows little time for one to appreciate the true quality of anything for long. To characterize this general attitudinal state, Australian immigrant and research psychologist Dr. John E. S. Lawrence has judged that Americans suffer from "soul pollution."

Although there are certain aspects of American life which the migrants like, Australians are "knockers" at heart; therefore they do not mind voicing honest criticism about the United States. What they criticize today are the same things which Australian immigrants to this country criticized 100 years ago, such as too much violence and too much of an emphasis on material things.[37] To most of the Aussies who come to the United States, the nation is simply overrated. They feel the cost of medical care is too high, the quality of newspapers and television is too low; and they feel there is still a sense of perpetual crisis here.[38]

In comparing the United States to their homeland, the migrants also have very definite opinions, especially concerning the areas of food, housing, education, business and labor, economics, and the quality of life. Pertaining to food, they notice a greater variety of brand-name products in groceries, and that there are more restaurants and quick-eat establishments in the United States. Americans seem to eat more beef and less lamb than do Australians, but the migrants attest that Australian beer is better than the American varieties. Regarding their comparisons of housing, they feel that the average American house is larger and more comfortable; lots in the United States are larger on the average; and the average American apartment is superior to the Australian flat, as it is called there.

Unlike American schools, many Australian schools are segregated by sex; and it is the general feeling among many of the immigrants that American education is not as challenging. Because there is less discipline in American schools, there are more frequent distractions from an academic learning experience. While it is true that fewer Australians in their native land graduate from high school, it should be stressed that many of those who decide to leave school do so because they have failed to pass a rigorous examination; whereas American students have come to expect eventual graduation for "social reasons," regardless of their level of academic achievement, if only they are willing to remain in school long enough.[39] Similarly in higher education, only about 15 percent of Australian students attend university compared to the almost 50 percent of American students who attend a college or university; however, it is generally conceded that the B.A. degree in Australia is equivalent to the M.A. in the United States.

With respect to business and labor, Australian migrants in this country feel that business here is more "pressure-cooked," but there are fewer strikes.[40] In the Southwest Pacific continent, the trade unions are far more powerful than in the United States, probably because of the difference in the migratory histories of the people of both nations. For example, European nationals desiring to emigrate would first attempt to gain admittance to the United States. Those not allowed to enter, usually of the lower classes, then would attempt to migrate to Australia. Although this is certainly an oversimplification, and one should not infer that Australia is inhabited entirely by American "rejects," it is a generally accurate statement that the United States on the average has received a "higher class" of immigrant. The point of all this, of course, is that those of the lower as opposed to upper class tend to unionize to a greater extent. Both nations, however, have a remarkably similar distribution of work forces (Table 6).

Economically, Australia has held down inflation far more successfully over the years than has the United States (1978 rate of inflation in Australia was under 8 percent while in the United States the annual rate was 8.8 percent). The migrants find that the average weekly wage in both nations is approximately the same, yet the cost of living in the United States seems considerably less. Clothing, certain food products like poultry, and manufactured items in general, are all less expensive in America. On the other hand, the migrants do find that beef, pork, vegetables,

Table 6
Work Force Distribution in Australia and the United States
(Work Force in Industry as a Percentage of Total Work Force)

Industry	Australia (Percentage)	United States (Percentage)
Agriculture (including fishing and forestry)	13.4	12.5
Mining and Quarrying	1.7	1.7
Manufacturing (including electricity, gas, and water supply	30.0	28.9
Building and Construction	8.9	6.4
Transportation and Communication	9.2	7.2
Commerce	18.5	19.0
Other Industries	18.3	24.3

Source: Australian News and Information Bureau, *Australia, an Economic and Investment Reference* (Canberra: Australian Government Publishing Service, 1961), p. 15.

Note: Since 1961 the absolute figures in this table obviously have changed, such as the decline in the percentages of workers engaged in "Agriculture" in both countries; the purpose of this table, however, is only to demonstrate the similarity between the two nations in work force distribution.

and food overall are more expensive in the United States. In addition, although the migrants have Social Security deductions, sales, utilities, separate capital gains and state income taxes in the United States which they did not have in Australia, they discover to their great pleasure that the total tax burden in their new land is less because of the extremely high federal income tax in the land from which they departed (though it must be noted that on a national level, taxes as a percentage of the gross national product appear to be actually higher in the United States; see Table 7).

Table 7

Taxes as a Percentage of Gross National Product

Year	Australia (Percentage)	United States (Percentage)
1965	23.9	25.3
1968	25.4	26.3
1972	24.3	28.1

Source: Dennis Laurence Cuddy, *The Yanks are Coming: American Immigration to Australia* (San Francisco: R & E Research Associates, Inc., 1977). p. 98.

The Australian tax system, however, more evenly distributes the wealth of that nation; therefore the Australian migrants here note the greater proportions of extremely rich and extremely poor individuals residing in this country compared with the nation from which they departed. Perhaps because of the greater proportion of wealthy people in the United States, the migrants find the American standard of living higher; and they also find a greater emphasis here on "culture"—art, music, dance, and the theater.

In general, then, depending on the area under consideration, the immigrants feel that America is the same as, or different from, or better or worse than their homeland, the antipodean continent in the Southwest Pacific.[41] It would probably be best not to pass qualitative judgment on which nation is better, but simply say that to many of the migrants the United States is different enough to be stimulating, yet enough like Australia to be convenient.[42]

In addition to the migrants' specific comparisons between the two countries, there are quite a few comparisons which can be made with respect to the peoples of both lands. The inhabitants of each nation are relatively young for the most part, with nearly 40 percent of all Australians under twenty-one years old, and over one third of the population of the United States under twenty years of age.[43] Probably the most obvious comparison made by the migrants is the larger number of nonwhites in America, and it is also noted that Americans do not seem to see nonwhites as individuals but rather as one of a group; this is different from the attitude of Australians toward nonwhites there, where less racism is evident. Another distinct comparison is made by female migrants who find that they are treated with greater respect in the United States, a less male-dominated country than their homeland.

Overall, Americans appear to be more articulate but naive, more efficient, competitive, and more hard-working than Australians who toil daily from only 9:00 to 5:00 and annually receive four weeks vacation from the time they become employed.[44] Americans are also considered by the immigrants as more nationalistic, independent, individualistic, and more friendly than the inhabitants of Australia. According to Alan Ashbolt in his "An American Experience," ". . . we Australians are not a people capable of large enthusiasms. We lack the optimism of most Americans and the generosity of the best Americans. We grow up in cynicism."[45] Judging themselves, Australians are found more family oriented, sociable, loyal to friends, frugal, well read, participatory, and collective in spirit and efforts than are Americans, who share and exchange things to a lesser degree than do Australians.[46] Thus, while it is readily apparent that Aussies and "Yanks," as Americans in Australia are called, have different attributes and qualities, it should be added as a final note that the people of both lands are actually quite similar, especially when compared to those of other nations.

Whether the migrants are eventually satisfied or dissatisfied with life in the United States depends in large measure on whether their desires for immigration (e.g., for greater economic opportunity) are fulfilled. For the Australian war brides who arrived during and after World War II, fewer were eventually satisfied than dissatisfied. Many were deserted by their husbands or found themselves in poverty due to the inability of their husbands to find gainful employment. Others felt shunned by in-laws who might have thought their sons had been "trapped" into marriage; while still others found that in Australia their future husbands had merely fed them the glamorous but inaccurate illusions of Hollywood films that everyone was or became financially secure in America.[47] There have been, however, many immigrants to the United States who, for example, have found greater economic opportunity. Penny Pulz, for instance, a professional golfer who was the leading money-winner in Australia with only $14,000 per year, immigrated to America to improve her financial status and has been quite successful. Furthermore, she now attests about her new homeland: "I really love this country now. I'd never go back to Australia. California is just super. The climate is perfect and you can go to the desert, the water or the mountains."[48]

For the most part, there have been two consistent themes regarding Australians in the United States. First, there has been a general appreciation for "the noble experiment" even with its difficulties; and second, there has been an eagerness on the part of many Australians here to learn from America what to do, as well as what not to do.[49] Although it is recognized that the United States has its problems, the majority of them are seen as only minor blemishes. Besides, most of the newcomers realize that America is a large country, and feel there are always places they can settle where there are no weekly riots in the streets or daily drug-related murders, for example. Nevertheless,

Table 8

Australian Immigration to the United States and Naturalization

Periods	Number of Immigrants (By Birth)	Number of Earlier Immigrants Naturalized During This Same Period
1950–1959	5,943*	3,398
1959–1968	8,031	2,884
1967–1976	13,700	2,400

* This figure also includes immigrants from New Zealand.

Source: United States Immigration and Naturalization Service Annual Reports.

while many of the migrants become fond of America, many also become more proud of being Australian.[50] Thus, over the past three decades, though the number of Australians choosing the United States as the place in which to live has risen considerably, the number of migrants who have chosen to become naturalized Americans has simultaneously declined (Table 8).

Concerning possible resettlement in Australia, while it is true that numerous Australians remain in America, available statistics tend to indicate that most of those who have migrated to the United States eventually resettle in their homeland in the Southwest Pacific (Table 9). Historically, laborer James H. Kelly wrote to the *Bulletin* in Australia in 1891 that he hated life in the United States and was returning to the land from which he had left. He wrote: "Altogether for a labouring man this place is, in my opinion, a long way behind Australia, and I would strongly advise miners and labourers to stay by the country whose workmen's motto is, 'eight hours for manly labour, eight hours for balmy sleep, eight hours for recreation and our triple eight hours we keep.' "[51]

Table 9
Return to Australia of Australian Migrants to the United States

Australian Residents Departing:
Country of Intended Residence, U.S.

Year	Former settlers departing permanently	Other residents departing permanently	Australian residents departing one year or more but not permanently	Australian residents returning after one year or more abroad; country of last residence or where most time spent, U.S.
1971	1,176	950	2,603	3,772
1972	1,923	994	2,868	3,775
1973	2,229	1,090	2,772	3,986
1974	1,333	949	3,781	3,311
6 months Jan.–June 1975	510	456	1,856	1,432

Source: Letter from the Australian Department of Immigration and Ethnic Affairs, June 16, 1976.

Later, a report was produced in 1947 which indicated that "80 percent of the 10,000 war brides in the United States at that time wanted to return to their homeland with their husbands and families."[52] One such bride advised other Australian women: "Stay home! Marry Australians! America might be fine if you had lots of money, but it's a terrible place if you happen to be poor," as many Australian war brides unfortunately were.[53] It was remarked earlier, however, that more recently Australian women felt they were treated somewhat better in this country than in their own. Why, then, would any of them want to leave America? The answer perhaps lies in the rather strong family ties among Australians, and the ties between women and their families are among the strongest of these.

Pertaining to resettlement in general, it should be noted that many of the migrants probably return to their continental home because they never intended to leave permanently anyway! Also, for those who were not really dissatisfied with life in Australia when they left, the likelihood is greater that they will eventually return to the land which nurtured and molded them. In a word, for them Australia is "home." More specifically, many of the migrants returned to Australia because they did not like the rat race which they found here, and they did not care for the feeling that they were merely IBM numbers in an impersonalized society. Perhaps some returnees, looking toward the future of the United States, also had determined that with a population approaching 225 million, it would be far more difficult for the United States to solve its current and future problems than it is or will be for Australia to solve its problems with a population of under 15 million in approximately the same size land mass as America's.

The future of the United States appears to be fraught with economic difficulties such as continuing inflation and unemployment as well as international crises and periodic social upheavals with only temporary respites in between.[54] Although America is certainly not on the verge of collapse by any stretch of the imagination, it is interesting that research scientist David Goodman has found that of George Orwell's 137 predictions offered in *1984,* exactly 100 had already occurred by 1979![55] Goodman's findings are especially ominous given the relatively recent activities of the American Reverend Jim Jones in Guyana and Australian D. J. O'Hearn's foreboding observation in the United States in 1974 that America seemed obsessed with rituals. Writing in 1975, O'Hearn stated:

These public forms of ritual (evangelist meetings, mass parades, marching girls, graduation ceremonies and stylized political meetings) seem to cater to a deep-set individual need; they are a public reassurance against the mass of individual phobias: an assertion of togetherness against the inner loneliness, a public surrogate for the private insecurity. And if this is true they are immensely worrying for they bespeak a nation waiting for a leader, a nation fascinated by demagoguery of the most unsubtle kind, a nation seeking a great cause.[56]

In "An American Experience," Alan Ashbolt asked, "Will it [America] be a society in which honesty, kindliness and open-heartedness continue to be undermined by greed, fraud, criminality, murder and assassination? The answer is vital to all of us. . . ."[57] Although Ashbolt's remarks remain today applicable to the future of American society, many of the migrants feel that the United States remains "the grand experiment," and it is still the great hope of the future.[58] In fact, many of them view America as what Australia will eventually become in the positive sense.[59]

Like the future of the United States, however, the future of Australia is also somewhat uncertain. Politically, the Labor party will proably not remain out of power for another twenty-three years. What will happen most likely is that Labor and the Liberal-National Country coalition will alternate control as the needs of that country shift. For example, when inflation is finally controlled because of Liberal party conservative fiscal policies, social needs will once again become the major issue and Labor in all likelihood will then return to power. Concerning population, the total for Australia by the year 2000 possibly will reach 19 million, with Sydney and Melbourne each having perhaps just under 5 million inhabitants. The people of the Southwest Pacific continent will tend to become increasingly nationalistic, turning inward and taking their national character from their own unique environment and reflecting it. Internationally, as the United States focuses more upon the Pacific and its new relations with the People's Republic of China, Australia might attempt to enlarge its security from ANZUS to include a "Pacific Pact," comprised not only of Australia, New Zealand, and the United States, but also of Canada and Japan.[60] In an essay of this short length, it is impossible to deal fully with the economic historical, social, and political relations between Australia and the United States and the futures of both nations; however, these topics are covered in greater detail in this writer's current book, *Contemporary Australian-American Relations*.[61]

With respect to the future of Australian immigration to the United States, it will probably continue to grow, even during periods of mild social turmoil and economic difficulties in America, just as it did between 1964 and 1970. Regarding business here, the large retailer David Jones Ltd. has already planned a major expansion in the United States between 1980 and 1982. And pertaining to the average migrant, distance, and the expense of immigration have in the past proved prohibitive; but as of February 1, 1979, the air fare from Sydney to San Francisco became only $450 (Australian) which was $500 (Australian) cheaper than the formerly lowest available fare. Thus, a future increase in immigration from the continent under the Southern Cross to the United States should be assured; but then, only the passing of time—the future itself—will verify the validity of the prognostications offered in the latter part of this essay.

NOTES

1. Dennis Cuddy, *The Yanks are Coming: American Immigration to Australia* (San Francisco: R & E Research Associates, Inc., 1977), p. 94; and United States Immigration and Naturalization Service Annual Reports.

2. Charles Price, Department of Demography, Research School

of Social Sciences, The Australian National University, Canberra, from essay "Migration to and from Australia," p. 8, to be published in London as part of a book on migration within the British Commonwealth.

3. Dennis Cuddy, *The Yanks Are Coming*, p. 4.

4. William Bromwell, *History of Immigration to the United States* (New York: Arno Press, 1969), p. 104.

5. Jay Monaghan, *Australians and the Gold Rush* (Berkeley: University of California Press, 1966), p. 121.

6. J. H. Moore, ed., *Australians in America, 1876–1976* (St. Lucia: University of Queensland Press, 1977), p. 87.

7. Ibid., pp. 87, 56, 25.

8. Ray Aitchison, *Americans in Australia* (New York: Scribner's, 1972), p. 19.

9. J. H. Moore, *Australians in America*, p. 50.

10. Charles Price, "Migration from Australia," p. 8.

11. Dennis Cuddy, *The Yanks Are Coming*, p. xii.

12. J. H. Moore, *Australians in America*, p. 173.

13. Ibid., p. 162.

14. Charles Price, "Migration from Australia," p. 8.

15. Lawrence Davies, "From Old World (America) to New (Australia)," *New York Times Magazine*, September 14, 1947, p. 66.

16. J. H. Moore, *Australians in America*, p. 234.

17. Stewart Cockburn, "Jack Kennedy's America," in *Australians in America*, pp. 275–76.

18. Kenneth Read, "Letter from Seattle," in *Australians in America*, p. 259.

19. Alan Ashbolt, "An American Experience," in *Australians in America*, p. 304.

20. Stewart Cockburn, "Jack Kennedy's America," pp. 263, 267.

21. Ibid., pp. 280–81.

22. Howard Beale, "Reflections Upon a Wounded Giant," in *Australians in America*, p. 306.

23. J. H. Moore, *Australians in America*, p. 311.

24. Sam Lipski, "America Has *Not* Been Cancelled," in *Australians in America*, p. 319.

25. Charles Price, "Migration from Australia," p. 37.

26. Dennis Cuddy, *The Yanks Are Coming*, p. 169.

27. Ibid.; and " 'Happiness' Is Escape from Aust. Taxes," *News* (Adelaide), May 14, 1975, p. 16.

28. Laura Faulk and Odie Faulk, *The Australian Alternative* (New Rochelle, N.Y.; Arlington House Publishers, 1975), p. 90.

29. J. H. Moore, *Australians in America*, p. 32.

30. Ibid., p. 7.

31. Dennis Cuddy, *The Yanks Are Coming*, p. 170.

32. Kenneth Read, "Letter from Seattle," p. 258.

33. Ray Polkinghorne, "Land of Upturned Palms," *Advertiser* (Adelaide), November 30, 1978, p. 4.

34. Charles Price, "Migration from Australia," pp. 8, 37.

35. Craig McGregor, *Profile of Australia* (Ringwood, Victoria: Penguin Books Ltd., 1968), p. 376.

36. Dennis Cuddy, *The Yanks Are Coming*, p. 162.

37. J. H. Moore, *Australians in America*, p. 211.

38. Laura Faulk and Odie Faulk, *The Australian Alternative*, p. 179.

39. Dennis Cuddy, *The Yanks Are Coming*, p. 99.

40. Ray Aitchison, *Americans in Australia*, p. 105; and Dennis Cuddy, *The Yanks Are Coming*, p. 91.

41. Dennis Cuddy, *The Yanks Are Coming*, p. 100.

42. Ibid., p. 101.

43. Craig McGregor, *Profile of Australia*, p. 377; and Dennis Cuddy, *The Yanks Are Coming*, p. 103.

44. Laura Faulk and Odie Faulk, *The Australian Alternative*, p. 133.

45. Alan Ashbolt, "An American Experience," p. 294.

46. Frank Hopkins, "The American Image of Australia," in *Pacific Orbit*, ed. Norman Harper (Melbourne: F. W. Cheshire, 1968), p. 234; and Dennis Cuddy, *The Yanks Are Coming*, pp. 104–5.

47. Lon Jones, "Disillusioned Brides in America," in *Australians in America*, p. 240.

48. Joe Tiede, "Self-Made Penny Pulz: Rising Star on Tour," *News and Observer* (Raleigh, N.C.), April 20, 1978, p. 31.

49. J. H. Moore, *Australians in America*, p. 1.

50. Ibid., p. 7.

51. James Kelly, "A Labourer's Complaint," in *Australians in America*, p. 89.

52. "Emigration of Americans Welcomed by Australians," *New York Times*, September 16, 1947, p. 28.

53. Lon Jones, "Disillusioned Brides in America," p. 242.

54. Dennis Cuddy, *The Yanks Are Coming*, pp. 170–77 passim.

55. "Trib-Bits," *Decatur Tribune*, February 14, 1979, p. 2.

56. D. J. O'Hearn, "Ritualism and Racism," in *Australians in America*, p. 324.

57. Alan Ashbolt, "An American Experience," p. 304.

58. J. H. Moore, *Australians in America*, p. 211.

59. Ibid., p. 7.

60. Dennis Cuddy, *The Yanks Are Coming*, pp. 172–73.

61. Dennis Cuddy, *Contemporary Australian-American Relations* (Palo Alto, Calif.: Century Twenty One Publishing, 1981).